Mathematics Today

Curriculum and Instruction

Janet S. Abbott

Coordinator of Mathematics
Chula Vista City School District
Chula Vista, California

David W. Wells

Director of Instruction
  and Mathematics Education
Oakland Schools
Pontiac, Michigan

Consulting Educators

Dr. Barbara Branch

Principal
Bellevue Junior High School
Memphis, Tennessee

Dr. Philip E. Duren

Mathematics Consultant, K-12
Stark County,
Ohio

Dr. E. Alma Flagg

Educational Consultant
Newark, New Jersey

Betty Jean Gould

Learning Development Specialist
Sachem Central School District
Holbrook, New York

William Ezra Hansen

Supervisor of Math and Science/
  Kindergarten through 12
Davis County School District
Farmington, Utah

Terri Katsulis

Administrator
Chicago Public Schools
Chicago, Illinois

Kathy Lanigan

Kindergarten Teacher
Blanton Elementary School
Carrollton Farmers Branch ISD
Carrollton, Texas

Alice D. Lombardi

Mathematics Specialist
Division of Curriculum & Instruction
New York City Board of Education

Charlotte Sabatino

Elementary School Teacher
Half Hollow Hills School District
Dix Hills, New York

Yvonne Tomlinson

Jefferson Parish Educational
  Service Center
Harvey, Louisiana

Mathematics Today

 Harcourt Brace Jovanovich, Publishers

Orlando   New York   Chicago   San Diego   Atlanta   Dallas

PHOTO CREDITS
Ken Karp: Cover
Ray Hoover: 1, 34, 37, 65, 89, 113, 132, 135, 167, 195, 225, 249, 277, 299

ART CREDITS
Key: Top (t); Bottom (b)

Olivia Cole: 9, 10, 21, 22, 35, 36, 42, 73, 74, 83, 101, 102, 108, 125, 126, 145, 146, 203, 204, 215, 216, 230, 261, 262, 281, 303, 304, 318, 319, 320. *Bill Colrus*: 2, 11, 12, 19, 20, 31, 32, 44, 57, 75, 79, 80, 97, 98, 121, 170, 174, 180, 205, 206, 213, 214, 222, 248, 263, 264, 287, 288, 300, 301, 302, 313, 314. *Ethel Gold*: 3, 4, 15(b), 16, 23, 24, 29, 30, 51, 52, 69, 70, 91, 92, 103, 104, 175, 176, 183, 184, 211, 212, 233, 293, 294, 310. *Denman Hampson*: 7, 17, 18, 33, 47, 67, 68, 81, 82, 177, 178, 209, 210, 305, 306. *Bill Hartman*: 5(b), 6, 13, 14, 25, 26, 50, 71, 72, 93, 105, 106, 187, 188, 189, 198, 208, 283, 291, 307, 308, 321, 322. *Bob Shein*: 5(t), 15, 28, 55(t), 243, 296, 315, 316.

PRODUCTION AND LAYOUT
Thomas Vroman Associates, Inc.

Printed in the United States of America

ISBN: 0-15-350703-9

CONTENTS

chapter **4** Addition and Subtraction Facts to 18

chapter **5** Place Value to 1,000

chapter **6** Time and Money

chapter **7** Addition of Two-Digit Numbers

chapter **8** Subtraction of Two-Digit Numbers

chapter **9** Geometry and Fractions

Addition and Subtraction Facts to 10

CHAPTER 1

GETTING STARTED

How many are there? Write the numbers.

a.

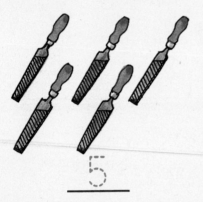

5
___

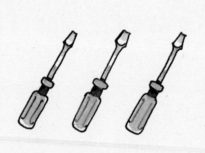

___

___

b.

___

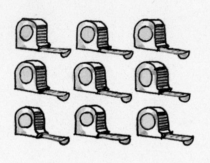

___

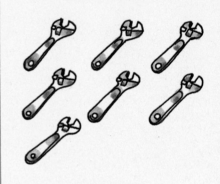

___

c.

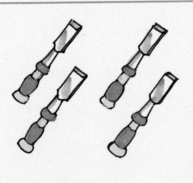

___

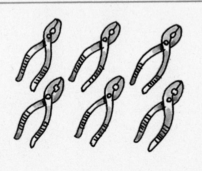

___

___

d.

___

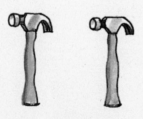

___

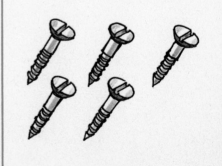

___

2

Order to 10

Write the numbers in order.

		zero	0	0		
	one	1				
	two	2				
	three	3				
	four	4				
	five	5				
	six	6				
	seven	7				
	eight	8				
	nine	9				
	ten	10				

Write the missing numbers.

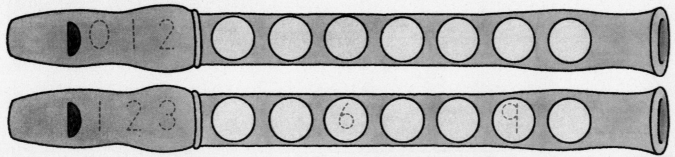

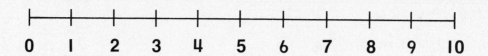

0 1 2 3 4 5 6 7 8 9 10

Write the missing numbers.

a. 1 2 3   0 _ 2   _ 1 2

b. 4 5 _   1 _ 3   _ 6 7

c. 2 3 _   3 _ 5   _ 8 9

d. 7 8 _   5 _ 7   _ 5 6

e. 8 9 _   7 _ 9   _ 9 10

f. 1 2 3 _ _ _ _ 8

g. 3 4 _ _ _ _ 9

4

Sums to 6

$$4 + 2 = 6$$

addition sentence

Complete the addition sentences.

a.

$3 + 2 = \underline{5}$

$2 + 1 = \underline{\hspace{1cm}}$

b.

$1 + 0 = \underline{\hspace{1cm}}$

$3 + 3 = \underline{\hspace{1cm}}$

c. $1 + 1 = \underline{2}$ $1 + 3 = \underline{\hspace{1cm}}$ $1 + 4 = \underline{\hspace{1cm}}$

d. $5 + 1 = \underline{\hspace{1cm}}$ $2 + 0 = \underline{\hspace{1cm}}$ $2 + 2 = \underline{\hspace{1cm}}$

e. $3 + 1 = \underline{\hspace{1cm}}$ $4 + 1 = \underline{\hspace{1cm}}$ $0 + 3 = \underline{\hspace{1cm}}$

f. $4 + 2 = \underline{\hspace{1cm}}$ $1 + 2 = \underline{\hspace{1cm}}$ $4 + 0 = \underline{\hspace{1cm}}$

g. $2 + 3 = \underline{\hspace{1cm}}$ $0 + 6 = \underline{\hspace{1cm}}$ $1 + 5 = \underline{\hspace{1cm}}$

Addition in Any Order

Complete the addition sentences.

a.

$$5 + 1 = \underline{6}$$

$$3 + 2 = \underline{}$$

$$1 + 5 = \underline{}$$

$$2 + 3 = \underline{}$$

b.

$$3 + 1 = \underline{}$$

$$2 + 4 = \underline{}$$

$$1 + 3 = \underline{}$$

$$4 + 2 = \underline{}$$

c.

$$1 + 4 = \underline{} \qquad 0 + 5 = \underline{} \qquad 1 + 5 = \underline{}$$

$$4 + 1 = \underline{} \qquad 5 + 0 = \underline{} \qquad 5 + 1 = \underline{}$$

d.

$$1 + 2 = \underline{} \qquad 0 + 4 = \underline{} \qquad 1 + 3 = \underline{}$$

$$2 + 1 = \underline{} \qquad 4 + 0 = \underline{} \qquad 3 + 1 = \underline{}$$

e.

$$4 + 2 = \underline{} \qquad 4 + 1 = \underline{} \qquad 0 + 6 = \underline{}$$

$$2 + 4 = \underline{} \qquad 1 + 4 = \underline{} \qquad 6 + 0 = \underline{}$$

Vertical Addition

$$2 + 4 = \underset{\uparrow\ \text{sum}}{\underline{6}}$$

$$\begin{array}{r} 2 \\ +4 \\ \hline \underset{\uparrow\ \text{sum}}{6} \end{array}$$

Find the sums.

a.
$$\begin{array}{r} 3 \\ +2 \\ \hline 5 \end{array} \qquad \begin{array}{r} 2 \\ +2 \\ \hline \end{array} \qquad \begin{array}{r} 0 \\ +3 \\ \hline \end{array} \qquad \begin{array}{r} 5 \\ +1 \\ \hline \end{array} \qquad \begin{array}{r} 6 \\ +0 \\ \hline \end{array} \qquad \begin{array}{r} 1 \\ +2 \\ \hline \end{array} \qquad \begin{array}{r} 1 \\ +4 \\ \hline \end{array}$$

b.
$$\begin{array}{r} 1 \\ +1 \\ \hline \end{array} \qquad \begin{array}{r} 1 \\ +0 \\ \hline \end{array} \qquad \begin{array}{r} 3 \\ +3 \\ \hline \end{array} \qquad \begin{array}{r} 0 \\ +0 \\ \hline \end{array} \qquad \begin{array}{r} 3 \\ +1 \\ \hline \end{array} \qquad \begin{array}{r} 0 \\ +4 \\ \hline \end{array} \qquad \begin{array}{r} 2 \\ +3 \\ \hline \end{array}$$

c.
$$\begin{array}{r} 1 \\ +2 \\ \hline \end{array} \qquad \begin{array}{r} 2 \\ +0 \\ \hline \end{array} \qquad \begin{array}{r} 1 \\ +3 \\ \hline \end{array} \qquad \begin{array}{r} 3 \\ +2 \\ \hline \end{array} \qquad \begin{array}{r} 4 \\ +0 \\ \hline \end{array} \qquad \begin{array}{r} 4 \\ +1 \\ \hline \end{array} \qquad \begin{array}{r} 1 \\ +5 \\ \hline \end{array}$$

d.
$$\begin{array}{r} 0 \\ +6 \\ \hline \end{array} \qquad \begin{array}{r} 2 \\ +1 \\ \hline \end{array} \qquad \begin{array}{r} 2 \\ +4 \\ \hline \end{array} \qquad \begin{array}{r} 2 \\ +2 \\ \hline \end{array} \qquad \begin{array}{r} 5 \\ +0 \\ \hline \end{array} \qquad \begin{array}{r} 3 \\ +1 \\ \hline \end{array} \qquad \begin{array}{r} 0 \\ +1 \\ \hline \end{array}$$

e.
$$\begin{array}{r} 3 \\ +0 \\ \hline \end{array} \qquad \begin{array}{r} 4 \\ +2 \\ \hline \end{array} \qquad \begin{array}{r} 3 \\ +3 \\ \hline \end{array} \qquad \begin{array}{r} 0 \\ +5 \\ \hline \end{array} \qquad \begin{array}{r} 1 \\ +4 \\ \hline \end{array} \qquad \begin{array}{r} 0 \\ +2 \\ \hline \end{array} \qquad \begin{array}{r} 5 \\ +1 \\ \hline \end{array}$$

Find the sums.

a.
$$\begin{array}{r} 2 \\ +3 \\ \hline 5 \end{array}$$
$$\begin{array}{r} 1 \\ +3 \\ \hline \end{array}$$
$$\begin{array}{r} 0 \\ +2 \\ \hline \end{array}$$
$$\begin{array}{r} 2 \\ +2 \\ \hline \end{array}$$
$$\begin{array}{r} 2 \\ +4 \\ \hline \end{array}$$
$$\begin{array}{r} 4 \\ +1 \\ \hline \end{array}$$
$$\begin{array}{r} 3 \\ +0 \\ \hline \end{array}$$

b.
$$\begin{array}{r} 3 \\ +3 \\ \hline \end{array}$$
$$\begin{array}{r} 1 \\ +4 \\ \hline \end{array}$$
$$\begin{array}{r} 3 \\ +2 \\ \hline \end{array}$$
$$\begin{array}{r} 0 \\ +1 \\ \hline \end{array}$$
$$\begin{array}{r} 1 \\ +3 \\ \hline \end{array}$$
$$\begin{array}{r} 5 \\ +0 \\ \hline \end{array}$$
$$\begin{array}{r} 4 \\ +2 \\ \hline \end{array}$$

c.
$$\begin{array}{r} 1 \\ +2 \\ \hline \end{array}$$
$$\begin{array}{r} 0 \\ +3 \\ \hline \end{array}$$
$$\begin{array}{r} 5 \\ +1 \\ \hline \end{array}$$
$$\begin{array}{r} 3 \\ +1 \\ \hline \end{array}$$
$$\begin{array}{r} 0 \\ +4 \\ \hline \end{array}$$
$$\begin{array}{r} 1 \\ +5 \\ \hline \end{array}$$
$$\begin{array}{r} 6 \\ +0 \\ \hline \end{array}$$

d.
$$\begin{array}{r} 0 \\ +6 \\ \hline \end{array}$$
$$\begin{array}{r} 1 \\ +4 \\ \hline \end{array}$$
$$\begin{array}{r} 2 \\ +0 \\ \hline \end{array}$$
$$\begin{array}{r} 1 \\ +1 \\ \hline \end{array}$$
$$\begin{array}{r} 2 \\ +1 \\ \hline \end{array}$$
$$\begin{array}{r} 0 \\ +5 \\ \hline \end{array}$$
$$\begin{array}{r} 4 \\ +0 \\ \hline \end{array}$$

Skills Maintenance

Write the missing numbers.

1   3   4

5   6   9

Sums to 8

Find the sums.

a.

$$6 + 1 = \underline{7}$$

$$5 + 2 = \underline{}$$

b.

$$4 + 3 = \underline{}$$

$$7 + 1 = \underline{}$$

c.

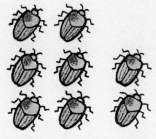

$$6 + 2 = \underline{}$$

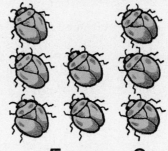

$$5 + 3 = \underline{}$$

d. $4 + 4 = \underline{}$ $0 + 7 = \underline{}$ $1 + 6 = \underline{}$

e. $1 + 7 = \underline{}$ $2 + 6 = \underline{}$ $8 + 0 = \underline{}$

f. $3 + 4 = \underline{}$ $5 + 1 = \underline{}$ $2 + 3 = \underline{}$

g. $2 + 5 = \underline{}$ $3 + 5 = \underline{}$ $4 + 2 = \underline{}$

h. $4 + 1 = \underline{}$ $2 + 2 = \underline{}$ $3 + 3 = \underline{}$

Find the sums.

a.
$$5 + 3 = 8$$ $$4 + 2$$ $$7 + 1$$ $$0 + 8$$ $$2 + 5$$ $$5 + 0$$ $$6 + 2$$

b.
$$5 + 1$$ $$2 + 3$$ $$2 + 2$$ $$4 + 3$$ $$6 + 1$$ $$1 + 7$$ $$4 + 4$$

c.
$$1 + 1$$ $$2 + 6$$ $$4 + 1$$ $$2 + 4$$ $$3 + 3$$ $$3 + 2$$ $$5 + 2$$

d.
$$1 + 7$$ $$1 + 6$$ $$3 + 5$$ $$4 + 4$$ $$2 + 1$$ $$8 + 0$$ $$1 + 4$$

PROBLEM SOLVING

How many in all?

e.

_____

f.

_____

10

Sums to 10

Add.

a.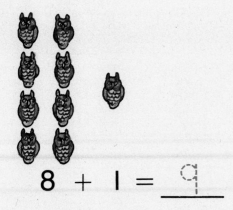

$8 + 1 = \underline{9}$

$7 + 2 = \underline{}$

b.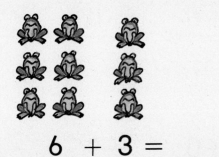

$6 + 3 = \underline{}$

$9 + 1 = \underline{}$

c.

$8 + 2 = \underline{}$

$7 + 3 = \underline{}$

d. $4 + 5 = \underline{}$ $4 + 6 = \underline{}$ $3 + 6 = \underline{}$

e. $2 + 7 = \underline{}$ $5 + 5 = \underline{}$ $0 + 9 = \underline{}$

f. $1 + 9 = \underline{}$ $5 + 4 = \underline{}$ $3 + 5 = \underline{}$

g. $1 + 8 = \underline{}$ $6 + 4 = \underline{}$ $2 + 8 = \underline{}$

h. $5 + 2 = \underline{}$ $4 + 4 = \underline{}$ $3 + 7 = \underline{}$

Add.

a.
$$\begin{array}{r} 4 \\ +6 \\ \hline 10 \end{array}$$
$$\begin{array}{r} 1 \\ +8 \\ \hline \end{array}$$
$$\begin{array}{r} 1 \\ +7 \\ \hline \end{array}$$
$$\begin{array}{r} 7 \\ +3 \\ \hline \end{array}$$
$$\begin{array}{r} 3 \\ +6 \\ \hline \end{array}$$

b.
$$\begin{array}{r} 0 \\ +8 \\ \hline \end{array}$$
$$\begin{array}{r} 6 \\ +1 \\ \hline \end{array}$$
$$\begin{array}{r} 6 \\ +3 \\ \hline \end{array}$$
$$\begin{array}{r} 8 \\ +2 \\ \hline \end{array}$$
$$\begin{array}{r} 2 \\ +7 \\ \hline \end{array}$$
$$\begin{array}{r} 6 \\ +4 \\ \hline \end{array}$$
$$\begin{array}{r} 5 \\ +3 \\ \hline \end{array}$$

c.
$$\begin{array}{r} 7 \\ +3 \\ \hline \end{array}$$
$$\begin{array}{r} 8 \\ +1 \\ \hline \end{array}$$
$$\begin{array}{r} 3 \\ +5 \\ \hline \end{array}$$
$$\begin{array}{r} 5 \\ +5 \\ \hline \end{array}$$
$$\begin{array}{r} 3 \\ +6 \\ \hline \end{array}$$
$$\begin{array}{r} 4 \\ +4 \\ \hline \end{array}$$
$$\begin{array}{r} 2 \\ +8 \\ \hline \end{array}$$

d.
$$\begin{array}{r} 2 \\ +6 \\ \hline \end{array}$$
$$\begin{array}{r} 9 \\ +1 \\ \hline \end{array}$$
$$\begin{array}{r} 7 \\ +2 \\ \hline \end{array}$$
$$\begin{array}{r} 3 \\ +4 \\ \hline \end{array}$$
$$\begin{array}{r} 9 \\ +0 \\ \hline \end{array}$$
$$\begin{array}{r} 1 \\ +9 \\ \hline \end{array}$$
$$\begin{array}{r} 4 \\ +5 \\ \hline \end{array}$$

★ Challenge

Add across or down.
Ring the pairs that add up to 10.

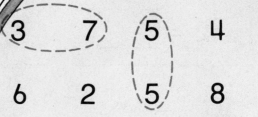

3	7	5	4	6
6	2	5	8	1
4	9	1	6	8
0	1	5	5	2

12

PROBLEM SOLVING

Addition

Solve.

a.

2 small

6 big

How many in all?

$$\begin{array}{r} 2 \\ +6 \\ \hline 8 \end{array}$$

b.

4  are there.

2 more 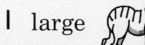 come.

How many in all?

c.

4 are eating.

6 are sleeping.

How many in all?

d.

4 small

1 large

How many in all?

e.

Bob brings 4 .

Sam brings 4 .

How many in all?

f.

Susan eats 7 .

She eats 3 more .

How many in all?

g.

Mrs. Ross buys 4 .

She buys 3 more .

How many in all?

h.

Mr. Davis makes 5 .

He makes 3 more .

How many in all?

Solve.

a.

See 4 .

See 5 .

How many in all?

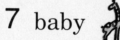

b.

9 blue

1 green

How many in all?

c.

5 large

5 small

How many in all?

d.

1 big

7 baby

How many in all?

e.

Peggy finds 4 .

She finds 3 more .

How many in all?

f.

Wanda sees 3 .

She sees 6 .

How many in all?

g.

Mrs. Long buys 7 .

She buys 2 more.

How many in all?

h.

Tim eats 3.

Joe eats 5.

How many in all?

14

Subtraction Facts to 6

$$6 - 2 = 4$$

subtraction sentence

Complete the subtraction sentences.

a.

$$4 - 3 = \underline{\ 1\ }$$

$$5 - 2 = \underline{\qquad}$$

b.

$$3 - 0 = \underline{\qquad}$$

$$6 - 1 = \underline{\qquad}$$

c. $6 - 4 = \underline{\qquad}$ $4 - 1 = \underline{\qquad}$ $5 - 1 = \underline{\qquad}$

d. $2 - 1 = \underline{\qquad}$ $6 - 6 = \underline{\qquad}$ $4 - 3 = \underline{\qquad}$

e. $6 - 3 = \underline{\qquad}$ $5 - 3 = \underline{\qquad}$ $5 - 0 = \underline{\qquad}$

f. $5 - 2 = \underline{\qquad}$ $6 - 1 = \underline{\qquad}$ $3 - 1 = \underline{\qquad}$

g. $3 - 2 = \underline{\qquad}$ $5 - 4 = \underline{\qquad}$ $3 - 3 = \underline{\qquad}$

Subtract.

a.

$6 - 2 = \underline{4}$

$4 - 0 = \underline{}$

$6 - 4 = \underline{}$

$4 - 4 = \underline{}$

b.

$5 - 2 = \underline{}$

$3 - 2 = \underline{}$

$5 - 3 = \underline{}$

$3 - 1 = \underline{}$

c. $5 - 1 = \underline{}$ $\qquad$ $6 - 5 = \underline{}$ $\qquad$ $5 - 3 = \underline{}$

$5 - 4 = \underline{}$ $\qquad$ $6 - 1 = \underline{}$ $\qquad$ $5 - 2 = \underline{}$

d. $6 - 0 = \underline{}$ $\qquad$ $4 - 3 = \underline{}$ $\qquad$ $3 - 0 = \underline{}$

$6 - 6 = \underline{}$ $\qquad$ $4 - 1 = \underline{}$ $\qquad$ $3 - 3 = \underline{}$

e. $2 - 0 = \underline{}$ $\qquad$ $3 - 2 = \underline{}$ $\qquad$ $6 - 4 = \underline{}$

$2 - 2 = \underline{}$ $\qquad$ $3 - 1 = \underline{}$ $\qquad$ $6 - 2 = \underline{}$

Vertical Subtraction

$5 - 2 =$ ___3___

↑
difference

$$\begin{array}{r} 5 \\ -2 \\ \hline 3 \end{array}$$

↑
difference

Find the differences.

a.
$$\begin{array}{r} 6 \\ -5 \\ \hline \end{array}$$
$$\begin{array}{r} 3 \\ -3 \\ \hline \end{array}$$
$$\begin{array}{r} 6 \\ -3 \\ \hline \end{array}$$
$$\begin{array}{r} 4 \\ -2 \\ \hline \end{array}$$
$$\begin{array}{r} 6 \\ -6 \\ \hline \end{array}$$
$$\begin{array}{r} 3 \\ -1 \\ \hline \end{array}$$
$$\begin{array}{r} 1 \\ -1 \\ \hline \end{array}$$

b.
$$\begin{array}{r} 6 \\ -1 \\ \hline \end{array}$$
$$\begin{array}{r} 2 \\ -1 \\ \hline \end{array}$$
$$\begin{array}{r} 5 \\ -3 \\ \hline \end{array}$$
$$\begin{array}{r} 6 \\ -1 \\ \hline \end{array}$$
$$\begin{array}{r} 5 \\ -4 \\ \hline \end{array}$$
$$\begin{array}{r} 6 \\ -2 \\ \hline \end{array}$$
$$\begin{array}{r} 4 \\ -0 \\ \hline \end{array}$$

c.
$$\begin{array}{r} 4 \\ -3 \\ \hline \end{array}$$
$$\begin{array}{r} 2 \\ -0 \\ \hline \end{array}$$
$$\begin{array}{r} 6 \\ -4 \\ \hline \end{array}$$
$$\begin{array}{r} 5 \\ -0 \\ \hline \end{array}$$
$$\begin{array}{r} 6 \\ -3 \\ \hline \end{array}$$
$$\begin{array}{r} 3 \\ -2 \\ \hline \end{array}$$
$$\begin{array}{r} 6 \\ -6 \\ \hline \end{array}$$

d.
$$\begin{array}{r} 5 \\ -5 \\ \hline \end{array}$$
$$\begin{array}{r} 4 \\ -1 \\ \hline \end{array}$$
$$\begin{array}{r} 6 \\ -0 \\ \hline \end{array}$$
$$\begin{array}{r} 5 \\ -2 \\ \hline \end{array}$$
$$\begin{array}{r} 4 \\ -4 \\ \hline \end{array}$$
$$\begin{array}{r} 5 \\ -1 \\ \hline \end{array}$$
$$\begin{array}{r} 3 \\ -0 \\ \hline \end{array}$$

e.
$$\begin{array}{r} 2 \\ -2 \\ \hline \end{array}$$
$$\begin{array}{r} 6 \\ -2 \\ \hline \end{array}$$
$$\begin{array}{r} 1 \\ -0 \\ \hline \end{array}$$
$$\begin{array}{r} 6 \\ -3 \\ \hline \end{array}$$
$$\begin{array}{r} 6 \\ -5 \\ \hline \end{array}$$
$$\begin{array}{r} 5 \\ -4 \\ \hline \end{array}$$
$$\begin{array}{r} 4 \\ -2 \\ \hline \end{array}$$

Find the differences.

a.
$$6 - 4 = 2$$ $$2 - 0 =$$ $$5 - 2 =$$ $$3 - 1 =$$ $$6 - 0 =$$ $$4 - 3 =$$ $$5 - 4 =$$

b.
$$3 - 0 =$$ $$6 - 5 =$$ $$5 - 5 =$$ $$1 - 1 =$$ $$4 - 0 =$$ $$3 - 2 =$$ $$2 - 2 =$$

c.
$$5 - 2 =$$ $$4 - 1 =$$ $$6 - 1 =$$ $$5 - 3 =$$ $$6 - 3 =$$ $$6 - 2 =$$ $$5 - 4 =$$

d.
$$2 - 1 =$$ $$4 - 2 =$$ $$3 - 3 =$$ $$4 - 4 =$$ $$6 - 6 =$$ $$5 - 1 =$$ $$3 - 2 =$$

Midchapter Review

Add.

$$3 + 5 =$$ $$4 + 2 =$$ $$2 + 2 =$$ $$9 + 1 =$$ $$0 + 5 =$$ $$3 + 4 =$$ $$7 + 2 =$$

Subtracting from 7 and 8

Find the differences.

a.

$$\begin{array}{r} 7 \\ -1 \\ \hline 6 \end{array}$$

$$\begin{array}{r} 7 \\ -2 \\ \hline \end{array}$$

b.

$$\begin{array}{r} 7 \\ -3 \\ \hline \end{array}$$

$$\begin{array}{r} 8 \\ -1 \\ \hline \end{array}$$

c.

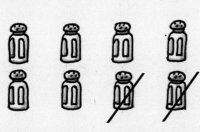

$$\begin{array}{r} 8 \\ -2 \\ \hline \end{array}$$

$$\begin{array}{r} 8 \\ -3 \\ \hline \end{array}$$

d.

$$\begin{array}{r} 7 \\ -4 \\ \hline \end{array} \qquad \begin{array}{r} 7 \\ -5 \\ \hline \end{array} \qquad \begin{array}{r} 7 \\ -6 \\ \hline \end{array} \qquad \begin{array}{r} 7 \\ -7 \\ \hline \end{array} \qquad \begin{array}{r} 8 \\ -0 \\ \hline \end{array} \qquad \begin{array}{r} 8 \\ -4 \\ \hline \end{array} \qquad \begin{array}{r} 8 \\ -5 \\ \hline \end{array}$$

e.

$$\begin{array}{r} 8 \\ -6 \\ \hline \end{array} \qquad \begin{array}{r} 8 \\ -7 \\ \hline \end{array} \qquad \begin{array}{r} 8 \\ -8 \\ \hline \end{array} \qquad \begin{array}{r} 7 \\ -0 \\ \hline \end{array} \qquad \begin{array}{r} 6 \\ -3 \\ \hline \end{array} \qquad \begin{array}{r} 5 \\ -1 \\ \hline \end{array} \qquad \begin{array}{r} 8 \\ -2 \\ \hline \end{array}$$

f.

$$\begin{array}{r} 7 \\ -1 \\ \hline \end{array} \qquad \begin{array}{r} 6 \\ -2 \\ \hline \end{array} \qquad \begin{array}{r} 5 \\ -4 \\ \hline \end{array} \qquad \begin{array}{r} 8 \\ -3 \\ \hline \end{array} \qquad \begin{array}{r} 6 \\ -6 \\ \hline \end{array} \qquad \begin{array}{r} 7 \\ -2 \\ \hline \end{array} \qquad \begin{array}{r} 8 \\ -4 \\ \hline \end{array}$$

Find the differences.

a.
$$8 - 6 = 2$$ $$6 - 2 =$$ $$7 - 7 =$$ $$8 - 5 =$$ $$6 - 3 =$$ $$7 - 2 =$$ $$8 - 4 =$$

b.
$$7 - 5 =$$ $$5 - 0 =$$ $$7 - 1 =$$ $$6 - 5 =$$ $$5 - 2 =$$ $$5 - 4 =$$ $$7 - 3 =$$

c.
$$6 - 0 =$$ $$7 - 2 =$$ $$8 - 2 =$$ $$8 - 8 =$$ $$7 - 4 =$$ $$8 - 1 =$$ $$8 - 3 =$$

d.
$$4 - 2 =$$ $$5 - 5 =$$ $$6 - 1 =$$ $$8 - 0 =$$ $$7 - 6 =$$ $$6 - 2 =$$ $$4 - 4 =$$

e.
$$6 - 6 =$$ $$7 - 1 =$$ $$7 - 0 =$$ $$8 - 7 =$$ $$5 - 1 =$$ $$8 - 2 =$$ $$7 - 4 =$$

f.
$$5 - 3 =$$ $$6 - 4 =$$ $$8 - 5 =$$ $$8 - 6 =$$

Subtracting from 9 and 10

Subtract.

a.
$$\begin{array}{r} 9 \\ -\,1 \\ \hline 8 \end{array}$$

$$\begin{array}{r} 9 \\ -\,2 \\ \hline \end{array}$$

b.
$$\begin{array}{r} 9 \\ -\,3 \\ \hline \end{array}$$

$$\begin{array}{r} 10 \\ -\,1 \\ \hline \end{array}$$

c.
$$\begin{array}{r} 10 \\ -\,2 \\ \hline \end{array}$$

$$\begin{array}{r} 10 \\ -\,3 \\ \hline \end{array}$$

d.
$$\begin{array}{r} 9 \\ -\,4 \\ \hline \end{array}\qquad \begin{array}{r} 9 \\ -\,5 \\ \hline \end{array}\qquad \begin{array}{r} 10 \\ -\,4 \\ \hline \end{array}\qquad \begin{array}{r} 9 \\ -\,6 \\ \hline \end{array}\qquad \begin{array}{r} 10 \\ -\,5 \\ \hline \end{array}\qquad \begin{array}{r} 10 \\ -\,6 \\ \hline \end{array}\qquad \begin{array}{r} 9 \\ -\,0 \\ \hline \end{array}$$

e.
$$\begin{array}{r} 10 \\ -\,7 \\ \hline \end{array}\qquad \begin{array}{r} 10 \\ -\,8 \\ \hline \end{array}\qquad \begin{array}{r} 9 \\ -\,7 \\ \hline \end{array}\qquad \begin{array}{r} 9 \\ -\,8 \\ \hline \end{array}\qquad \begin{array}{r} 9 \\ -\,9 \\ \hline \end{array}\qquad \begin{array}{r} 10 \\ -\,9 \\ \hline \end{array}\qquad \begin{array}{r} 9 \\ -\,1 \\ \hline \end{array}$$

f.
$$\begin{array}{r} 8 \\ -\,6 \\ \hline \end{array}\qquad \begin{array}{r} 9 \\ -\,3 \\ \hline \end{array}\qquad \begin{array}{r} 10 \\ -\,2 \\ \hline \end{array}\qquad \begin{array}{r} 8 \\ -\,3 \\ \hline \end{array}\qquad \begin{array}{r} 9 \\ -\,2 \\ \hline \end{array}\qquad \begin{array}{r} 7 \\ -\,1 \\ \hline \end{array}\qquad \begin{array}{r} 10 \\ -\,3 \\ \hline \end{array}$$

Find the differences.

a.
$$10 - 7 = 3$$
$$9 - 4 =$$
$$9 - 7 =$$
$$10 - 2 =$$
$$9 - 0 =$$
$$8 - 1 =$$
$$10 - 4 =$$

b.
$$9 - 5 =$$
$$8 - 4 =$$
$$10 - 9 =$$
$$9 - 2 =$$
$$8 - 8 =$$
$$7 - 3 =$$
$$10 - 5 =$$

c.
$$9 - 9 =$$
$$8 - 0 =$$
$$7 - 7 =$$
$$7 - 5 =$$
$$6 - 5 =$$
$$10 - 8 =$$
$$10 - 6 =$$

d.
$$10 - 1 =$$
$$9 - 8 =$$
$$9 - 6 =$$
$$10 - 3 =$$
$$8 - 5 =$$
$$9 - 3 =$$
$$9 - 1 =$$

PROBLEM SOLVING

Color to continue the pattern.

e.

f.

g.

PROBLEM SOLVING

Subtraction

Solve.

a.

6

3 are planted.

How many are left?

$$6$$
$$-3$$
$$\overline{3}$$

b.

8 big

Todd picks 6.

How many are left?

c.

10 blue

2 are broken.

How many are left?

d.

5

4 are eaten.

How many are left?

e.

9

3 are sold.

How many are left?

f.

7

3 are picked.

How many are left?

g.

Marcia grows 10 .

She sells 4.

How many are left?

h.

Tara has 10 .

She plants 5 .

How many are left?

Solve.

a.

Mrs. Brown has 9 .

She gives 5 away.

How many are left?

b.

Linda grows 8 .

She sells 1 .

How many are left?

c.

Carlos grows 6 .

He sells 2 .

How many are left?

d.

Mr. Lee buys 7 .

He eats 5 .

How many are left?

e.

Mr. Santos grows 9 .

He eats 2 .

How many are left?

f.

Sam has 10 .

He sells 3 .

How many are left?

g.

There are 10 .

6 are sold.

How many are left?

h.

9 are in the store.

4 are sold.

How many are left?

Addition Facts Drill

Add.

a.
$\begin{array}{r} 1 \\ +8 \\ \hline 9 \end{array}$
$\begin{array}{r} 8 \\ +2 \\ \hline \end{array}$
$\begin{array}{r} 5 \\ +1 \\ \hline \end{array}$
$\begin{array}{r} 2 \\ +7 \\ \hline \end{array}$
$\begin{array}{r} 4 \\ +2 \\ \hline \end{array}$

b.
$\begin{array}{r} 6 \\ +4 \\ \hline \end{array}$
$\begin{array}{r} 7 \\ +1 \\ \hline \end{array}$
$\begin{array}{r} 3 \\ +6 \\ \hline \end{array}$
$\begin{array}{r} 2 \\ +1 \\ \hline \end{array}$
$\begin{array}{r} 3 \\ +4 \\ \hline \end{array}$
$\begin{array}{r} 5 \\ +4 \\ \hline \end{array}$
$\begin{array}{r} 6 \\ +2 \\ \hline \end{array}$

c.
$\begin{array}{r} 2 \\ +8 \\ \hline \end{array}$
$\begin{array}{r} 1 \\ +6 \\ \hline \end{array}$
$\begin{array}{r} 4 \\ +4 \\ \hline \end{array}$
$\begin{array}{r} 3 \\ +5 \\ \hline \end{array}$
$\begin{array}{r} 7 \\ +3 \\ \hline \end{array}$
$\begin{array}{r} 6 \\ +2 \\ \hline \end{array}$
$\begin{array}{r} 1 \\ +5 \\ \hline \end{array}$

d.
$\begin{array}{r} 0 \\ +9 \\ \hline \end{array}$
$\begin{array}{r} 8 \\ +1 \\ \hline \end{array}$
$\begin{array}{r} 4 \\ +6 \\ \hline \end{array}$
$\begin{array}{r} 3 \\ +3 \\ \hline \end{array}$
$\begin{array}{r} 1 \\ +9 \\ \hline \end{array}$
$\begin{array}{r} 1 \\ +4 \\ \hline \end{array}$
$\begin{array}{r} 2 \\ +6 \\ \hline \end{array}$

e.
$\begin{array}{r} 2 \\ +5 \\ \hline \end{array}$
$\begin{array}{r} 5 \\ +3 \\ \hline \end{array}$
$\begin{array}{r} 7 \\ +0 \\ \hline \end{array}$
$\begin{array}{r} 1 \\ +7 \\ \hline \end{array}$
$\begin{array}{r} 2 \\ +2 \\ \hline \end{array}$
$\begin{array}{r} 8 \\ +0 \\ \hline \end{array}$
$\begin{array}{r} 5 \\ +5 \\ \hline \end{array}$

f.
$\begin{array}{r} 4 \\ +5 \\ \hline \end{array}$
$\begin{array}{r} 5 \\ +2 \\ \hline \end{array}$
$\begin{array}{r} 3 \\ +2 \\ \hline \end{array}$
$\begin{array}{r} 1 \\ +3 \\ \hline \end{array}$
$\begin{array}{r} 3 \\ +7 \\ \hline \end{array}$
$\begin{array}{r} 7 \\ +2 \\ \hline \end{array}$
$\begin{array}{r} 9 \\ +1 \\ \hline \end{array}$

Subtraction Facts Drill

Subtract.

a.
$$\begin{array}{r} 9 \\ -3 \\ \hline \end{array}$$ 6
$$\begin{array}{r} 8 \\ -1 \\ \hline \end{array}$$
$$\begin{array}{r} 10 \\ -5 \\ \hline \end{array}$$
$$\begin{array}{r} 8 \\ -6 \\ \hline \end{array}$$
$$\begin{array}{r} 10 \\ -7 \\ \hline \end{array}$$
$$\begin{array}{r} 7 \\ -7 \\ \hline \end{array}$$
$$\begin{array}{r} 5 \\ -4 \\ \hline \end{array}$$

b.
$$\begin{array}{r} 10 \\ -9 \\ \hline \end{array}$$
$$\begin{array}{r} 9 \\ -0 \\ \hline \end{array}$$
$$\begin{array}{r} 7 \\ -3 \\ \hline \end{array}$$
$$\begin{array}{r} 8 \\ -5 \\ \hline \end{array}$$
$$\begin{array}{r} 5 \\ -5 \\ \hline \end{array}$$
$$\begin{array}{r} 9 \\ -5 \\ \hline \end{array}$$
$$\begin{array}{r} 6 \\ -2 \\ \hline \end{array}$$

c.
$$\begin{array}{r} 10 \\ -4 \\ \hline \end{array}$$
$$\begin{array}{r} 9 \\ -4 \\ \hline \end{array}$$
$$\begin{array}{r} 10 \\ -2 \\ \hline \end{array}$$
$$\begin{array}{r} 8 \\ -4 \\ \hline \end{array}$$
$$\begin{array}{r} 7 \\ -5 \\ \hline \end{array}$$
$$\begin{array}{r} 6 \\ -5 \\ \hline \end{array}$$
$$\begin{array}{r} 8 \\ -7 \\ \hline \end{array}$$

d.
$$\begin{array}{r} 9 \\ -8 \\ \hline \end{array}$$
$$\begin{array}{r} 10 \\ -6 \\ \hline \end{array}$$
$$\begin{array}{r} 6 \\ -6 \\ \hline \end{array}$$
$$\begin{array}{r} 3 \\ -2 \\ \hline \end{array}$$
$$\begin{array}{r} 10 \\ -1 \\ \hline \end{array}$$
$$\begin{array}{r} 6 \\ -3 \\ \hline \end{array}$$
$$\begin{array}{r} 2 \\ -2 \\ \hline \end{array}$$

e.
$$\begin{array}{r} 5 \\ -2 \\ \hline \end{array}$$
$$\begin{array}{r} 8 \\ -2 \\ \hline \end{array}$$
$$\begin{array}{r} 7 \\ -6 \\ \hline \end{array}$$
$$\begin{array}{r} 4 \\ -2 \\ \hline \end{array}$$
$$\begin{array}{r} 9 \\ -1 \\ \hline \end{array}$$
$$\begin{array}{r} 8 \\ -3 \\ \hline \end{array}$$
$$\begin{array}{r} 2 \\ -1 \\ \hline \end{array}$$

f.
$$\begin{array}{r} 9 \\ -7 \\ \hline \end{array}$$
$$\begin{array}{r} 10 \\ -3 \\ \hline \end{array}$$
$$\begin{array}{r} 10 \\ -8 \\ \hline \end{array}$$
$$\begin{array}{r} 7 \\ -1 \\ \hline \end{array}$$
$$\begin{array}{r} 9 \\ -2 \\ \hline \end{array}$$

26

Families of Facts

Add or subtract.

a.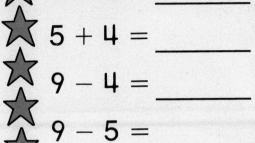
4 + 5 = _9_

5 + 4 = _____

9 − 4 = _____

9 − 5 = _____

b.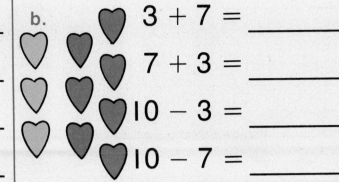
3 + 7 = _____

7 + 3 = _____

10 − 3 = _____

10 − 7 = _____

c.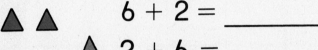
6 + 2 = _____

2 + 6 = _____

8 − 6 = _____

8 − 2 = _____

d.
8 + 1 = _____

1 + 8 = _____

9 − 8 = _____

9 − 1 = _____

e.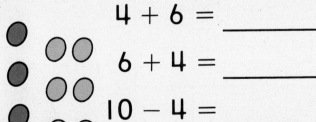
4 + 6 = _____

6 + 4 = _____

10 − 4 = _____

10 − 6 = _____

f.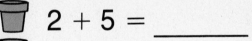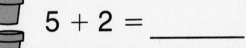
2 + 5 = _____

5 + 2 = _____

7 − 2 = _____

7 − 5 = _____

g.
3 + 3 = _____

6 − 3 = _____

h.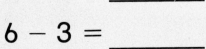
5 + 5 = _____

10 − 5 = _____

Addition and Subtraction Practice

Add or subtract.
Use the code to solve.

0	1	2	3	4	5
K	B	H	U	G	L

6	7	8	9	10
O	T	M	E	A

6 +1	3 +7	8 −8	5 +4	4 +4	10 −1
7 T					

8 −2	5 −2	4 +3	10 −3	1 +5

7 +0	9 −7	8 +1	8 −7	6 +4	10 −5	1 +4

7 −3	8 +2	9 −1	2 +7

28

Copyright © 1985 by Harcourt Brace Jovanovich, Inc.

Names for Numbers

Ring each name for the number.

10

(5 + 5)

3 + 6

(6 + 4)

1 + 5

8

4 + 3

9 − 1

6 + 2

8 − 0

9

10 − 1

6 + 3

7 + 3

6 + 2

7

5 + 2

10 − 3

3 + 4

4 + 2

9

10 − 2

5 + 4

2 + 7

9 − 6

6

8 − 3

10 − 2

7 − 1

9 − 3

8

1 + 7

10 − 2

8 + 0

7 + 2

10

4 + 5

3 + 7

1 + 9

2 + 8

7

1 + 6

4 + 4

9 − 2

7 − 0

More Addition and Subtraction Practice

Add or subtract.

Color **5**  red . Color **7** green .

Color **6** blue . Color **8** yellow .

1 +5	8 −2	5 +3	4 +2
8 −1	7 −0	6 −1	1 +4
	3 +4		
6 −0		0 +7	7 −1
0 +5	3 +2	8 −3	4 +1	0 +8
5 +2		1 +7	6 +2
2 +4	3 +3	8 −0	2 +6	2 +5
	6 +1		7 −2	4 +4

30

Copyright © 1985 by Harcourt Brace Jovanovich, Inc.

Three Addends

Add.

$$\begin{array}{r}3 \\ 2 \\ +5 \\ \hline 10\end{array}\;5\quad$$ 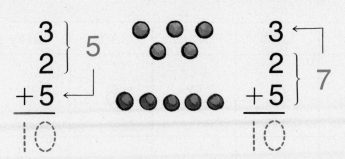 $$\quad\begin{array}{r}3 \\ 2 \\ +5 \\ \hline 10\end{array}\;7$$

You can add up.

You can add down.

a.

$$\begin{array}{r}2\\4\\+3\\\hline 9\end{array}\qquad\begin{array}{r}2\\3\\+3\\\hline\end{array}\qquad\begin{array}{r}6\\2\\+1\\\hline\end{array}\qquad\begin{array}{r}2\\5\\+1\\\hline\end{array}\qquad\begin{array}{r}5\\0\\+5\\\hline\end{array}\qquad\begin{array}{r}1\\3\\+4\\\hline\end{array}\qquad\begin{array}{r}2\\3\\+2\\\hline\end{array}$$

b.

$$\begin{array}{r}2\\5\\+3\\\hline\end{array}\qquad\begin{array}{r}5\\2\\+2\\\hline\end{array}\qquad\begin{array}{r}4\\5\\+1\\\hline\end{array}\qquad\begin{array}{r}3\\3\\+3\\\hline\end{array}\qquad\begin{array}{r}1\\1\\+8\\\hline\end{array}\qquad\begin{array}{r}1\\2\\+3\\\hline\end{array}\qquad\begin{array}{r}2\\3\\+4\\\hline\end{array}$$

c.

$$\begin{array}{r}3\\2\\+3\\\hline\end{array}\qquad\begin{array}{r}4\\2\\+1\\\hline\end{array}\qquad\begin{array}{r}3\\0\\+7\\\hline\end{array}\qquad\begin{array}{r}3\\1\\+5\\\hline\end{array}\qquad\begin{array}{r}3\\3\\+4\\\hline\end{array}\qquad\begin{array}{r}4\\2\\+2\\\hline\end{array}\qquad\begin{array}{r}1\\5\\+4\\\hline\end{array}$$

d.

$$\begin{array}{r}5\\1\\+1\\\hline\end{array}\qquad\begin{array}{r}6\\2\\+2\\\hline\end{array}\qquad\begin{array}{r}4\\1\\+3\\\hline\end{array}\qquad\begin{array}{r}2\\3\\+1\\\hline\end{array}\qquad\begin{array}{r}3\\5\\+1\\\hline\end{array}\qquad\begin{array}{r}2\\4\\+4\\\hline\end{array}\qquad\begin{array}{r}6\\3\\+1\\\hline\end{array}$$

PROBLEM SOLVING

The children count the animals
they see at the zoo.

Complete the table. Write how many in all.

	Diego	Marsha	Glenn	Ling	Rosa	Jack	May
Bears	3	2	3	5	2	5	4
Seals	1	5	3	1	1	2	3
Monkeys	3	1	4	3	3	3	2
In all	7						

Color the chart to show how many.

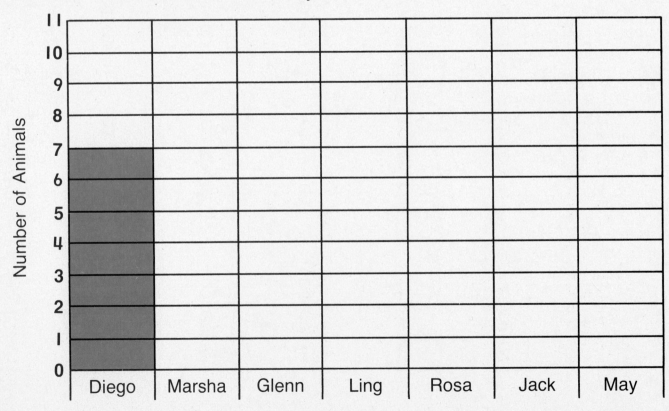

32

Add. (pages 5–12, 31–32)

a.
$$\begin{array}{r} 3 \\ +5 \\ \hline \end{array} \qquad \begin{array}{r} 4 \\ +2 \\ \hline \end{array} \qquad \begin{array}{r} 6 \\ +1 \\ \hline \end{array} \qquad \begin{array}{r} 7 \\ +2 \\ \hline \end{array} \qquad \begin{array}{r} 1 \\ +8 \\ \hline \end{array} \qquad \begin{array}{r} 4 \\ +1 \\ \hline \end{array} \qquad \begin{array}{r} 6 \\ +2 \\ \hline \end{array}$$

b.
$$\begin{array}{r} 3 \\ 2 \\ +1 \\ \hline \end{array} \qquad \begin{array}{r} 4 \\ 2 \\ +4 \\ \hline \end{array} \qquad \begin{array}{r} 3 \\ 1 \\ +5 \\ \hline \end{array} \qquad \begin{array}{r} 2 \\ 4 \\ +1 \\ \hline \end{array} \qquad \begin{array}{r} 3 \\ 4 \\ +3 \\ \hline \end{array} \qquad \begin{array}{r} 5 \\ 0 \\ +3 \\ \hline \end{array} \qquad \begin{array}{r} 3 \\ 5 \\ +1 \\ \hline \end{array}$$

Subtract. (pages 15–22)

c.
$$\begin{array}{r} 10 \\ -6 \\ \hline \end{array} \qquad \begin{array}{r} 9 \\ -9 \\ \hline \end{array} \qquad \begin{array}{r} 6 \\ -4 \\ \hline \end{array} \qquad \begin{array}{r} 7 \\ -3 \\ \hline \end{array} \qquad \begin{array}{r} 10 \\ -5 \\ \hline \end{array} \qquad \begin{array}{r} 9 \\ -2 \\ \hline \end{array} \qquad \begin{array}{r} 8 \\ -4 \\ \hline \end{array}$$

d.
$$\begin{array}{r} 9 \\ -7 \\ \hline \end{array} \qquad \begin{array}{r} 8 \\ -0 \\ \hline \end{array} \qquad \begin{array}{r} 10 \\ -3 \\ \hline \end{array} \qquad \begin{array}{r} 5 \\ -1 \\ \hline \end{array} \qquad \begin{array}{r} 7 \\ -2 \\ \hline \end{array} \qquad \begin{array}{r} 10 \\ -8 \\ \hline \end{array} \qquad \begin{array}{r} 9 \\ -4 \\ \hline \end{array}$$

Solve. (pages 13-14, 23-24)

e.

Robin has 9 .

She gives 2 away.

How many are left?

f.

The boys make 3 .

The girls make 6 .

How many in all?

Score 10

You need:

2 3 4 5 6

Write $+2, +2, +3, +3, +4, +4$ on the .

Write $-0, -1, -2, -3, -4, -4$ on the .

Play this game with a friend.

Turn all face down.

Pick one .

Roll and add the number

to your .

Roll and subtract from your sum.

The answer is your score.

Put your back. Now your friend has

a turn.

Whoever has the highest score gets one point.
The first player to get ten points is the winner.

TEST

Add.

a.
6	4	2	3	1	5	0
+4	+4	+7	+3	+7	+5	+9

b.
3	5	0	2	4	3	0
2	1	6	2	3	3	1
+5	+3	+1	+5	+3	+2	+7

Subtract.

c.
10	8	10	7	9	7	6
− 9	−4	− 7	−5	−2	−3	−2

d.
9	10	6	8	7	9	10
−5	− 4	−5	−8	−0	−1	− 5

Solve.

e. Cindy has 4 🐚.
She finds 6 more.
How many in all?

f. Pedro has 8 🏆.
He breaks 2.
How many are left?

name

ENRICHMENT

Missing Numbers

Find the missing numbers.

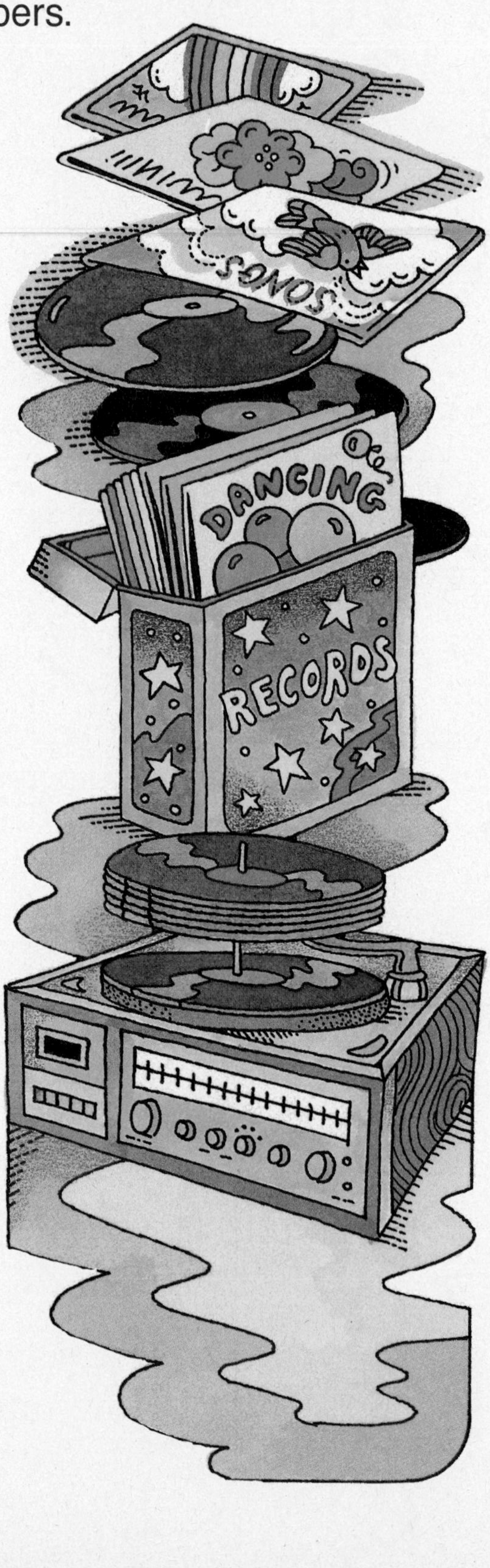

(4) + 3 = 7

7 + ◯ = 9

4 + ◯ = 10

◯ + 0 = 5

3 + 3 = ◯

◯ + 2 = 7

2 + ◯ = 8

◯ + 6 = 9

8 + 2 = ◯

◯ + 1 = 8

4 + ◯ = 6

◯ + 2 = 5

8 − (6) = 2

10 − ◯ = 7

◯ − 5 = 4

◯ − 6 = 1

6 − 0 = ◯

8 − ◯ = 5

◯ − 4 = 1

10 − ◯ = 1

8 − 4 = ◯

◯ − 1 = 8

7 − ◯ = 0

◯ − 5 = 1

Place Value to 100

GETTING STARTED

Color 10.

a.

b.

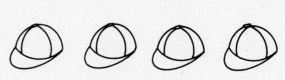

c.

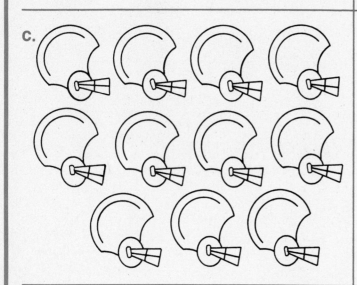

d.

e.

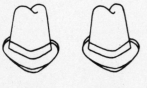

f.

Numbers 10 to 19

10 ones make 1 ten.

Write the numbers.

a.

ten _____ 10

b.

eleven _____

c.

twelve _____

d.

thirteen _____

e.

fourteen _____

f.

fifteen _____

g.

sixteen _____

h.

seventeen _____

i.

eighteen _____

j.

nineteen _____

Write the numbers.

a.

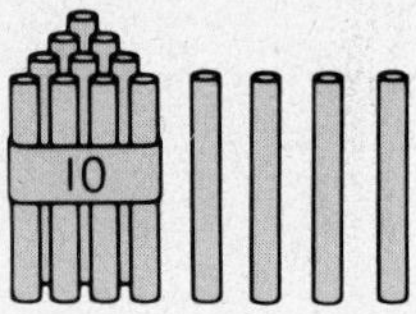

14

b.

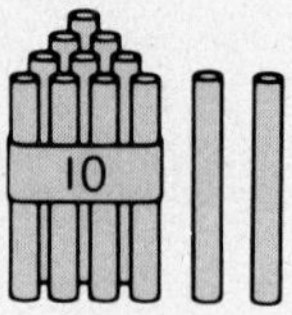

_____

c.

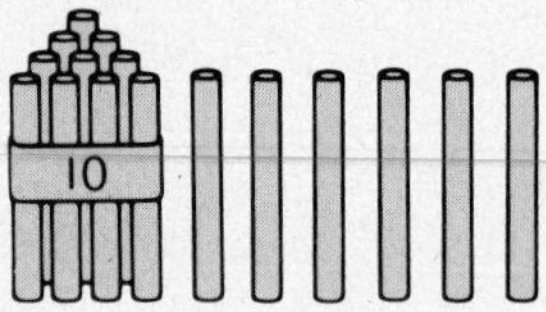

_____

d.

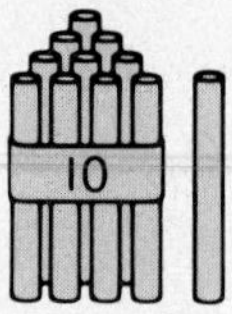

_____

e.

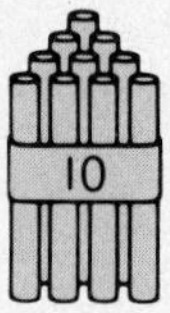

_____

f.

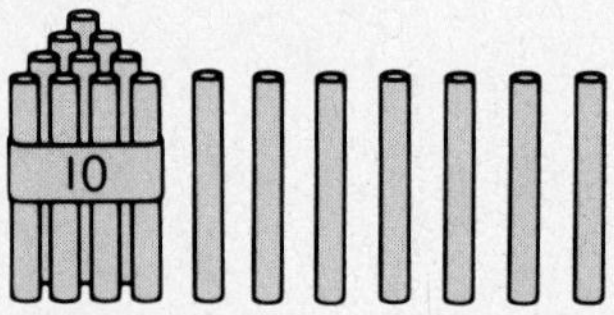

_____

g.

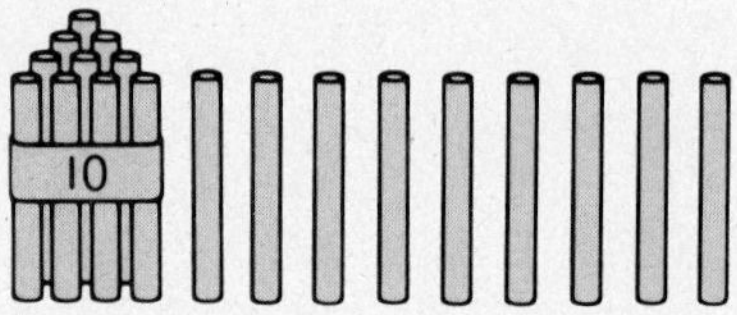

_____

h.

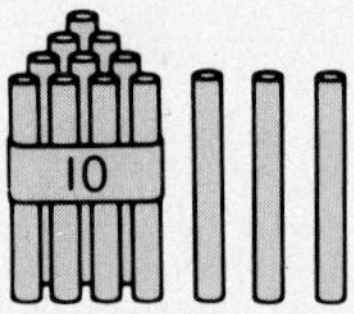

_____

i.

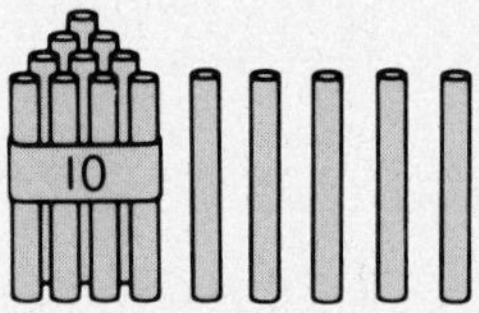

_____

j.

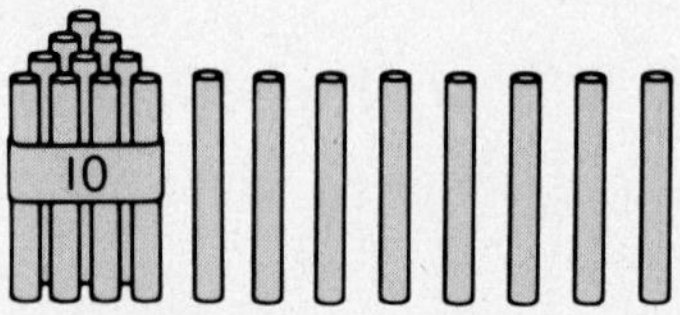

_____

k.

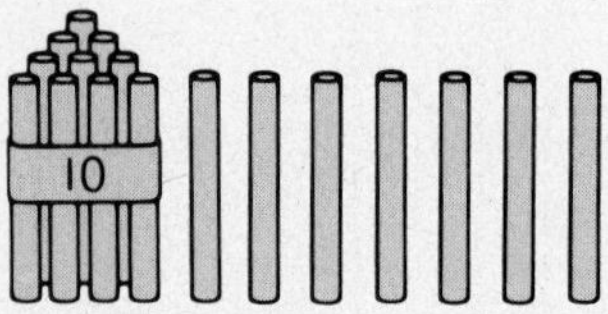

_____

l.

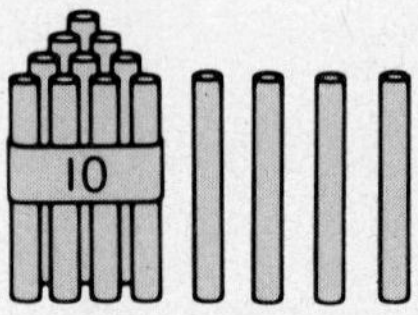

_____

Tens

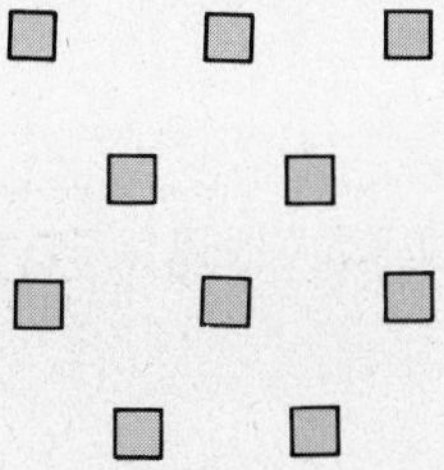

10 ones   make 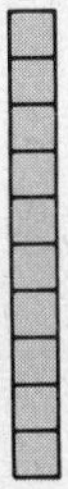   1 ten.

Write how many tens.
Write the numbers.

a.

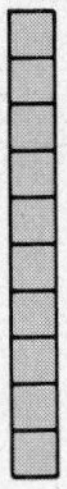

_____1_____ ten

_____10_____

b.

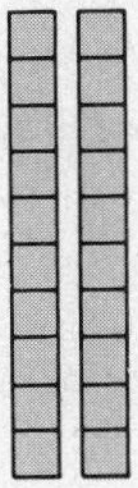

_____ tens

_____

c.

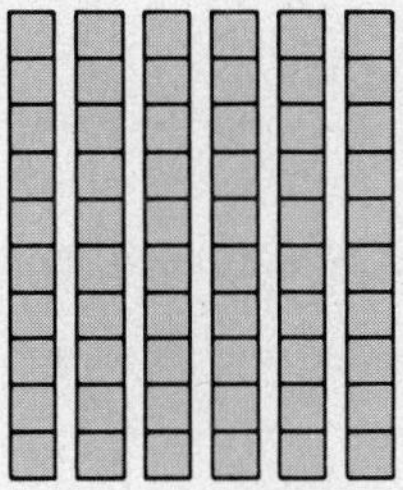

_____ tens

_____

d.

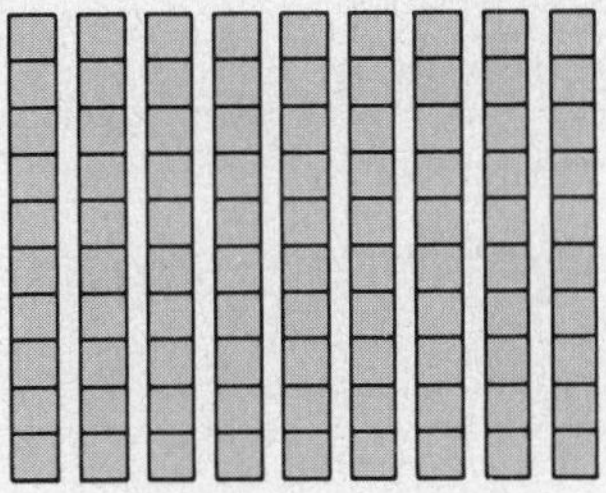

_____ tens

_____

e.

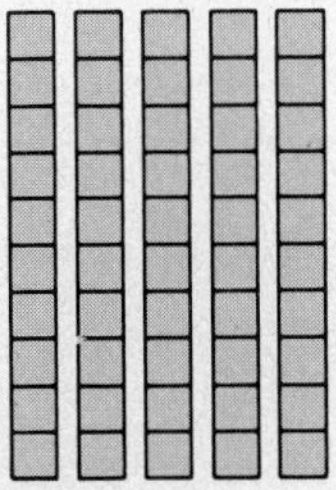

_____ tens

_____

f.

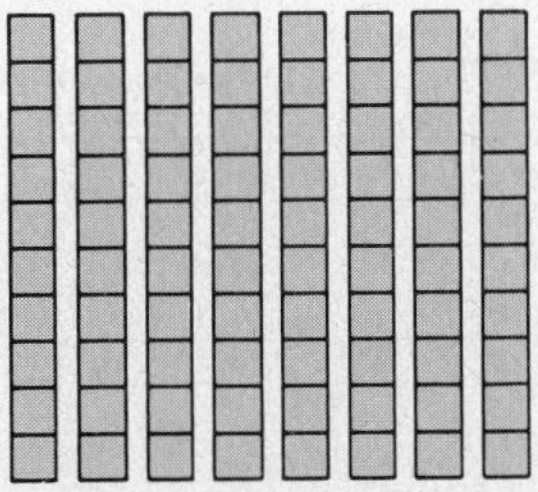

_____ tens

_____

g.

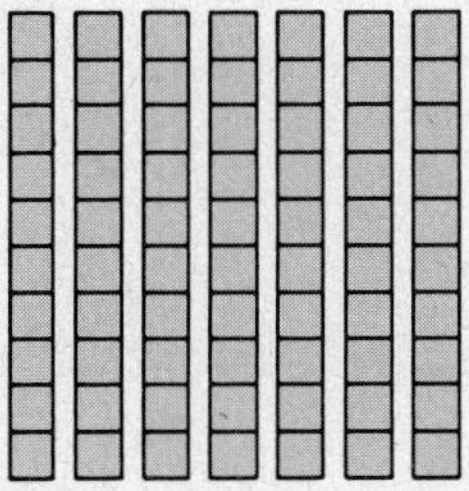

_____ tens

_____

h.

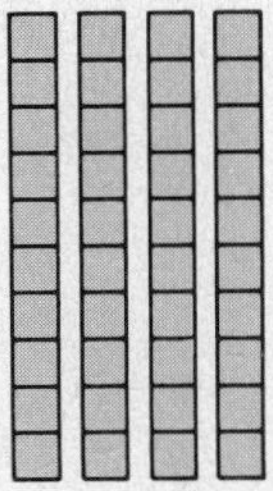

_____ tens

_____

Write the numbers.

a. _30_

b. _____

c. _____

d. _____

e. _____

f. _____

g. _____

h. _____

Connect the dots in order.

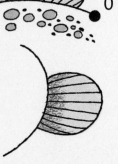

90   0

80   20

70   10

60   30

50   40

42

Tens and Ones

Write how many tens and ones.

Write the numbers.

a.

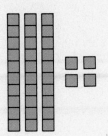

tens	ones
3	4

34

b.

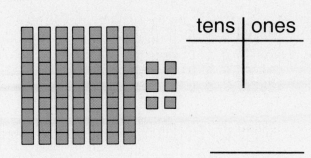

tens	ones

_____

c.

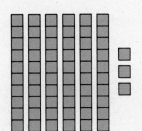

tens	ones

_____

d.

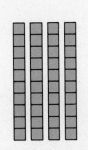

tens	ones

_____

e.

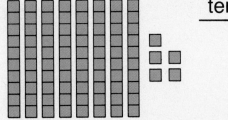

tens	ones

_____

f.

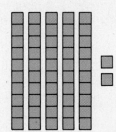

tens	ones

_____

g.

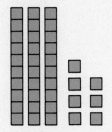

tens	ones

_____

h.

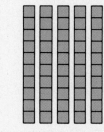

tens	ones

_____

Match each picture to the correct number.

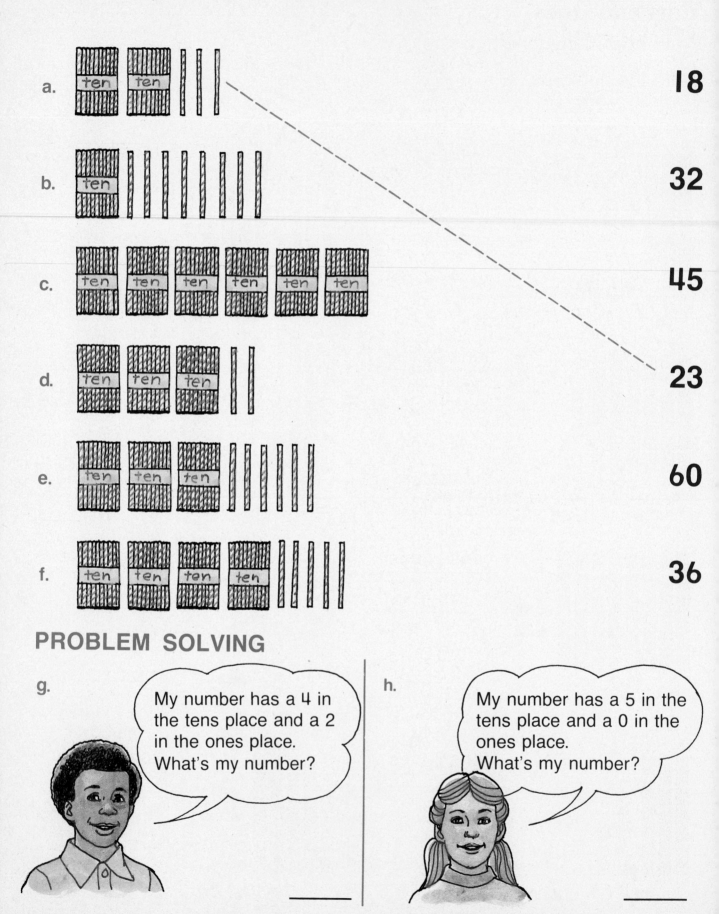

a.   18

b.   32

c.   45

d.   23

e.   60

f.   36

PROBLEM SOLVING

g.

My number has a 4 in the tens place and a 2 in the ones place. What's my number?

_____

h.

My number has a 5 in the tens place and a 0 in the ones place. What's my number?

_____

More About Tens and Ones

Write the numbers.

a.

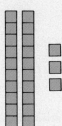

23

b.

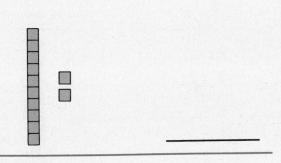

_____

c.

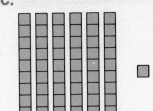

_____

d.

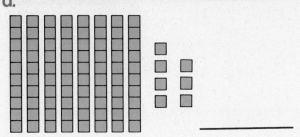

_____

e.

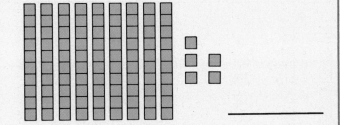

_____

f.

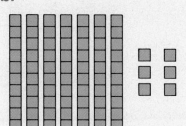

_____

g.

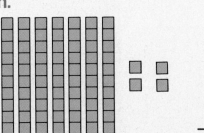

_____

h.

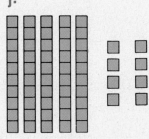

_____

i.

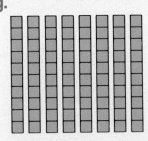

_____

j.

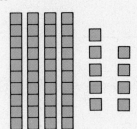

_____

45

Write the numbers.

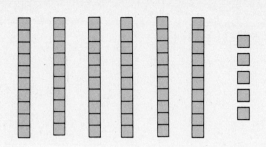

6 tens   5 ones = <u>65</u>

a. 9 tens   2 ones = _____   8 tens   8 ones = _____

b. 6 tens   4 ones = _____   3 tens   6 ones = _____

c. 8 tens   0 ones = _____   2 tens   3 ones = _____

d. 1 ten   7 ones = _____   7 tens   9 ones = _____

e. 3 tens   5 ones = _____   2 tens   1 one   = _____

Complete.

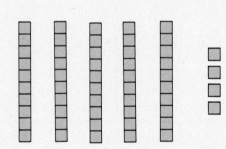

54 = <u>5</u> tens <u>4</u> ones

f. 19 = _____ ten _____ ones   95 = _____ tens _____ ones

g. 76 = _____ tens _____ ones   30 = _____ tens _____ ones

h. 32 = _____ tens _____ ones   67 = _____ tens _____ ones

i. 85 = _____ tens _____ ones   24 = _____ tens _____ ones

j. 50 = _____ tens _____ ones   41 = _____ tens _____ one

46

Order to 100   Complete the chart.

		3						9	
11									20
		24							
				36					
					48				
			55						
								70	
					77				
	82								
								100	

10 tens is 100.

Write the missing numbers.

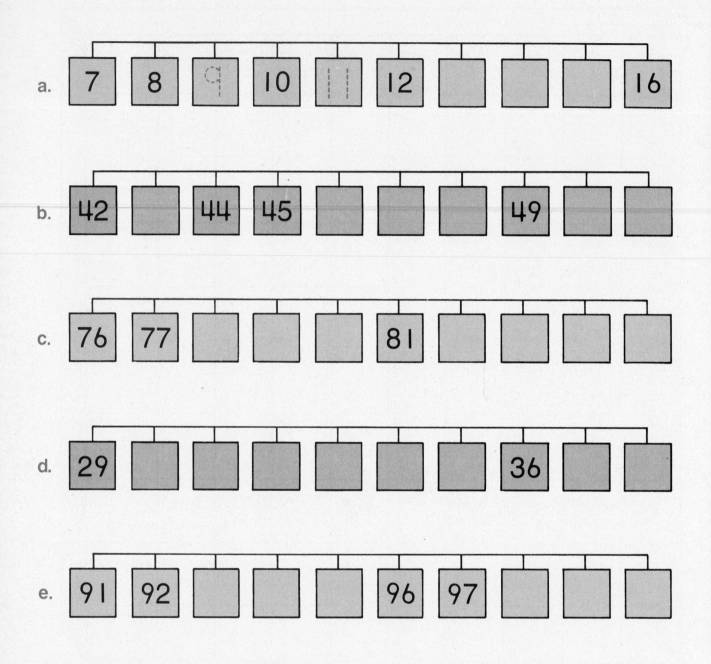

a. | 7 | 8 | 9 | 10 | 11 | 12 | | | | 16 |

b. | 42 | | 44 | 45 | | | | 49 | | |

c. | 76 | 77 | | | 81 | | | | |

d. | 29 | | | | | | | 36 | |

e. | 91 | 92 | | | | 96 | 97 | | |

Midchapter Review

Write the numbers.

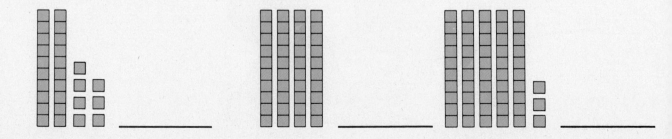

_____   _____   _____

Counting Patterns
Complete the chart.

1	2	3	4	5	6	7	8	9	10
11	12	13	14		16	17	18	19	
21	22	23	24		26	27	28	29	
31	32	33	34		36	37	38	39	
41	42	43	44		46	47	48	49	
51	52	53	54		56	57	58	59	
61	62	63	64		66	67	68	69	
71	72	73	74		76	77	78	79	
81	82	83	84		86	87	88	89	
91	92	93	94		96	97	98	99	

Count by fives.

_____, _____, 15, _____, _____, _____, _____,

40, _____, _____, _____, _____, 65, _____

Count by tens.

30, _____, _____, _____, 70, _____, _____

49

Complete the chart.

1	2	3	4	5		7		9	
11		13		15		17		19	
21		23		25		27		29	
31		33		35		37		39	
41		43		45		47		49	

Count by twos.
Connect the dots.

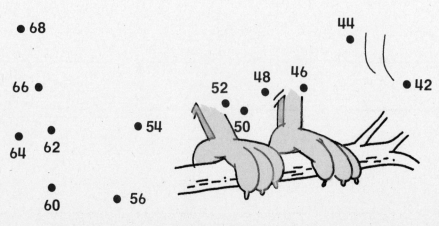

name

PROBLEM SOLVING

Choosing the Operation

Write + or −.

a.

How many  in all?

5 ⊕ 2 = 7

b.

How many  are left?

6 ◯ 1 = 5

c.

How many  are left?

8 ◯ 2 = 6

d.

How many  in all?

3 ◯ 6 = 9

e.

How many  in all?

4 ◯ 6 = 10

f.

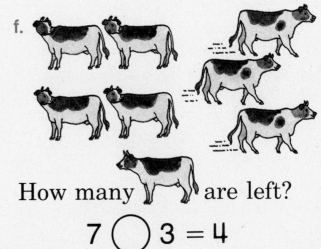

How many are left?

7 ◯ 3 = 4

a.

$$3 \oplus 5 = 8 \qquad 7 \ominus 3 = 4$$

Write + or −.

b. $1 \oplus 5 = 6$ $8 \bigcirc 1 = 7$ $3 \bigcirc 3 = 6$

c. $2 \bigcirc 6 = 8$ $5 \bigcirc 2 = 7$ $1 \bigcirc 7 = 8$

d. $8 \bigcirc 7 = 1$ $2 \bigcirc 3 = 5$ $8 \bigcirc 2 = 6$

e. $6 \bigcirc 1 = 5$ $7 \bigcirc 5 = 2$ $3 \bigcirc 4 = 7$

f. $4 \bigcirc 2 = 2$ $8 \bigcirc 8 = 0$ $7 \bigcirc 2 = 5$

g. $5 \bigcirc 3 = 8$ $4 \bigcirc 4 = 8$ $6 \bigcirc 2 = 8$

h. $1 \bigcirc 3 = 4$ $1 \bigcirc 6 = 7$ $5 \bigcirc 1 = 4$

i. $2 \bigcirc 7 = 9$ $7 \bigcirc 4 = 3$ $8 \bigcirc 2 = 10$

j. $9 \bigcirc 6 = 3$ $4 \bigcirc 6 = 10$ $9 \bigcirc 5 = 4$

k. $7 \bigcirc 7 = 0$ $1 \bigcirc 8 = 9$ $3 \bigcirc 7 = 10$

name

Greater Than and Less Than

Ring the number that is greater.

a. 12 ▭ ▫   36 ▭ ▫

(15) ▭ ▫   28 ▭ ▫

b.

14	29	20	44	57	23	12	4
11	38	22	41	49	25	10	9

c.

56	84	73	95	58	59	63	60
64	87	70	89	61	55	77	50

Ring the number that is less.

d. (13) ▭ ▫   31 ▭ ▫

17 ▭ ▫   24 ▭ ▫

e.

6	13	27	65	48	39	66	34
8	15	24	54	46	40	68	35

f.

30	9	42	72	98	64	53	76
32	7	47	74	99	67	52	80

Write the number that is 1 more.

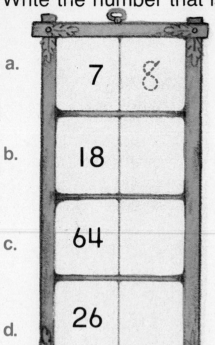
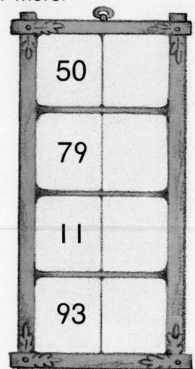
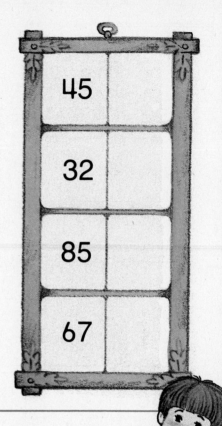

a.	7 8	50	45
b.	18	79	32
c.	64	11	85
d.	26	93	67

Write the number that is 1 less.

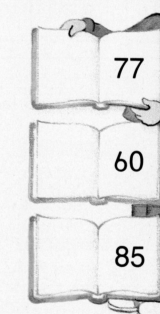

e.	13 14	68	77
f.	29	31	60
g.	40	53	85

Skills Maintenance

Add.

$$\begin{array}{r} 2 \\ +7 \\ \hline \end{array} \qquad \begin{array}{r} 5 \\ +5 \\ \hline \end{array} \qquad \begin{array}{r} 3 \\ +5 \\ \hline \end{array} \qquad \begin{array}{r} 4 \\ +6 \\ \hline \end{array} \qquad \begin{array}{r} 6 \\ +1 \\ \hline \end{array} \qquad \begin{array}{r} 0 \\ +9 \\ \hline \end{array} \qquad \begin{array}{r} 2 \\ +6 \\ \hline \end{array}$$

54

Comparing Numbers

6 is **greater** than **3** .

6 > 3

3 is **less** than **6** .

3 < 6

Write the numbers.
Write > or < .

a.

6 ⊘> 5
___   ___

b.

___ ◯ ___

c.

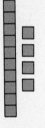
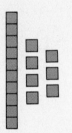

___ ◯ ___

d.

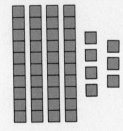
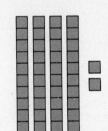

___ ◯ ___

e.

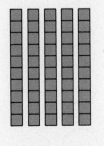
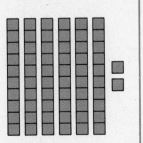

___ ◯ ___

f.

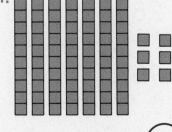
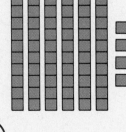

___ ◯ ___

Write > or <.

a.

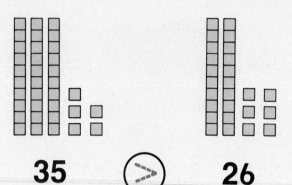

35 (**>**) **26**

is greater than

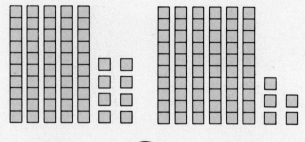

58 (**<**) **65**

is less than

b. 18 (>) 15	13 ◯ 19	22 ◯ 17
c. 47 ◯ 53	36 ◯ 32	52 ◯ 43
d. 61 ◯ 57	59 ◯ 62	40 ◯ 42
e. 80 ◯ 66	73 ◯ 78	67 ◯ 55
f. 76 ◯ 82	60 ◯ 90	92 ◯ 96
g. 70 ◯ 56	83 ◯ 77	75 ◯ 76
h. 44 ◯ 49	87 ◯ 72	97 ◯ 99
i. 38 ◯ 28	75 ◯ 80	46 ◯ 48
j. 92 ◯ 95	64 ◯ 54	27 ◯ 26
k. 84 ◯ 91	59 ◯ 77	99 ◯ 89

Ordinals

first second third fourth fifth sixth seventh eighth ninth tenth

Ring the correct position for each.

a. second   third   (fourth)   fifth

b. seventh   eighth   ninth   tenth

c. first   second   fourth   sixth

d. seventh   eighth   ninth   tenth

e. fourth   fifth   sixth   seventh

f. third   fifth   seventh   ninth

g. sixth   seventh   eighth   ninth

Color the correct objects.

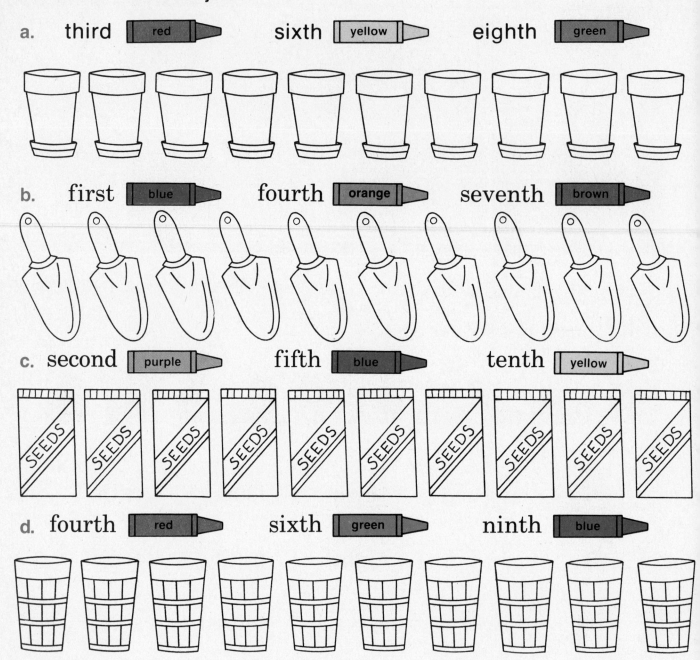

a. third [red]   sixth [yellow]   eighth [green]

b. first [blue]   fourth [orange]   seventh [brown]

c. second [purple]   fifth [blue]   tenth [yellow]

d. fourth [red]   sixth [green]   ninth [blue]

PROBLEM SOLVING

Write 1, 2, and 3 to show what happened first, second, and third.

e.

_____   _____   _____

Write how many tens and ones. (pages 41-46)
Write the numbers.

a.

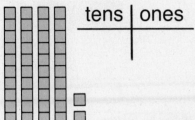 | tens | ones

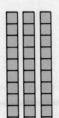 | tens | ones

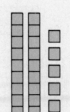 | tens | ones

_____ _____ _____

(pages 49-50)

b. Count by fives. 20 25 ◯ ◯ ◯ 45

c. Count by twos. 16 18 ◯ 22 ◯ ◯

Write + or −. (pages 51-52)

d. $2 \bigcirc 6 = 8$ $\qquad 7 \bigcirc 3 = 4$ $\qquad 5 \bigcirc 1 = 6$

Write > or <. (pages 55-56)

e. $12 \bigcirc 9$ $\qquad 47 \bigcirc 74$ $\qquad 86 \bigcirc 79$

Ring the correct position for each. (pages 57-58)

f. first second third fourth

g. fifth sixth seventh eighth

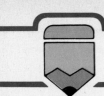

PROJECT

Secret Numbers

You need:

a red crayon  a green crayon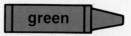

Each secret number will have two rings.
Find each secret number and write it in the box.

Ring with [red] if inside
the △ .

Ring with [green] if less
than **70** .

71   50

78

62   81

Ring with [red] if outside
the ○ .

Ring with [green] if greater
than 35 .

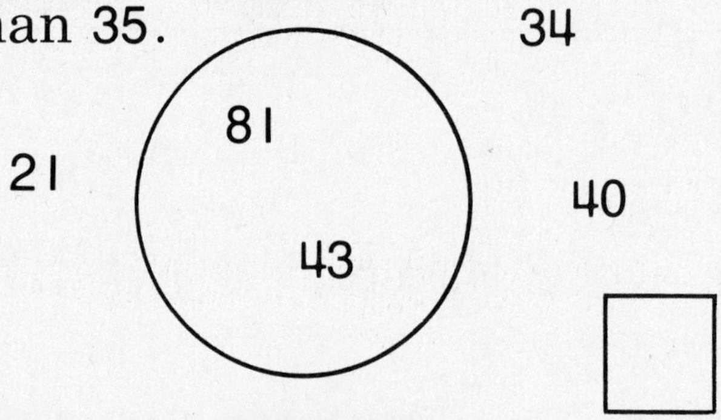

34

81

21

43

40

Ring with [red] if you say
it when you count by twos.

Ring with [green] if **3** is in
the tens place.

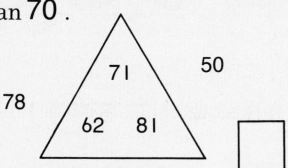

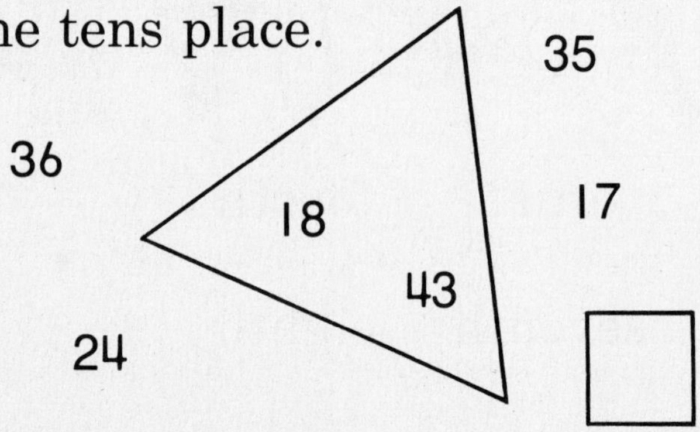

36   35

18   17

43

24

Ring with [red] if you say
it when you count by fives.

Ring with [green] if **2** is in
the tens place.

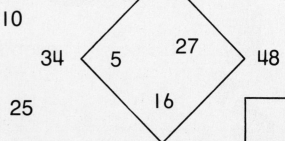

35

10

34   5   27   48

25   16

Write the numbers.

a.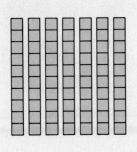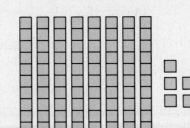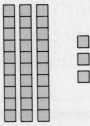

_____   _____   _____

b. Count by fives.

c. Count by twos.

| 55 | 60 | | | | | |

| 42 | 44 | | | | 52 | |

Write + or −.

d. $8 \bigcirc 3 = 5$ $4 \bigcirc 2 = 6$ $7 \bigcirc 2 = 5$

Write > or <.

e. $18 \bigcirc 13$ $54 \bigcirc 64$ $42 \bigcirc 45$

Ring the correct position for each.

f.   first   second   third   fourth

g.   seventh   eighth   ninth   tenth

ENRICHMENT

Solve the Riddle

Write each letter inside
the correct box
to solve the riddle.

W is 16
16 is between 10 and 20.
Write the letter
inside the box [W]
10   20

What runs but cannot walk?

	W					
0	10	20	30	40	50	60	70

$$W = 16 \quad R = 54 \quad T = 31 \quad A = 22 \quad E = 48$$

The more you take away from it, the bigger
it gets. What is it?

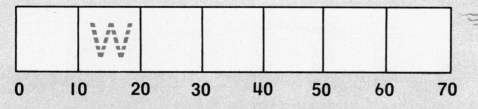

0	10	20	30	40	50	60	70

$$H = 25 \quad L = 43 \quad E = 51 \quad A = 2 \quad O = 39$$

What has ears but cannot hear?

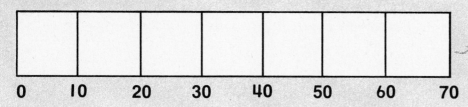

0	10	20	30	40	50	60	70	80	90	100	110

$$F = 67 \quad L = 93 \quad C = 21 \quad A = 4 \quad E = 86$$

$$D = 105 \quad O = 33 \quad I = 75 \quad R = 48 \quad N = 52$$

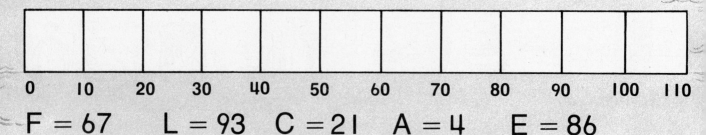

Choose the correct answers.

1.

$2 + 4 =$ _____

- (A) 2
- **(B) 6**
- (C) 5
- (D) not here

2.

$\begin{array}{r} 6 \\ +4 \\ \hline \end{array}$

- (A) 10
- (B) 9
- (C) 2
- (D) not here

3.

$\begin{array}{r} 6 \\ +1 \\ \hline \end{array}$

- (A) 3
- (B) 5
- (C) 8
- (D) not here

4.

$5 + 3 =$ _____

- (A) 7
- (B) 10
- (C) 8
- (D) not here

5.

$\begin{array}{r} 7 \\ +2 \\ \hline \end{array}$

- (A) 10
- (B) 8
- (C) 9
- (D) not here

6.

$\begin{array}{r} 3 \\ 5 \\ +2 \\ \hline \end{array}$

- (A) 8
- (B) 10
- (C) 7
- (D) not here

7.

$8 - 6 =$ _____

- (A) 4
- (B) 1
- (C) 3
- (D) not here

8.

$\begin{array}{r} 9 \\ -1 \\ \hline \end{array}$

- (A) 9
- (B) 7
- (C) 8
- (D) not here

9.

$\begin{array}{r} 10 \\ -5 \\ \hline \end{array}$

- (A) 4
- (B) 5
- (C) 6
- (D) not here

10.

$7 - 4 =$ _____

- (A) 3
- (B) 4
- (C) 2
- (D) not here

11.

$\begin{array}{r} 10 \\ -8 \\ \hline \end{array}$

- (A) 1
- (B) 0
- (C) 4
- (D) not here

12.

$\begin{array}{r} 7 \\ -0 \\ \hline \end{array}$

- (A) 7
- (B) 0
- (C) 3
- (D) not here

Choose the correct answers.

13.

The girls counted

7 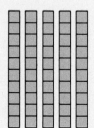 .

4 flew away.

How many are left?

(A) 2
(B) 3
(C) 4
(D) not here

14.

4 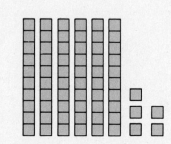 are inside.

5 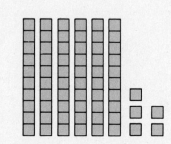 are outside.

How many in all?

(A) 8
(B) 10
(C) 9
(D) not here

15.

(A) 50
(B) 40
(C) 60
(D) not here

16.

(A) 56
(B) 65
(C) 75
(D) not here

17.

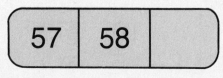

(A) 59
(B) 56
(C) 57
(D) not here

18.

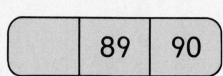

(A) 85
(B) 87
(C) 88
(D) not here

19.

Count by tens.

60, 70, 80, _____

(A) 80
(B) 85
(C) 95
(D) not here

20.

Count by fives.

40, 45, 50, _____

(A) 45
(B) 50
(C) 55
(D) not here

64

Addition and Subtraction Facts to 14

CHAPTER 3

GETTING STARTED

Add.

a.
$$\begin{array}{r} 4 \\ +5 \\ \hline 9 \end{array}$$
$$\begin{array}{r} 5 \\ +3 \\ \hline \end{array}$$
$$\begin{array}{r} 6 \\ +4 \\ \hline \end{array}$$
$$\begin{array}{r} 5 \\ +2 \\ \hline \end{array}$$
$$\begin{array}{r} 3 \\ +7 \\ \hline \end{array}$$
$$\begin{array}{r} 2 \\ +6 \\ \hline \end{array}$$
$$\begin{array}{r} 6 \\ +1 \\ \hline \end{array}$$

b.
$$\begin{array}{r} 8 \\ +2 \\ \hline \end{array}$$
$$\begin{array}{r} 2 \\ +4 \\ \hline \end{array}$$
$$\begin{array}{r} 8 \\ +0 \\ \hline \end{array}$$
$$\begin{array}{r} 5 \\ +5 \\ \hline \end{array}$$
$$\begin{array}{r} 3 \\ +4 \\ \hline \end{array}$$
$$\begin{array}{r} 1 \\ +8 \\ \hline \end{array}$$
$$\begin{array}{r} 7 \\ +2 \\ \hline \end{array}$$

c.
$$\begin{array}{r} 1 \\ +9 \\ \hline \end{array}$$
$$\begin{array}{r} 3 \\ +6 \\ \hline \end{array}$$
$$\begin{array}{r} 7 \\ +1 \\ \hline \end{array}$$
$$\begin{array}{r} 4 \\ +4 \\ \hline \end{array}$$
$$\begin{array}{r} 9 \\ +0 \\ \hline \end{array}$$
$$\begin{array}{r} 5 \\ +1 \\ \hline \end{array}$$
$$\begin{array}{r} 5 \\ +4 \\ \hline \end{array}$$

Subtract.

d.
$$\begin{array}{r} 10 \\ -7 \\ \hline 3 \end{array}$$
$$\begin{array}{r} 9 \\ -8 \\ \hline \end{array}$$
$$\begin{array}{r} 7 \\ -5 \\ \hline \end{array}$$
$$\begin{array}{r} 8 \\ -2 \\ \hline \end{array}$$
$$\begin{array}{r} 10 \\ -5 \\ \hline \end{array}$$
$$\begin{array}{r} 8 \\ -7 \\ \hline \end{array}$$
$$\begin{array}{r} 9 \\ -4 \\ \hline \end{array}$$

e.
$$\begin{array}{r} 7 \\ -7 \\ \hline \end{array}$$
$$\begin{array}{r} 10 \\ -1 \\ \hline \end{array}$$
$$\begin{array}{r} 9 \\ -2 \\ \hline \end{array}$$
$$\begin{array}{r} 8 \\ -5 \\ \hline \end{array}$$
$$\begin{array}{r} 9 \\ -6 \\ \hline \end{array}$$
$$\begin{array}{r} 7 \\ -2 \\ \hline \end{array}$$
$$\begin{array}{r} 10 \\ -8 \\ \hline \end{array}$$

f.
$$\begin{array}{r} 10 \\ -6 \\ \hline \end{array}$$
$$\begin{array}{r} 8 \\ -0 \\ \hline \end{array}$$
$$\begin{array}{r} 9 \\ -9 \\ \hline \end{array}$$
$$\begin{array}{r} 10 \\ -9 \\ \hline \end{array}$$
$$\begin{array}{r} 8 \\ -4 \\ \hline \end{array}$$
$$\begin{array}{r} 9 \\ -3 \\ \hline \end{array}$$
$$\begin{array}{r} 7 \\ -4 \\ \hline \end{array}$$

Sums to 12

Add.

a.

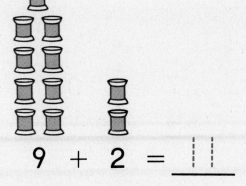

$9 + 2 = \underline{11}$ $8 + 3 = \underline{}$

b.

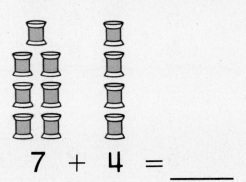

$7 + 4 = \underline{}$ $9 + 3 = \underline{}$

c.

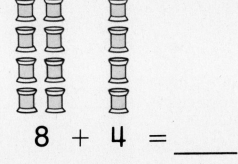

$8 + 4 = \underline{}$ $7 + 5 = \underline{}$

d. $5 + 6 = \underline{}$ $6 + 6 = \underline{}$ $2 + 9 = \underline{}$

e. $4 + 8 = \underline{}$ $5 + 7 = \underline{}$ $6 + 5 = \underline{}$

f. $3 + 8 = \underline{}$ $6 + 4 = \underline{}$ $3 + 9 = \underline{}$

g. $4 + 7 = \underline{}$ $3 + 7 = \underline{}$ $6 + 6 = \underline{}$

Add.

a.
$$\begin{array}{r} 2 \\ +9 \\ \hline \end{array}$$
11

$$\begin{array}{r} 5 \\ +7 \\ \hline \end{array}$$

$$\begin{array}{r} 8 \\ +3 \\ \hline \end{array}$$

$$\begin{array}{r} 4 \\ +6 \\ \hline \end{array}$$

$$\begin{array}{r} 6 \\ +3 \\ \hline \end{array}$$

$$\begin{array}{r} 4 \\ +7 \\ \hline \end{array}$$

$$\begin{array}{r} 6 \\ +2 \\ \hline \end{array}$$

b.
$$\begin{array}{r} 2 \\ +8 \\ \hline \end{array}$$

$$\begin{array}{r} 6 \\ +5 \\ \hline \end{array}$$

$$\begin{array}{r} 3 \\ +9 \\ \hline \end{array}$$

$$\begin{array}{r} 6 \\ +6 \\ \hline \end{array}$$

$$\begin{array}{r} 7 \\ +4 \\ \hline \end{array}$$

$$\begin{array}{r} 0 \\ +9 \\ \hline \end{array}$$

$$\begin{array}{r} 8 \\ +1 \\ \hline \end{array}$$

c.
$$\begin{array}{r} 7 \\ +3 \\ \hline \end{array}$$

$$\begin{array}{r} 2 \\ +9 \\ \hline \end{array}$$

$$\begin{array}{r} 7 \\ +5 \\ \hline \end{array}$$

$$\begin{array}{r} 4 \\ +8 \\ \hline \end{array}$$

$$\begin{array}{r} 5 \\ +6 \\ \hline \end{array}$$

$$\begin{array}{r} 6 \\ +4 \\ \hline \end{array}$$

$$\begin{array}{r} 9 \\ +1 \\ \hline \end{array}$$

d.
$$\begin{array}{r} 8 \\ +4 \\ \hline \end{array}$$

$$\begin{array}{r} 3 \\ +8 \\ \hline \end{array}$$

$$\begin{array}{r} 8 \\ +2 \\ \hline \end{array}$$

$$\begin{array}{r} 9 \\ +3 \\ \hline \end{array}$$

$$\begin{array}{r} 5 \\ +5 \\ \hline \end{array}$$

$$\begin{array}{r} 9 \\ +2 \\ \hline \end{array}$$

$$\begin{array}{r} 5 \\ +7 \\ \hline \end{array}$$

e.
$$\begin{array}{r} 6 \\ +6 \\ \hline \end{array}$$

$$\begin{array}{r} 1 \\ +7 \\ \hline \end{array}$$

$$\begin{array}{r} 3 \\ +7 \\ \hline \end{array}$$

$$\begin{array}{r} 4 \\ +5 \\ \hline \end{array}$$

$$\begin{array}{r} 3 \\ +5 \\ \hline \end{array}$$

$$\begin{array}{r} 3 \\ +9 \\ \hline \end{array}$$

$$\begin{array}{r} 4 \\ +7 \\ \hline \end{array}$$

PROBLEM SOLVING

Solve.

f.
5 small

7 large

How many in all?

g.
8 red

3 blue

How many in all?

Subtracting from 11 and 12

Subtract.

a.

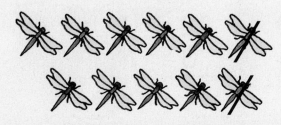 

$11 - 2 = \underline{9}$ $11 - 3 = \underline{}$

b.

$11 - 4 = \underline{}$ $12 - 3 = \underline{}$

c.

 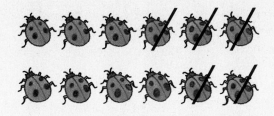

$12 - 4 = \underline{}$ $12 - 5 = \underline{}$

d. $11 - 5 = \underline{}$ $11 - 6 = \underline{}$ $11 - 7 = \underline{}$

e. $12 - 6 = \underline{}$ $12 - 7 = \underline{5}$ $11 - 8 = \underline{}$

f. $11 - 9 = \underline{}$ $12 - 9 = \underline{}$ $11 - 2 = \underline{}$

g. $12 - 3 = \underline{}$ $11 - 4 = \underline{}$ $12 - 5 = \underline{}$

Subtract.

a.
$$12 - 7 = 5$$ $$11 - 5$$ $$11 - 9$$ $$10 - 3$$ $$12 - 3$$

b.
$$10 - 2$$ $$11 - 8$$ $$12 - 9$$ $$9 - 5$$ $$11 - 2$$ $$9 - 7$$ $$12 - 6$$

c.
$$11 - 6$$ $$10 - 4$$ $$12 - 8$$ $$11 - 7$$ $$9 - 1$$ $$10 - 2$$ $$11 - 5$$

d.
$$12 - 4$$ $$9 - 0$$ $$12 - 5$$ $$11 - 6$$ $$12 - 3$$ $$12 - 7$$ $$11 - 3$$

e.
$$11 - 4$$ $$10 - 7$$ $$9 - 3$$ $$12 - 8$$ $$10 - 6$$ $$9 - 4$$ $$12 - 9$$

PROBLEM SOLVING

f. Alma has 11 ⚾ .
4 roll away.
How many are left?

g. Leon has 12 🎈 .
4 break .
How many are left?

Sums to 14

Add.

a.

$9 + 4 = \underline{13}$

$8 + 5 = \underline{}$

b.

$7 + 6 = \underline{}$

$9 + 5 = \underline{}$

c.

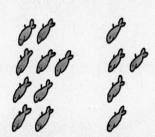

$8 + 6 = \underline{}$

$7 + 7 = \underline{}$

d. $5 + 8 = \underline{}$ $8 + 6 = \underline{}$ $7 + 4 = \underline{}$

e. $7 + 5 = \underline{}$ $7 + 6 = \underline{}$ $5 + 7 = \underline{}$

f. $9 + 5 = \underline{}$ $4 + 9 = \underline{}$ $7 + 7 = \underline{}$

g. $6 + 7 = \underline{}$ $5 + 9 = \underline{}$ $6 + 8 = \underline{}$

$$\begin{array}{r} 9 \\ +5 \\ \hline 14 \end{array}$$
$$\begin{array}{r} 7 \\ +3 \\ \hline \end{array}$$
$$\begin{array}{r} 3 \\ +9 \\ \hline \end{array}$$
$$\begin{array}{r} 5 \\ +2 \\ \hline \end{array}$$
$$\begin{array}{r} 4 \\ +7 \\ \hline \end{array}$$
$$\begin{array}{r} 0 \\ +5 \\ \hline \end{array}$$
$$\begin{array}{r} 7 \\ +6 \\ \hline \end{array}$$
$$\begin{array}{r} 4 \\ +5 \\ \hline \end{array}$$

Add.

Color 11 [yellow].
Color 12 [orange].
Color 13 [green].
Color 14 [red].

$$\begin{array}{r} 4 \\ +9 \\ \hline \end{array}$$
$$\begin{array}{r} 6 \\ +8 \\ \hline \end{array}$$
$$\begin{array}{r} 8 \\ +1 \\ \hline \end{array}$$
$$\begin{array}{r} 6 \\ +5 \\ \hline \end{array}$$
$$\begin{array}{r} 7 \\ +2 \\ \hline \end{array}$$
$$\begin{array}{r} 7 \\ +7 \\ \hline \end{array}$$
$$\begin{array}{r} 2 \\ +4 \\ \hline \end{array}$$
$$\begin{array}{r} 8 \\ +3 \\ \hline \end{array}$$

$$\begin{array}{r} 9 \\ +4 \\ \hline \end{array}$$
$$\begin{array}{r} 4 \\ +6 \\ \hline \end{array}$$
$$\begin{array}{r} 8 \\ +6 \\ \hline \end{array}$$
$$\begin{array}{r} 3 \\ +4 \\ \hline \end{array}$$
$$\begin{array}{r} 8 \\ +4 \\ \hline \end{array}$$
$$\begin{array}{r} 6 \\ +3 \\ \hline \end{array}$$
$$\begin{array}{r} 8 \\ +6 \\ \hline \end{array}$$
$$\begin{array}{r} 9 \\ +2 \\ \hline \end{array}$$

Midchapter Review

Add or subtract.

$$\begin{array}{r} 4 \\ +7 \\ \hline \end{array}$$
$$\begin{array}{r} 6 \\ +6 \\ \hline \end{array}$$
$$\begin{array}{r} 12 \\ -5 \\ \hline \end{array}$$
$$\begin{array}{r} 9 \\ +4 \\ \hline \end{array}$$
$$\begin{array}{r} 11 \\ -2 \\ \hline \end{array}$$
$$\begin{array}{r} 12 \\ -8 \\ \hline \end{array}$$
$$\begin{array}{r} 5 \\ +9 \\ \hline \end{array}$$

Subtracting from 13 and 14

Subtract.

a.

$$\begin{array}{r} 13 \\ -\ 4 \\ \hline 9 \end{array}$$

$$\begin{array}{r} 13 \\ -\ 5 \\ \hline \end{array}$$

$$\begin{array}{r} 13 \\ -\ 6 \\ \hline \end{array}$$

b.

$$\begin{array}{r} 14 \\ -\ 5 \\ \hline \end{array}$$

$$\begin{array}{r} 14 \\ -\ 6 \\ \hline \end{array}$$

$$\begin{array}{r} 14 \\ -\ 7 \\ \hline \end{array}$$

c.

13	14	13	13	14	14
− 7	− 6	− 9	− 4	− 5	− 8

d.

13	14	13	14	13	12
− 8	− 9	− 5	− 7	− 6	− 8

e.

11	13	12	14	12	11
− 5	− 4	− 6	− 5	− 3	− 7

f.

14	13	14	12	13	14
− 6	− 9	− 8	− 7	− 7	− 9

Mixed Practice

Add or subtract. Watch the signs.

a.
$$6 + 8 = 14$$ $$5 + 8$$ $$14 - 7$$ $$12 - 6$$ $$10 - 3$$ $$9 + 5$$ $$12 - 9$$

b.
$$14 - 9$$ $$8 + 6$$ $$14 - 8$$ $$13 - 5$$ $$14 - 5$$ $$6 + 8$$ $$13 - 8$$

c.
$$11 - 3$$ $$9 + 4$$ $$13 - 6$$ $$12 - 4$$ $$9 + 3$$ $$13 - 9$$ $$14 - 5$$

d.
$$7 + 7$$ $$14 - 6$$ $$13 - 4$$ $$8 + 5$$ $$13 - 7$$ $$8 + 4$$ $$13 - 5$$

★ Challenge

Write an addition sentence and a subtraction sentence
for each group of numbers.

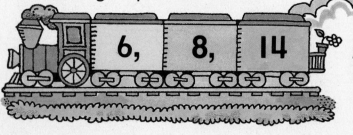

6, 8, 14   9, 4, 13

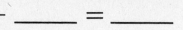

____ + ____ = ____   ____ + ____ = ____

____ − ____ = ____   ____ − ____ = ____

Families of Facts

Add or subtract.

a.

$3 + 8 = \underline{11}$ $4 + 9 = \underline{\hspace{1cm}}$ $5 + 8 = \underline{\hspace{1cm}}$

$8 + 3 = \underline{\hspace{1cm}}$ $9 + 4 = \underline{\hspace{1cm}}$ $8 + 5 = \underline{\hspace{1cm}}$

$11 - 3 = \underline{\hspace{1cm}}$ $13 - 4 = \underline{\hspace{1cm}}$ $13 - 5 = \underline{\hspace{1cm}}$

$11 - 8 = \underline{\hspace{1cm}}$ $13 - 9 = \underline{\hspace{1cm}}$ $13 - 8 = \underline{\hspace{1cm}}$

b.

$6 + 7 = \underline{\hspace{1cm}}$ $5 + 7 = \underline{\hspace{1cm}}$ $5 + 6 = \underline{\hspace{1cm}}$

$7 + 6 = \underline{\hspace{1cm}}$ $7 + 5 = \underline{\hspace{1cm}}$ $6 + 5 = \underline{\hspace{1cm}}$

$13 - 6 = \underline{\hspace{1cm}}$ $12 - 5 = \underline{\hspace{1cm}}$ $11 - 5 = \underline{\hspace{1cm}}$

$13 - 7 = \underline{\hspace{1cm}}$ $12 - 7 = \underline{\hspace{1cm}}$ $11 - 6 = \underline{\hspace{1cm}}$

c.

$6 + 8 = \underline{\hspace{1cm}}$ $3 + 9 = \underline{\hspace{1cm}}$ $5 + 9 = \underline{\hspace{1cm}}$

$8 + 6 = \underline{\hspace{1cm}}$ $9 + 3 = \underline{\hspace{1cm}}$ $9 + 5 = \underline{\hspace{1cm}}$

$14 - 6 = \underline{\hspace{1cm}}$ $12 - 3 = \underline{\hspace{1cm}}$ $14 - 5 = \underline{\hspace{1cm}}$

$14 - 8 = \underline{\hspace{1cm}}$ $12 - 9 = \underline{\hspace{1cm}}$ $14 - 9 = \underline{\hspace{1cm}}$

Names for Numbers

Ring each name for the number.

 a. **13**   4 + 8   14 − 7   (7 + 6)   (4 + 9)

 b. **8**   14 − 6   12 − 6   5 + 3   13 − 5

 c. **11**   13 − 5   7 + 4   8 + 3   12 − 3

 d. **7**   13 − 6   12 − 5   7 + 0   6 + 2

 e. **5**   9 − 4   12 − 8   4 + 3   11 − 6

 f. **9**   9 − 0   8 + 1   13 − 4   11 − 2

 g. **12**   14 − 5   7 + 5   6 + 6   7 + 6

 h. **6**   14 − 8   4 + 2   5 + 2   13 − 7

 i. **10**   12 − 3   6 + 4   14 − 6   2 + 8

 j. **4**   13 − 9   12 − 8   2 + 6   11 − 7

name

Addition Practice

Add.

Write the missing numbers.

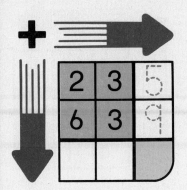

2	3	5
6	3	9

2	3	5
6	3	9
8	6	

2	3	5
6	3	9
8	6	14

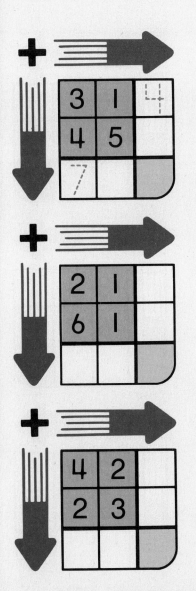

3	1	4
4	5	
7		

1	3	
4	3	

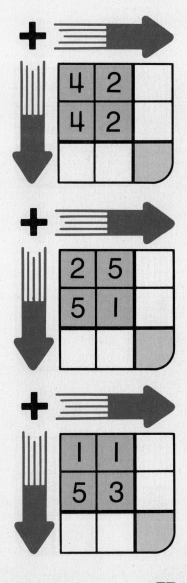

4	2	
4	2	

2	1	
6	1	

6	0	
0	8	

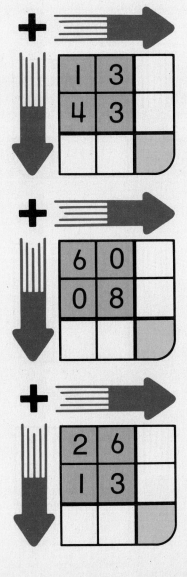

2	5	
5	1	

4	2	
2	3	

2	6	
1	3	

1	1	
5	3	

Subtraction Practice

Subtract.

Write the missing numbers.

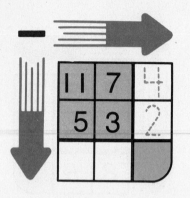

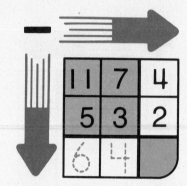

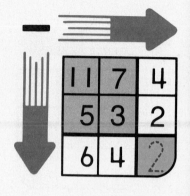

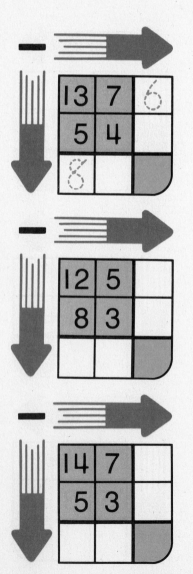

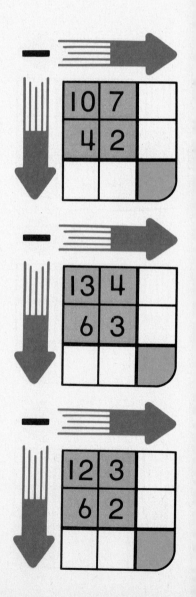

Missing Addends

2 + ____ = **7**   **2** + _5_ = **7**

Complete the addition sentences.

a.

4 + _6_ = 10

1 + ____ = 10

5 + ____ = 10

8 + ____ = 10

b.

3 + ____ = 8

4 + ____ = 8

8 + ____ = 8

6 + ____ = 8

c.

0 + ____ = 6

1 + ____ = 6

4 + ____ = 6

3 + ____ = 6

d.

7 + ____ = 9

1 + ____ = 9

9 + ____ = 9

4 + ____ = 9

Complete the addition sentences.

a. $2 + \underline{} = 6$ $2 + \underline{} = 7$ $5 + \underline{} = 5$

b. $6 + \underline{} = 10$ $3 + \underline{} = 5$ $8 + \underline{} = 9$

c. $1 + \underline{} = 8$ $2 + \underline{} = 9$ $5 + \underline{} = 7$

d. $6 + \underline{} = 9$ $5 + \underline{} = 8$ $5 + \underline{} = 6$

e. $1 + \underline{} = 5$ $4 + \underline{} = 7$ $2 + \underline{} = 10$

f. $4 + \underline{} = 7$ $0 + \underline{} = 8$ $6 + \underline{} = 7$

g. $5 + \underline{} = 11$ $4 + \underline{} = 13$ $8 + \underline{} = 12$

h. $7 + \underline{} = 10$ $6 + \underline{} = 14$ $7 + \underline{} = 12$

i. $9 + \underline{} = 11$ $8 + \underline{} = 13$ $7 + \underline{} = 14$

j. $6 + \underline{} = 12$ $4 + \underline{} = 11$ $6 + \underline{} = 13$

Skills Maintenance

Write the missing numbers.

83 84 ___ 86 ___ ___ ___

56 ___ 58 ___ ___ ___ 61

80

Addition Facts Drill

Add.

a.
$\begin{array}{r} 5 \\ +8 \\ \hline 13 \end{array}$
$\begin{array}{r} 7 \\ +7 \\ \hline \end{array}$
$\begin{array}{r} 9 \\ +3 \\ \hline \end{array}$
$\begin{array}{r} 8 \\ +6 \\ \hline \end{array}$
$\begin{array}{r} 6 \\ +5 \\ \hline \end{array}$
$\begin{array}{r} 5 \\ +7 \\ \hline \end{array}$
$\begin{array}{r} 9 \\ +4 \\ \hline \end{array}$

b.
$\begin{array}{r} 9 \\ +3 \\ \hline \end{array}$
$\begin{array}{r} 4 \\ +6 \\ \hline \end{array}$
$\begin{array}{r} 7 \\ +4 \\ \hline \end{array}$
$\begin{array}{r} 3 \\ +8 \\ \hline \end{array}$
$\begin{array}{r} 7 \\ +6 \\ \hline \end{array}$
$\begin{array}{r} 8 \\ +4 \\ \hline \end{array}$
$\begin{array}{r} 5 \\ +9 \\ \hline \end{array}$

c.
$\begin{array}{r} 7 \\ +7 \\ \hline \end{array}$
$\begin{array}{r} 5 \\ +7 \\ \hline \end{array}$
$\begin{array}{r} 5 \\ +8 \\ \hline \end{array}$
$\begin{array}{r} 6 \\ +6 \\ \hline \end{array}$
$\begin{array}{r} 3 \\ +9 \\ \hline \end{array}$
$\begin{array}{r} 9 \\ +5 \\ \hline \end{array}$
$\begin{array}{r} 9 \\ +2 \\ \hline \end{array}$

d.
$\begin{array}{r} 4 \\ +7 \\ \hline \end{array}$
$\begin{array}{r} 7 \\ +5 \\ \hline \end{array}$
$\begin{array}{r} 6 \\ +7 \\ \hline \end{array}$
$\begin{array}{r} 8 \\ +6 \\ \hline \end{array}$
$\begin{array}{r} 7 \\ +3 \\ \hline \end{array}$
$\begin{array}{r} 5 \\ +6 \\ \hline \end{array}$
$\begin{array}{r} 5 \\ +4 \\ \hline \end{array}$

e.
$\begin{array}{r} 6 \\ +8 \\ \hline \end{array}$
$\begin{array}{r} 7 \\ +6 \\ \hline \end{array}$
$\begin{array}{r} 8 \\ +2 \\ \hline \end{array}$
$\begin{array}{r} 4 \\ +9 \\ \hline \end{array}$
$\begin{array}{r} 9 \\ +0 \\ \hline \end{array}$
$\begin{array}{r} 8 \\ +5 \\ \hline \end{array}$
$\begin{array}{r} 7 \\ +4 \\ \hline \end{array}$

f.
$\begin{array}{r} 2 \\ +9 \\ \hline \end{array}$
$\begin{array}{r} 6 \\ +3 \\ \hline \end{array}$
$\begin{array}{r} 8 \\ +3 \\ \hline \end{array}$
$\begin{array}{r} 4 \\ +8 \\ \hline \end{array}$

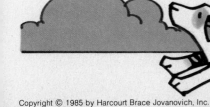

Subtraction Facts Drill

Subtract.

a.
$$\begin{array}{r} 12 \\ -4 \\ \hline 8 \end{array}$$
$$\begin{array}{r} 10 \\ -8 \\ \hline \end{array}$$
$$\begin{array}{r} 13 \\ -8 \\ \hline \end{array}$$
$$\begin{array}{r} 11 \\ -9 \\ \hline \end{array}$$
$$\begin{array}{r} 14 \\ -7 \\ \hline \end{array}$$
$$\begin{array}{r} 10 \\ -3 \\ \hline \end{array}$$
$$\begin{array}{r} 11 \\ -5 \\ \hline \end{array}$$

b.
$$\begin{array}{r} 11 \\ -8 \\ \hline \end{array}$$
$$\begin{array}{r} 12 \\ -7 \\ \hline \end{array}$$
$$\begin{array}{r} 13 \\ -6 \\ \hline \end{array}$$
$$\begin{array}{r} 11 \\ -7 \\ \hline \end{array}$$
$$\begin{array}{r} 14 \\ -5 \\ \hline \end{array}$$
$$\begin{array}{r} 9 \\ -4 \\ \hline \end{array}$$
$$\begin{array}{r} 9 \\ -0 \\ \hline \end{array}$$

c.
$$\begin{array}{r} 11 \\ -2 \\ \hline \end{array}$$
$$\begin{array}{r} 14 \\ -9 \\ \hline \end{array}$$
$$\begin{array}{r} 13 \\ -4 \\ \hline \end{array}$$
$$\begin{array}{r} 10 \\ -5 \\ \hline \end{array}$$
$$\begin{array}{r} 14 \\ -8 \\ \hline \end{array}$$
$$\begin{array}{r} 11 \\ -6 \\ \hline \end{array}$$
$$\begin{array}{r} 14 \\ -6 \\ \hline \end{array}$$

d.
$$\begin{array}{r} 9 \\ -9 \\ \hline \end{array}$$
$$\begin{array}{r} 14 \\ -7 \\ \hline \end{array}$$
$$\begin{array}{r} 12 \\ -8 \\ \hline \end{array}$$
$$\begin{array}{r} 12 \\ -6 \\ \hline \end{array}$$
$$\begin{array}{r} 10 \\ -6 \\ \hline \end{array}$$
$$\begin{array}{r} 12 \\ -5 \\ \hline \end{array}$$
$$\begin{array}{r} 13 \\ -7 \\ \hline \end{array}$$

e.
$$\begin{array}{r} 12 \\ -3 \\ \hline \end{array}$$
$$\begin{array}{r} 13 \\ -5 \\ \hline \end{array}$$
$$\begin{array}{r} 11 \\ -3 \\ \hline \end{array}$$
$$\begin{array}{r} 12 \\ -9 \\ \hline \end{array}$$
$$\begin{array}{r} 14 \\ -5 \\ \hline \end{array}$$
$$\begin{array}{r} 10 \\ -4 \\ \hline \end{array}$$
$$\begin{array}{r} 11 \\ -5 \\ \hline \end{array}$$

f.
$$\begin{array}{r} 13 \\ -9 \\ \hline \end{array}$$
$$\begin{array}{r} 11 \\ -4 \\ \hline \end{array}$$
$$\begin{array}{r} 10 \\ -9 \\ \hline \end{array}$$
$$\begin{array}{r} 11 \\ -7 \\ \hline \end{array}$$

82

PROBLEM SOLVING
Add or Subtract?

 school  bus children

 coat ticket 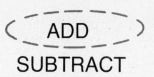 painting

Choose ADD or SUBTRACT. Then solve.

a. 4 buses are at the school.
6 more buses come.
How many buses in all?

(ADD)
SUBTRACT

$$\begin{array}{r} 6 \\ +\ 4 \\ \hline 10 \end{array}$$

---

b. 12 children are in line.
5 leave to get their coats.
How many children are left?

ADD
SUBTRACT

---

c. 6 girls have tickets.
5 boys have tickets.
How many tickets in all?

ADD
SUBTRACT

---

d. 11 children look at a painting.
4 children walk away.
How many children are left?

ADD
SUBTRACT

---

e. There are 10 buses.
6 buses drive away.
How many buses are left?

ADD
SUBTRACT

 boat

 car

 plane

truck

train

Choose ADD or SUBTRACT. Then solve.

a. 12 boats are in the water.
6 boats sail away.
How many boats are left?

ADD

(SUBTRACT)

$$\begin{array}{r} 12 \\ -6 \\ \hline 6 \end{array}$$

b. 5 cars are red.
4 cars are blue.
How many cars in all?

ADD

SUBTRACT

c. 12 trucks are parked.
8 trucks drive away.
How many trucks are left?

ADD

SUBTRACT

d. Beth counted 8 trains.
6 more trains come.
How many trains in all?

ADD

SUBTRACT

e. Mike sees 13 planes.
7 planes take off.
How many planes are left?

ADD

SUBTRACT

84

Add. (pages 67-68, 71-72)

a.
$$6 + 5$$
$$6 + 6$$
$$9 + 5$$
$$4 + 9$$
$$4 + 8$$
$$7 + 7$$

b.
$$7 + 6$$
$$4 + 7$$
$$6 + 8$$
$$9 + 3$$
$$8 + 5$$
$$8 + 3$$

Subtract. (pages 69-70, 73-74)

c.
$$12 - 7$$
$$14 - 5$$
$$13 - 9$$
$$11 - 6$$
$$14 - 8$$
$$11 - 2$$

d.
$$13 - 7$$
$$12 - 6$$
$$14 - 7$$
$$13 - 8$$
$$11 - 4$$
$$12 - 8$$

Complete the addition sentences. (pages 79-80)

e. $6 + \_\_\_ = 11$ $5 + \_\_\_ = 9$ $3 + \_\_\_ = 10$

f. $1 + \_\_\_ = 6$ $7 + \_\_\_ = 7$ $8 + \_\_\_ = 12$

Choose ADD or SUBTRACT. Then solve. (pages 83-84)

g. 14 flowers are in the garden.
8 are picked.
How many flowers are left?

ADD

SUBTRACT

Probability
You need:

3 red cards   **2** blue cards   **l** green card   **l** paper bag

Put the cards in a bag.
Pick one card.
Mark the chart with an × to show the
color you picked.
Put the card back in the bag.
Do this **l5** times.

First try with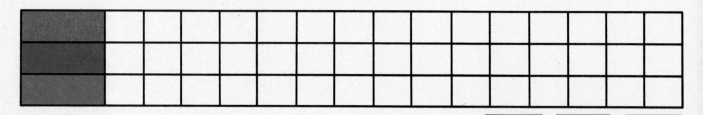

How many times did you pick each color?

Now try with

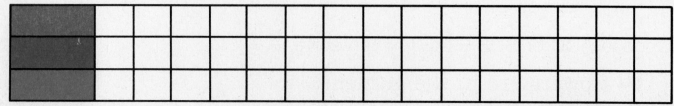

How many times did you pick each color?

Add.

a.
$$8 + 6$$ $$2 + 9$$ $$7 + 5$$ $$6 + 7$$ $$5 + 8$$ $$5 + 6$$

b.
$$3 + 8$$ $$5 + 7$$ $$9 + 2$$ $$6 + 8$$ $$9 + 5$$ $$8 + 5$$

Subtract.

c.
$$13 - 6$$ $$11 - 3$$ $$14 - 9$$ $$12 - 4$$ $$12 - 9$$ $$11 - 7$$

d.
$$14 - 7$$ $$11 - 5$$ $$13 - 5$$ $$14 - 6$$ $$12 - 7$$ $$13 - 4$$

Complete the addition sentences.

e. $5 + \underline{\hspace{1cm}} = 12$ $2 + \underline{\hspace{1cm}} = 10$ $9 + \underline{\hspace{1cm}} = 9$

f. $8 + \underline{\hspace{1cm}} = 14$ $1 + \underline{\hspace{1cm}} = 7$ $3 + \underline{\hspace{1cm}} = 11$

Choose ADD or SUBTRACT. Then solve.

g. Maria baked **8** rolls.
Chet baked **6** rolls.
How many rolls in all?

ADD

SUBTRACT

87

Number Sentences With <, >, or =

Fill in >, < or =.

4 + 8 is 12.
12 is greater than
10, and so I use
the > sign.

4 + 8 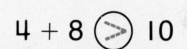 10

7 + 4 ◯ 13

11 − 6 ◯ 5

7 + 6 ◯ 11

12 − 9 ◯ 1

14 − 6 ◯ 10

6 + 4 ◯ 12

8 + 6 ◯ 14

13 − 4 ◯ 9

10 − 3 ◯ 7

5 + 8 ◯ 14

11 − 8 ◯ 1

14 − 9 ◯ 8

7 + 7 ◯ 14

7 + 5 ◯ 12

13 − 8 ◯ 10

2 + 9 ◯ 8

88

Addition and Subtraction Facts to 18

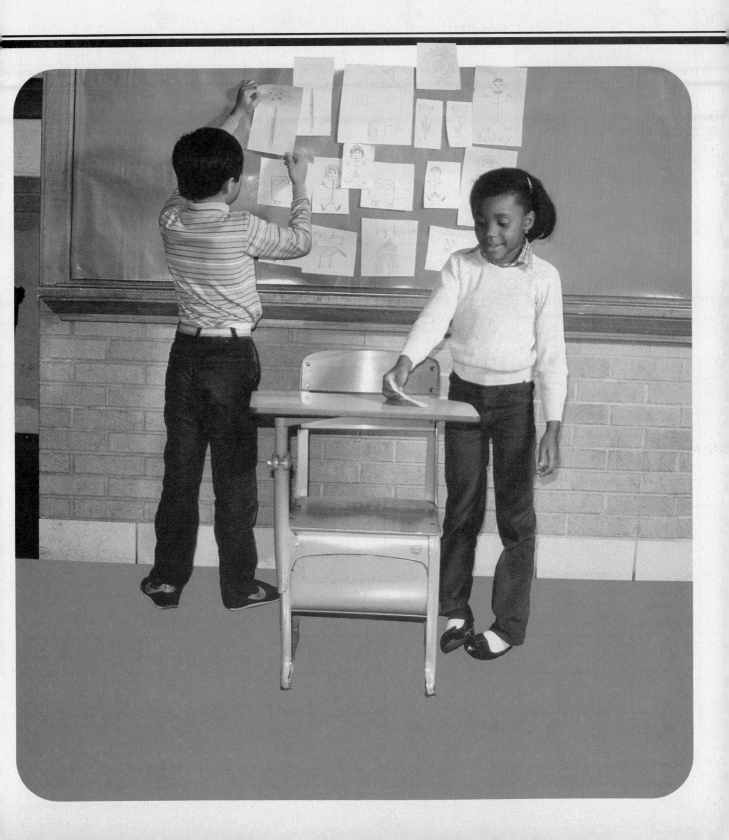

name

GETTING STARTED

Add or subtract.
Write the missing numbers.

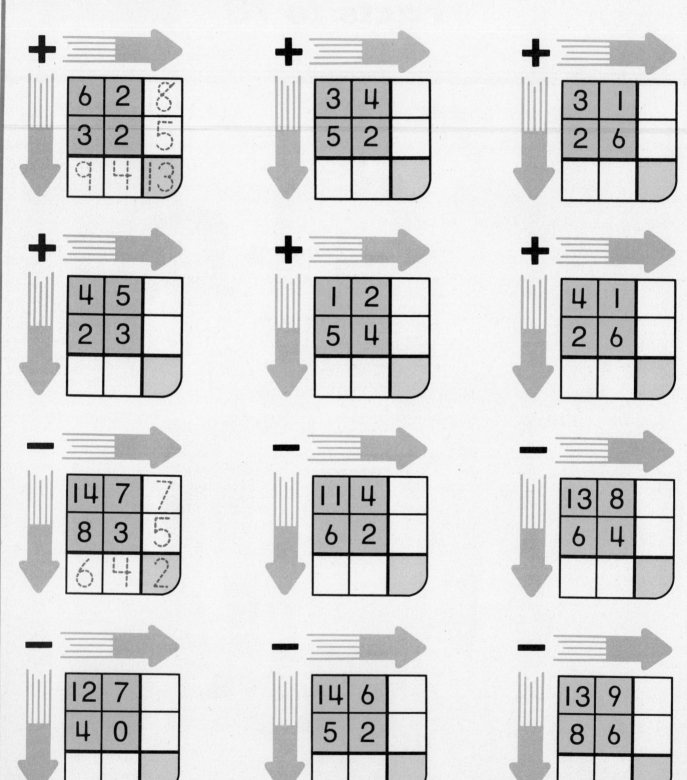

Sums to 18

Add.

a.

$$9 \ + \ 6 \ = \ \underline{15}$$

$$8 \ + \ 7 \ = \ \underline{\hspace{2cm}}$$

---

b.

$$9 \ + \ 7 \ = \ \underline{\hspace{2cm}}$$

$$8 \ + \ 8 \ = \ \underline{\hspace{2cm}}$$

---

c.

$$9 \ + \ 8 \ = \ \underline{\hspace{2cm}}$$

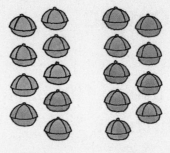

$$9 \ + \ 9 \ = \ \underline{\hspace{2cm}}$$

---

d. $8 + 7 = \underline{\hspace{1.5cm}}$ $9 + 7 = \underline{\hspace{1.5cm}}$ $9 + 8 = \underline{\hspace{1.5cm}}$

e. $7 + 9 = \underline{\hspace{1.5cm}}$ $9 + 6 = \underline{\hspace{1.5cm}}$ $8 + 9 = \underline{\hspace{1.5cm}}$

f. $9 + 9 = \underline{\hspace{1.5cm}}$ $7 + 7 = \underline{\hspace{1.5cm}}$ $6 + 9 = \underline{\hspace{1.5cm}}$

g. $8 + 8 = \underline{\hspace{1.5cm}}$ $7 + 8 = \underline{\hspace{1.5cm}}$ $6 + 7 = \underline{\hspace{1.5cm}}$

Add.

a.
$$9 + 7 = 16$$ $$6 + 9$$ $$7 + 8$$ $$9 + 9$$ $$7 + 7$$ $$8 + 5$$ $$7 + 9$$

b.
$$6 + 8$$ $$8 + 8$$ $$9 + 8$$ $$7 + 9$$ $$8 + 9$$ $$5 + 9$$ $$8 + 7$$

c.
$$7 + 8$$ $$9 + 5$$ $$9 + 4$$ $$5 + 8$$ $$6 + 9$$ $$4 + 9$$ $$7 + 7$$

d.
$$9 + 6$$ $$8 + 6$$ $$9 + 8$$ $$9 + 9$$ $$7 + 9$$ $$8 + 8$$ $$6 + 8$$

PROBLEM SOLVING

Solve.

e. 9 children are in the park.
8 more join them.
How many children are in
the park?

f. 8 girls are playing ball.
8 boys are playing ball.
How many children are
playing ball?

92

Subtracting from 15 to 18

Subtract.

a.

$15 - 6 = \underline{9}$

$15 - 7 = \underline{\hphantom{00}}$

b.

$16 - 7 = \underline{\hphantom{00}}$

$16 - 8 = \underline{\hphantom{00}}$

c.

$17 - 8 = \underline{\hphantom{00}}$

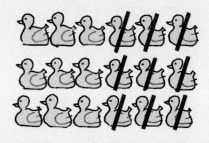

$18 - 9 = \underline{\hphantom{00}}$

d. $15 - 8 = \underline{\hphantom{00}}$ $15 - 9 = \underline{\hphantom{00}}$ $16 - 9 = \underline{\hphantom{00}}$

e. $17 - 9 = \underline{\hphantom{00}}$ $16 - 7 = \underline{\hphantom{00}}$ $18 - 9 = \underline{\hphantom{00}}$

f. $16 - 8 = \underline{\hphantom{00}}$ $14 - 6 = \underline{\hphantom{00}}$ $15 - 9 = \underline{\hphantom{00}}$

g. $14 - 7 = \underline{\hphantom{00}}$ $15 - 7 = \underline{\hphantom{00}}$ $17 - 8 = \underline{\hphantom{00}}$

Subtract.

a.
$$\begin{array}{r} 15 \\ -\ 9 \\ \hline 6 \end{array}$$
$$\begin{array}{r} 17 \\ -\ 9 \\ \hline \end{array}$$
$$\begin{array}{r} 14 \\ -\ 7 \\ \hline \end{array}$$
$$\begin{array}{r} 13 \\ -\ 8 \\ \hline \end{array}$$
$$\begin{array}{r} 18 \\ -\ 9 \\ \hline \end{array}$$
$$\begin{array}{r} 16 \\ -\ 7 \\ \hline \end{array}$$

b.
$$\begin{array}{r} 14 \\ -\ 8 \\ \hline \end{array}$$
$$\begin{array}{r} 16 \\ -\ 9 \\ \hline \end{array}$$
$$\begin{array}{r} 15 \\ -\ 8 \\ \hline \end{array}$$
$$\begin{array}{r} 17 \\ -\ 8 \\ \hline \end{array}$$
$$\begin{array}{r} 13 \\ -\ 7 \\ \hline \end{array}$$
$$\begin{array}{r} 16 \\ -\ 8 \\ \hline \end{array}$$

c.
$$\begin{array}{r} 13 \\ -\ 6 \\ \hline \end{array}$$
$$\begin{array}{r} 18 \\ -\ 9 \\ \hline \end{array}$$
$$\begin{array}{r} 15 \\ -\ 9 \\ \hline \end{array}$$
$$\begin{array}{r} 14 \\ -\ 5 \\ \hline \end{array}$$
$$\begin{array}{r} 17 \\ -\ 9 \\ \hline \end{array}$$
$$\begin{array}{r} 15 \\ -\ 6 \\ \hline \end{array}$$

d.
$$\begin{array}{r} 15 \\ -\ 7 \\ \hline \end{array}$$
$$\begin{array}{r} 17 \\ -\ 8 \\ \hline \end{array}$$
$$\begin{array}{r} 16 \\ -\ 8 \\ \hline \end{array}$$
$$\begin{array}{r} 13 \\ -\ 9 \\ \hline \end{array}$$
$$\begin{array}{r} 16 \\ -\ 7 \\ \hline \end{array}$$
$$\begin{array}{r} 14 \\ -\ 7 \\ \hline \end{array}$$

PROBLEM SOLVING

Solve.

e. 17 children are at the circus. 9 children go home. How many children are left?

f. 18 clowns are playing. 9 walk away. How many clowns are left?

Families of Facts

Add or subtract.

a.

7 + 8 = _15_

8 + 7 = _____

15 − 7 = _____

15 − 8 = _____

b.

9 + 8 = _____

8 + 9 = _____

17 − 9 = _____

17 − 8 = _____

c.

7 + 9 = _____

9 + 7 = _____

16 − 7 = _____

16 − 9 = _____

d.

6 + 9 = _____

9 + 6 = _____

15 − 6 = _____

15 − 9 = _____

e.

8 + 6 = _____

6 + 8 = _____

14 − 8 = _____

14 − 6 = _____

f.

9 + 4 = _____

4 + 9 = _____

13 − 9 = _____

13 − 4 = _____

g.

8 + 8 = _____

16 − 8 = _____

h.

9 + 9 = _____

18 − 9 = _____

Missing Addends

Complete the addition sentences.

a.

$6 + \underline{6} = 12$

$3 + \underline{} = 12$

$8 + \underline{} = 12$

$5 + \underline{} = 12$

$9 + \underline{} = 14$

$7 + \underline{} = 14$

$6 + \underline{} = 14$

$5 + \underline{} = 14$

b. $9 + \underline{} = 17 \qquad 9 + \underline{} = 18 \qquad 6 + \underline{} = 15$

c. $3 + \underline{} = 11 \qquad 9 + \underline{} = 11 \qquad 4 + \underline{} = 12$

d. $8 + \underline{} = 16 \qquad 7 + \underline{} = 12 \qquad 9 + \underline{} = 18$

e. $9 + \underline{} = 15 \qquad 9 + \underline{} = 16 \qquad 8 + \underline{} = 17$

f. $8 + \underline{} = 14 \qquad 5 + \underline{} = 11 \qquad 9 + \underline{} = 12$

g. $7 + \underline{} = 16 \qquad 8 + \underline{} = 15 \qquad 4 + \underline{} = 11$

Midchapter Review

Add or subtract.

$$\begin{array}{ccccccc}
8 & 15 & 17 & 8 & 6 & 18 & 9 \\
+9 & -6 & -9 & +8 & +9 & -9 & +7 \\
\hline
\end{array}$$

PROBLEM SOLVING

Two Uses of Subtraction

Draw lines to match.
Subtract to compare.

a. How many more  than 🍅 ?

$$\begin{array}{r} 10 \\ -8 \\ \hline 2 \end{array}$$

b. How many more 🍎 than 🍇 ?

c. How many more ☕ than ⬭ ?

d. How many more 🍴 than 🥄 ?

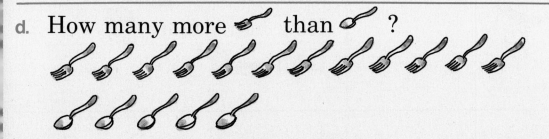

e. How many more 🥛 than 🏺 ?

Subtract to find how many are left.

John sees 17 .

9 are taken down.

How many are left?

$$\begin{array}{r} 17 \\ -\ 9 \\ \hline 8 \end{array}$$

8 are left.

Subtract to compare.

Sue has 14 .

She has 8.

How many more than ?

$$\begin{array}{r} 14 \\ -\ 8 \\ \hline 6 \end{array}$$

6 more .

Solve.

a.

There are 16 .

There are 7 .

How many more than ?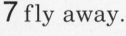

b.

Jerry cooks 18 .

9 are eaten.

How many are left?

c.

Lisa sees 14 .

7 fly away.

How many are left?

d.

There are 16 .

There are 8 .

How many more than ?

e.

Jerry counts 15 .

6 go hiking.

How many are left?

f.

Lisa finds 17 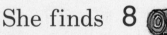.

She finds 8 .

How many more than 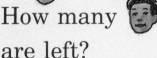   ?

98

Follow the Rule

Add. Complete the table.

Add 4	
6	10
5	9
7	

Add 8	
7	
0	
8	

Add 6	
5	
2	
6	

Add 9	
8	
6	
5	

Add 7	
6	
9	
8	

Add 5	
8	
7	
0	

Subtract. Complete the table.

Subtract 8	
10	2
9	1
15	

Subtract 9	
17	
15	
13	

Subtract 6	
13	
15	
10	

Subtract 5	
10	
9	
11	

Subtract 7	
16	
13	
15	

Subtract 4	
10	
12	
9	

Addition Table

Complete the addition table.

+	0	1	2	3	4	5	6	7	8	9
0										
1										
2								9		
3			5							
4										
5						10				
6										
7										
8			11							
9										

Skills Maintenance

Count by twos.

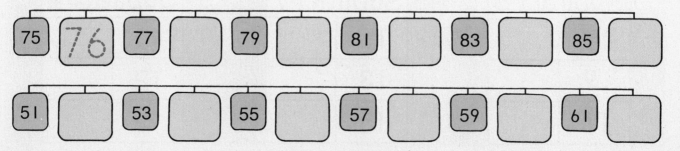

75 | 76 | 77 | | 79 | | 81 | | 83 | | 85 |

51 | | 53 | | 55 | | 57 | | 59 | | 61 |

100

Addition Facts Drill

Add.

a.
$$\begin{array}{r} 7 \\ +8 \\ \hline 15 \end{array}$$
$$\begin{array}{r} 9 \\ +5 \\ \hline \end{array}$$
$$\begin{array}{r} 9 \\ +8 \\ \hline \end{array}$$
$$\begin{array}{r} 7 \\ +7 \\ \hline \end{array}$$
$$\begin{array}{r} 9 \\ +7 \\ \hline \end{array}$$
$$\begin{array}{r} 7 \\ +6 \\ \hline \end{array}$$
$$\begin{array}{r} 9 \\ +4 \\ \hline \end{array}$$

b.
$$\begin{array}{r} 9 \\ +9 \\ \hline \end{array}$$
$$\begin{array}{r} 5 \\ +6 \\ \hline \end{array}$$
$$\begin{array}{r} 8 \\ +6 \\ \hline \end{array}$$
$$\begin{array}{r} 6 \\ +9 \\ \hline \end{array}$$
$$\begin{array}{r} 6 \\ +6 \\ \hline \end{array}$$
$$\begin{array}{r} 7 \\ +9 \\ \hline \end{array}$$
$$\begin{array}{r} 9 \\ +5 \\ \hline \end{array}$$

c.
$$\begin{array}{r} 8 \\ +5 \\ \hline \end{array}$$
$$\begin{array}{r} 5 \\ +9 \\ \hline \end{array}$$
$$\begin{array}{r} 8 \\ +7 \\ \hline \end{array}$$
$$\begin{array}{r} 8 \\ +3 \\ \hline \end{array}$$
$$\begin{array}{r} 8 \\ +8 \\ \hline \end{array}$$
$$\begin{array}{r} 9 \\ +6 \\ \hline \end{array}$$
$$\begin{array}{r} 0 \\ +6 \\ \hline \end{array}$$

d.
$$\begin{array}{r} 8 \\ +9 \\ \hline \end{array}$$
$$\begin{array}{r} 4 \\ +3 \\ \hline \end{array}$$
$$\begin{array}{r} 4 \\ +9 \\ \hline \end{array}$$
$$\begin{array}{r} 8 \\ +1 \\ \hline \end{array}$$
$$\begin{array}{r} 5 \\ +3 \\ \hline \end{array}$$
$$\begin{array}{r} 8 \\ +6 \\ \hline \end{array}$$
$$\begin{array}{r} 6 \\ +7 \\ \hline \end{array}$$

e.
$$\begin{array}{r} 7 \\ +1 \\ \hline \end{array}$$
$$\begin{array}{r} 9 \\ +6 \\ \hline \end{array}$$
$$\begin{array}{r} 5 \\ +7 \\ \hline \end{array}$$
$$\begin{array}{r} 8 \\ +8 \\ \hline \end{array}$$
$$\begin{array}{r} 9 \\ +9 \\ \hline \end{array}$$

f.
$$\begin{array}{r} 6 \\ +8 \\ \hline \end{array}$$
$$\begin{array}{r} 8 \\ +0 \\ \hline \end{array}$$
$$\begin{array}{r} 6 \\ +1 \\ \hline \end{array}$$
$$\begin{array}{r} 5 \\ +2 \\ \hline \end{array}$$
$$\begin{array}{r} 8 \\ +5 \\ \hline \end{array}$$

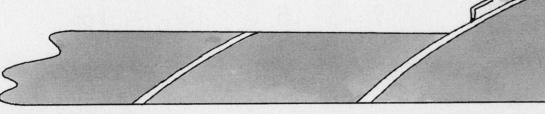

Subtraction Facts Drill

Subtract.

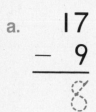

a.
$$\begin{array}{r} 17 \\ -\ 9 \\ \hline 8 \end{array}$$
$$\begin{array}{r} 14 \\ -\ 6 \\ \hline \end{array}$$
$$\begin{array}{r} 18 \\ -\ 9 \\ \hline \end{array}$$
$$\begin{array}{r} 16 \\ -\ 7 \\ \hline \end{array}$$
$$\begin{array}{r} 15 \\ -\ 9 \\ \hline \end{array}$$

b.
$$\begin{array}{r} 15 \\ -\ 6 \\ \hline \end{array}$$
$$\begin{array}{r} 11 \\ -\ 5 \\ \hline \end{array}$$
$$\begin{array}{r} 16 \\ -\ 8 \\ \hline \end{array}$$
$$\begin{array}{r} 12 \\ -\ 4 \\ \hline \end{array}$$
$$\begin{array}{r} 14 \\ -\ 8 \\ \hline \end{array}$$

c.
$$\begin{array}{r} 13 \\ -\ 9 \\ \hline \end{array}$$
$$\begin{array}{r} 14 \\ -\ 9 \\ \hline \end{array}$$
$$\begin{array}{r} 10 \\ -\ 5 \\ \hline \end{array}$$
$$\begin{array}{r} 17 \\ -\ 8 \\ \hline \end{array}$$
$$\begin{array}{r} 14 \\ -\ 7 \\ \hline \end{array}$$
$$\begin{array}{r} 15 \\ -\ 7 \\ \hline \end{array}$$
$$\begin{array}{r} 11 \\ -\ 7 \\ \hline \end{array}$$

d.
$$\begin{array}{r} 10 \\ -\ 7 \\ \hline \end{array}$$
$$\begin{array}{r} 15 \\ -\ 8 \\ \hline \end{array}$$
$$\begin{array}{r} 9 \\ -\ 3 \\ \hline \end{array}$$
$$\begin{array}{r} 16 \\ -\ 8 \\ \hline \end{array}$$
$$\begin{array}{r} 13 \\ -\ 7 \\ \hline \end{array}$$
$$\begin{array}{r} 9 \\ -\ 7 \\ \hline \end{array}$$
$$\begin{array}{r} 11 \\ -\ 3 \\ \hline \end{array}$$

e.
$$\begin{array}{r} 11 \\ -\ 9 \\ \hline \end{array}$$
$$\begin{array}{r} 18 \\ -\ 9 \\ \hline \end{array}$$
$$\begin{array}{r} 14 \\ -\ 5 \\ \hline \end{array}$$
$$\begin{array}{r} 8 \\ -\ 0 \\ \hline \end{array}$$
$$\begin{array}{r} 16 \\ -\ 7 \\ \hline \end{array}$$
$$\begin{array}{r} 12 \\ -\ 7 \\ \hline \end{array}$$
$$\begin{array}{r} 7 \\ -\ 4 \\ \hline \end{array}$$

f.
$$\begin{array}{r} 7 \\ -\ 2 \\ \hline \end{array}$$
$$\begin{array}{r} 13 \\ -\ 4 \\ \hline \end{array}$$
$$\begin{array}{r} 9 \\ -\ 9 \\ \hline \end{array}$$
$$\begin{array}{r} 15 \\ -\ 9 \\ \hline \end{array}$$
$$\begin{array}{r} 13 \\ -\ 5 \\ \hline \end{array}$$
$$\begin{array}{r} 16 \\ -\ 9 \\ \hline \end{array}$$
$$\begin{array}{r} 14 \\ -\ 8 \\ \hline \end{array}$$

PROBLEM SOLVING

Choosing the Operation

Ring the correct example for each question.
Then solve.

a.

There are **9** boys.
There are **8** girls.
How many children in all?

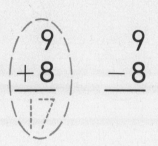

$$9 \atop +8 \over 17$$ $$9 \atop -8$$

b. Ramon has **9** books.
He reads **5** books.
How many books does he
have left to read?

$$9 \atop +5$$ $$9 \atop -5$$

c. Juanita has **8** crayons.
She has **6** pencils.
How many more crayons
than pencils does she have?

$$8 \atop +6$$ $$8 \atop -6$$

d. Kim finishes **8** math pages.
She finishes **7** reading pages.
How many pages has she
finished in all?

$$8 \atop +7$$ $$8 \atop -7$$

e.

There are **7** children reading.
6 children close their books.
How many are still reading?

$$7 \atop +6$$ $$7 \atop -6$$

basketball

jump rope

snacks

baseball

drinks

Solve.

a. Mrs. Wong has 17 snacks.
She gives 8 snacks away.
How many snacks are left?

17
- 8

9

b. There are 12 children.
There are 5 jump ropes.
How many more children than jump ropes?

c. 9 children play basketball.
9 children play tag.
How many children are playing in all?

d. There are 6 baseballs.
There are 9 basketballs.
How many balls in all?

e. 16 girls are in the yard.
8 boys are in the yard.
How many more girls than boys?

f. Sally brings 5 drinks.
Tommy brings 9 drinks.
How many drinks in all?

104

Names for Numbers

Ring each name for the number.

a.

8	**15**	**9**
(17 − 9)	18 − 9	6 + 7
9 + 2	7 + 8	18 − 9
(6 + 2)	5 + 6	15 − 6
15 − 9	9 + 6	9 + 0

b.

10	**6**	**4**	**5**
5 + 5	14 − 8	12 − 7	14 − 9
16 − 8	7 + 2	13 − 9	4 + 1
6 + 4	5 + 1	4 + 0	8 + 2
1 + 9	13 − 9	11 − 7	13 − 8

c.

13	**7**	**11**	**16**
17 − 8	8 + 2	5 + 6	8 + 8
9 + 5	16 − 9	3 + 8	17 − 8
5 + 8	6 + 1	2 + 6	9 + 7
4 + 9	15 − 8	15 − 7	8 + 5

Three Addends

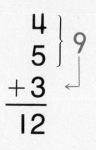

$$\left.\begin{array}{r} 4 \\ 5 \\ +3 \\ \hline 12 \end{array}\right\} 9$$

Add the first
two numbers.
Then add the third number.

Add.

a.
$$\begin{array}{r} 4 \\ 4 \\ +5 \\ \hline 13 \end{array}$$
$$\begin{array}{r} 6 \\ 2 \\ +3 \\ \hline \end{array}$$
$$\begin{array}{r} 2 \\ 7 \\ +7 \\ \hline \end{array}$$
$$\begin{array}{r} 5 \\ 2 \\ +5 \\ \hline \end{array}$$
$$\begin{array}{r} 4 \\ 3 \\ +5 \\ \hline \end{array}$$
$$\begin{array}{r} 3 \\ 2 \\ +8 \\ \hline \end{array}$$
$$\begin{array}{r} 4 \\ 5 \\ +7 \\ \hline \end{array}$$

b.
$$\begin{array}{r} 3 \\ 5 \\ +6 \\ \hline \end{array}$$
$$\begin{array}{r} 1 \\ 6 \\ +9 \\ \hline \end{array}$$
$$\begin{array}{r} 4 \\ 3 \\ +4 \\ \hline \end{array}$$
$$\begin{array}{r} 2 \\ 7 \\ +8 \\ \hline \end{array}$$
$$\begin{array}{r} 6 \\ 0 \\ +7 \\ \hline \end{array}$$
$$\begin{array}{r} 5 \\ 4 \\ +9 \\ \hline \end{array}$$
$$\begin{array}{r} 4 \\ 2 \\ +4 \\ \hline \end{array}$$

★ Challenge

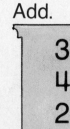

Add.

$$\begin{array}{r} 3 \\ 4 \\ 2 \\ +9 \\ \hline \end{array}$$
$$\begin{array}{r} 4 \\ 1 \\ 4 \\ +7 \\ \hline \end{array}$$
$$\begin{array}{r} 5 \\ 2 \\ 1 \\ +9 \\ \hline \end{array}$$
$$\begin{array}{r} 3 \\ 2 \\ 3 \\ +7 \\ \hline \end{array}$$
$$\begin{array}{r} 6 \\ 0 \\ 3 \\ +9 \\ \hline \end{array}$$
$$\begin{array}{r} 2 \\ 3 \\ 1 \\ +6 \\ \hline \end{array}$$
$$\begin{array}{r} 2 \\ 1 \\ 4 \\ +7 \\ \hline \end{array}$$

Add. (pages 91-92, 106)

a. 8 + 9 = _____   7 + 8 = _____   9 + 7 = _____

b.
$$\begin{array}{r} 9 \\ +9 \\ \hline \end{array} \qquad \begin{array}{r} 8 \\ +8 \\ \hline \end{array} \qquad \begin{array}{r} 8 \\ +7 \\ \hline \end{array} \qquad \begin{array}{r} 7 \\ +9 \\ \hline \end{array} \qquad \begin{array}{r} 9 \\ +6 \\ \hline \end{array} \qquad \begin{array}{r} 9 \\ +8 \\ \hline \end{array} \qquad \begin{array}{r} 6 \\ +9 \\ \hline \end{array}$$

c.
$$\begin{array}{r} 4 \\ 5 \\ +7 \\ \hline \end{array} \qquad \begin{array}{r} 6 \\ 2 \\ +9 \\ \hline \end{array} \qquad \begin{array}{r} 5 \\ 4 \\ +9 \\ \hline \end{array} \qquad \begin{array}{r} 5 \\ 3 \\ +7 \\ \hline \end{array} \qquad \begin{array}{r} 4 \\ 4 \\ +6 \\ \hline \end{array} \qquad \begin{array}{r} 8 \\ 1 \\ +3 \\ \hline \end{array} \qquad \begin{array}{r} 3 \\ 6 \\ +4 \\ \hline \end{array}$$

Subtract. (pages 93-94)

d. 16 − 9 = _____   18 − 9 = _____   15 − 7 = _____

e.
$$\begin{array}{r} 17 \\ -\ 9 \\ \hline \end{array} \qquad \begin{array}{r} 15 \\ -\ 8 \\ \hline \end{array} \qquad \begin{array}{r} 15 \\ -\ 9 \\ \hline \end{array} \qquad \begin{array}{r} 17 \\ -\ 8 \\ \hline \end{array} \qquad \begin{array}{r} 16 \\ -\ 8 \\ \hline \end{array} \qquad \begin{array}{r} 15 \\ -\ 6 \\ \hline \end{array} \qquad \begin{array}{r} 16 \\ -\ 7 \\ \hline \end{array}$$

Solve. (pages 97-98, 103-104)

f. Jean has 6 flowers.
She buys 9 more.
How many flowers
in all?

g. William has 16 pots.
He has 7 plants.
How many more
pots than plants?

PROJECT

Telephone Addition

 Use the to find a sum for each child.

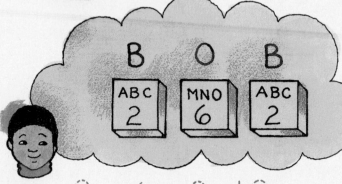

Bob $2 + 6 + 2 = 10$

 Pat _____

 **May** _____

 Amy _____

Lee _____

Kim _____

 Sam _____

Kin _____

 Meg _____

108

chapter

TEST

Add.

a. 9 + 6 = ____   9 + 9 = ____   7 + 8 = ____

b.
$$\begin{array}{ccccccc} 9 & 8 & 8 & 9 & 6 & 7 & 9 \\ +7 & +8 & +7 & +8 & +9 & +7 & +9 \end{array}$$

c.
$$\begin{array}{ccccccc} 4 & 5 & 3 & 1 & 4 & 2 & 2 \\ 5 & 3 & 5 & 7 & 4 & 4 & 0 \\ +7 & +7 & +9 & +8 & +6 & +8 & +9 \end{array}$$

Subtract.

d. 15 − 6 = ____   16 − 9 = ____   18 − 9 = ____

e.
$$\begin{array}{ccccccc} 17 & 15 & 16 & 15 & 18 & 16 & 15 \\ -\ 8 & -\ 8 & -\ 8 & -\ 9 & -\ 9 & -\ 7 & -\ 7 \end{array}$$

Solve.

f. Andy eats 16 cherries. He eats 9 grapes. How many more cherries than grapes?

g. Julia finds 8 shells. She finds 9 more shells. How many shells in all?

ENRICHMENT

Magic Squares

This is a magic square.

You can add →, ↓, or ↙ ↘
and get the same sum.
All the sums are 15.

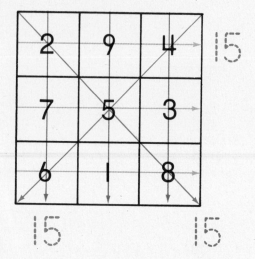

Complete these magic squares.

All the sums are 15.

	7	2
1	5	
8	3	4

	1	
7	5	3
	9	4

	9	2
3	5	
8		6

Put these numbers in the magic square.

0̸ 1̸ 2 3 4̸ 5 6 7 8

When you add →, ↓, or ↙ ↘
the sum should
be 12.

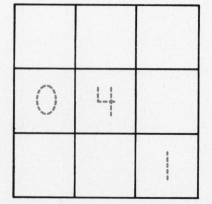

SKILLS MAINTENANCE

Choose the correct answers.

1.

$$\begin{array}{r} 7 \\ +1 \\ \hline \end{array}$$

(A) 7
(B) 8
(C) 6
(D) not here

2.

$$\begin{array}{r} 8 \\ +2 \\ \hline \end{array}$$

(A) 6
(B) 9
(C) 10
(D) not here

3.

$$\begin{array}{r} 4 \\ 3 \\ +2 \\ \hline \end{array}$$

(A) 9
(B) 5
(C) 7
(D) not here

4.

$$\begin{array}{r} 10 \\ -6 \\ \hline \end{array}$$

(A) 4
(B) 10
(C) 6
(D) not here

5.

$$\begin{array}{r} 9 \\ -3 \\ \hline \end{array}$$

(A) 3
(B) 4
(C) 5
(D) not here

6.

$$\begin{array}{r} 7 \\ -5 \\ \hline \end{array}$$

(A) 0
(B) 1
(C) 2
(D) not here

7.

$$\begin{array}{r} 7 \\ +5 \\ \hline \end{array}$$

(A) 10
(B) 12
(C) 13
(D) not here

8.

$$\begin{array}{r} 8 \\ +7 \\ \hline \end{array}$$

(A) 10
(B) 7
(C) 15
(D) not here

9.

$$\begin{array}{r} 9 \\ +8 \\ \hline \end{array}$$

(A) 14
(B) 16
(C) 18
(D) not here

10.

$$\begin{array}{r} 14 \\ -7 \\ \hline \end{array}$$

(A) 2
(B) 7
(C) 6
(D) not here

11.

$$\begin{array}{r} 16 \\ -8 \\ \hline \end{array}$$

(A) 8
(B) 10
(C) 9
(D) not here

12.

$$\begin{array}{r} 13 \\ -9 \\ \hline \end{array}$$

(A) 3
(B) 2
(C) 4
(D) not here

Choose the correct answers.

13.

43, 44, _____

(A) 42
(B) 45
(C) 46
(D) not here

14.

78, 79, _____

(A) 70
(B) 77
(C) 80
(D) not here

15.

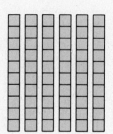

(A) 60
(B) 40
(C) 50
(D) not here

16.

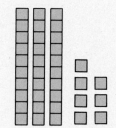

(A) 73
(B) 27
(C) 36
(D) not here

17.

Mrs. Hall buys 6  .

She uses 2.

How many are left?

(A) 2
(B) 4
(C) 6
(D) not here

18.

Teddy has 5  .

He buys 3 more.

How many in all?

(A) 8
(B) 2
(C) 7
(D) not here

19.

David brings 6 toys.

Randi brings 9 toys.

How many toys in all?

(A) 3
(B) 9
(C) 15
(D) not here

20.

There are 9 children.

There are 7 chairs.

How many more children than chairs?

(A) 9
(B) 2
(C) 7
(D) not here

Guess how many marbles there are.

GETTING STARTED

Write the numbers.

a.

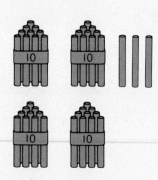

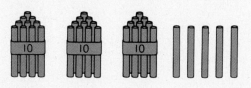

b.

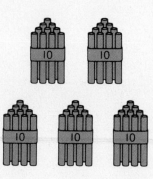

_____

c.

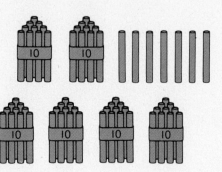

_____

d.

_____

e.

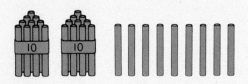

_____

f.

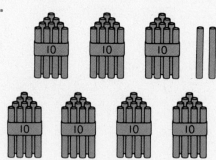

_____

g.

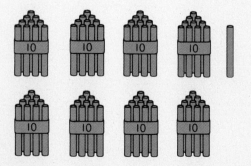

_____

h.

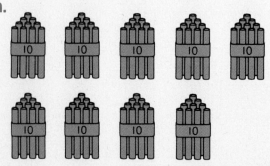

_____

Hundreds

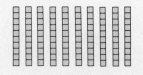

10 tens   make   **1** hundred.   **100**

Count the hundreds.
Write how many.

a.

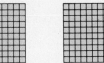

_____ **4** hundreds

_____ **400**

b.

_____ hundreds

_____

c.

_____ hundreds

_____

d.

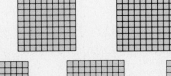

_____ hundreds

_____

e.

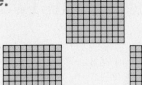 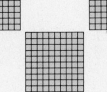

_____ hundreds

_____

Write the numbers.

a.

300 _____

_____

b.

_____

_____

c. 4 hundreds = _____   8 hundreds = _____

d. 1 hundred = _____   9 hundreds = _____

e. 6 hundreds = _____   3 hundreds = _____

PROBLEM SOLVING

Ring the best guess for each problem.

f. Arlene Brook's mother is

3, 30, 300

years old.

g. There are

3, 30, 300

pages in your math book.

h. There are **200** beans in one jar.
How many beans in two jars?

4, 40, 400

i. There are **20** pencils in one box.
How many pencils in two boxes?

4, 40, 400

116

Hundreds, Tens, and Ones

Write how many hundreds, tens, and ones.
Write the numbers.

a.

 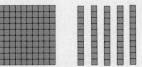

hundreds	tens	ones
2	5	0

250

b.

hundreds	tens	ones

_____

c.

hundreds	tens	ones

_____

d.

hundreds	tens	ones

_____

e.

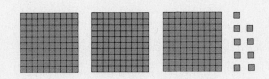

hundreds	tens	ones

_____

f.

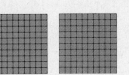 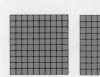

hundreds	tens	ones

_____

Write the numbers.

a.

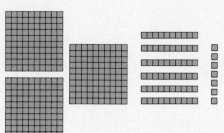

367

b.

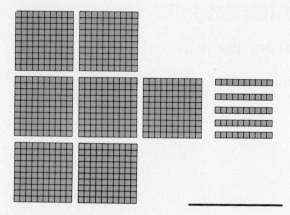

_____

c.

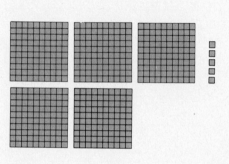

_____

d.

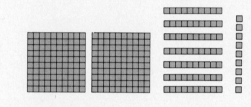

_____

e.

_____

f.

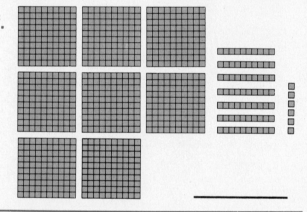

_____

PROBLEM SOLVING

g.

My number has a 4 in the hundreds place, a 3 in the tens place, and a 1 in the ones place. What's my number?

_____

h.

My number has a 6 in the hundreds place, a 0 in the tens place, and a 2 in the ones place. What's my number?

_____

118

More About Hundreds, Tens, and Ones

Write the numbers.

a.

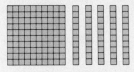

<u>150</u>

b.

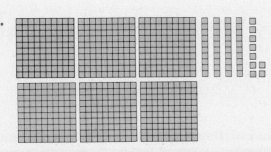

_____

c.

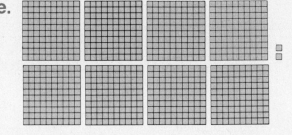

_____

d.

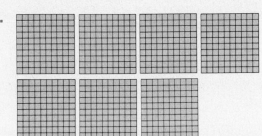

_____

e.

_____

f.

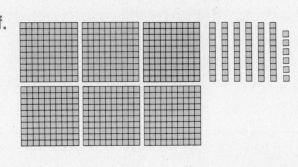

_____

g.

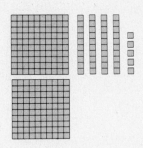

_____

h.

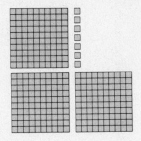

_____

Write the numbers.

a.   1 hundred   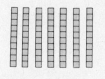   7 tens   9 ones = _179_

b. 7 hundreds   1 ten   3 ones = _____

c. 1 hundred   4 tens   0 ones = _____

d. 4 hundreds   7 tens   7 ones = _____

e. 5 hundreds   0 tens   5 ones = _____

f. 9 hundreds   9 tens   1 ones = _____

g. 3 hundreds   0 tens   0 ones = _____

Complete.

h. 765 = _7_ hundreds _6_ tens _5_ ones

i. 312 = _____ hundreds _____ ten _____ ones

j. 478 = _____ hundreds _____ tens _____ ones

k. 506 = _____ hundreds _____ tens _____ ones

l. 880 = _____ hundreds _____ tens _____ ones

m. 625 = _____ hundreds _____ tens _____ ones

n. 234 = _____ hundreds _____ tens _____ ones

120

Order to 1,000

Complete the chart.

101	102	103	104						110
111	112				116				120
121		123						129	
	132						138		
		144							150
151			155						
	162						169		
171						177			
	183						188		190
	192								200

Write the missing numbers.

a. | 251 | 252 | 253 | | | | 257 | | 259 |

b. | 631 | | | | 635 | | | | |

c. | 791 | | 793 | | | | | 798 | |

d. | 401 | | | 404 | | | 407 | | |

e. | 811 | 812 | | | | | | 818 | |

f. | 561 | | | | 565 | | | | 569 |

Midchapter Review

Write the numbers.

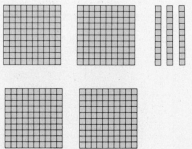

_____   _____

Counting Patterns

Count by fives.

a. 235   240   245   ___   ___   ___

b. 610   615   ___   ___   ___   ___

c. 780   785   ___   ___   800   ___

d. 965   ___   ___   980   ___   ___

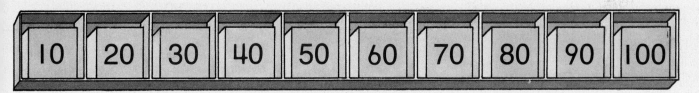

Count by tens.

e. 130   140   150   ___   ___   ___

f. 310   320   ___   ___   ___   360

g. 560   ___   ___   ___   600   ___

h. 840   850   ___   ___   ___   890

i. 930   ___   ___   960   ___   ___

50	100	150	200	250
300	350	400	450	500
550	600	650	700	750
800	850	900	950	1,000

Count by 50s.

a. __50__   __100__   __150__   _____   _____

b. __450__   _____   _____   __600__   _____

c. __800__   _____   __900__   _____   __1,000__

d. __250__   _____   _____   __400__   _____

Count by 100s.

e. __100__   __200__   _____   _____   _____

f. _____   __700__   _____   _____   __1,000__

Skills Maintenance

Add or subtract.

$$\begin{array}{ccccccc} 5 & 16 & 9 & 17 & 14 & 8 & 18 \\ +8 & -7 & +5 & -8 & -6 & +8 & -9 \\ \hline \end{array}$$

PROBLEM SOLVING
Reading Bar Graphs

The children counted the sports equipment in their school and made a graph.

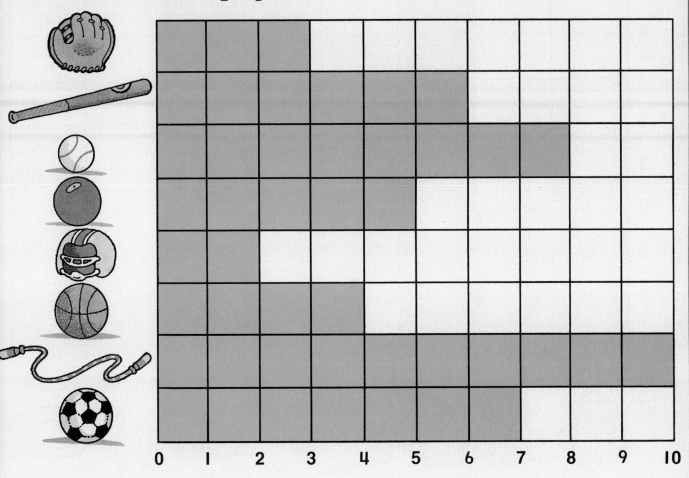

How many items did they count?

Mr. Cane counted the toys in his
store and made a graph.

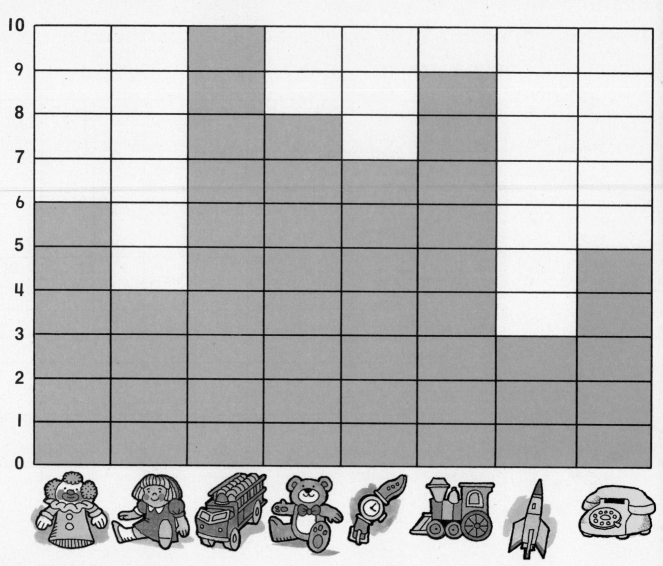

Write how many of each.
Ring the number that is greater.

Greater Than and Less Than

Ring the number that is greater.

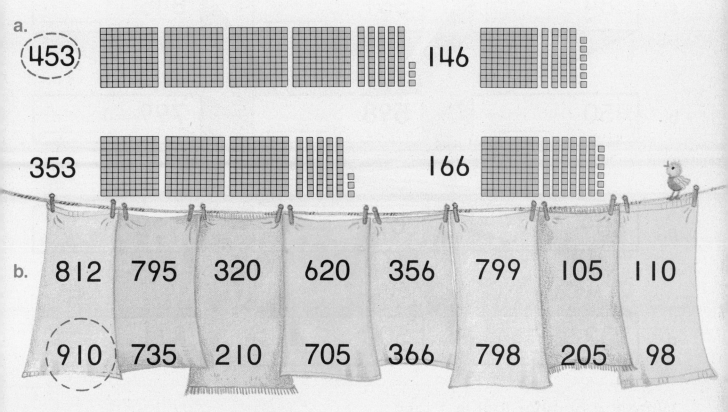

a. (453) 146

353 166

b. 812 795 320 620 356 799 105 110

(910) 735 210 705 366 798 205 98

Ring the number that is less.

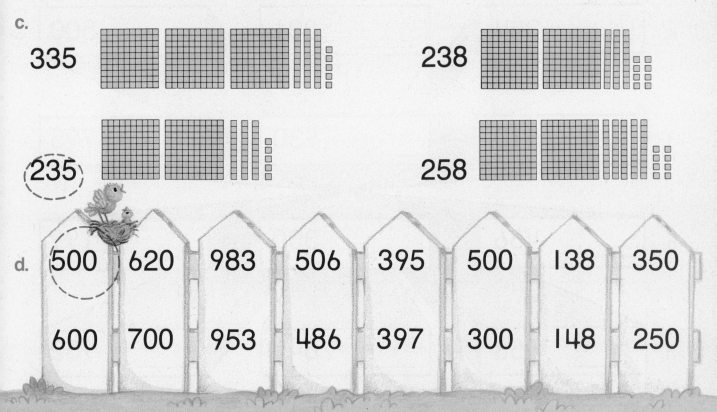

c. 335 238

(235) 258

d. (500) 620 983 506 395 500 138 350

600 700 953 486 397 300 148 250

Write the number that is 1 more.

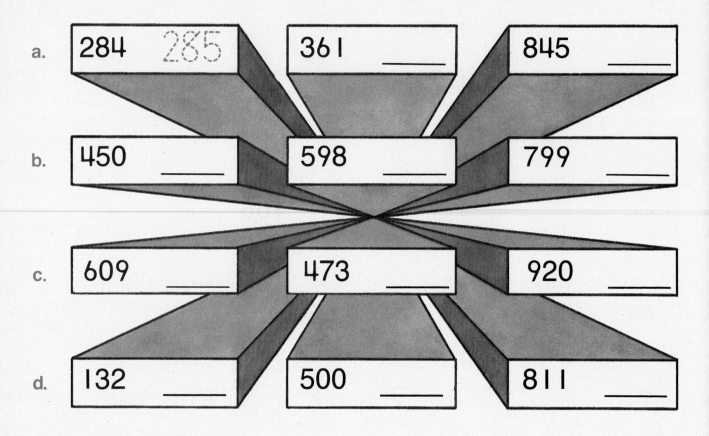

a. 284 [285]   361 ____   845 ____

b. 450 ____   598 ____   799 ____

c. 609 ____   473 ____   920 ____

d. 132 ____   500 ____   811 ____

Write the number that is 1 less.

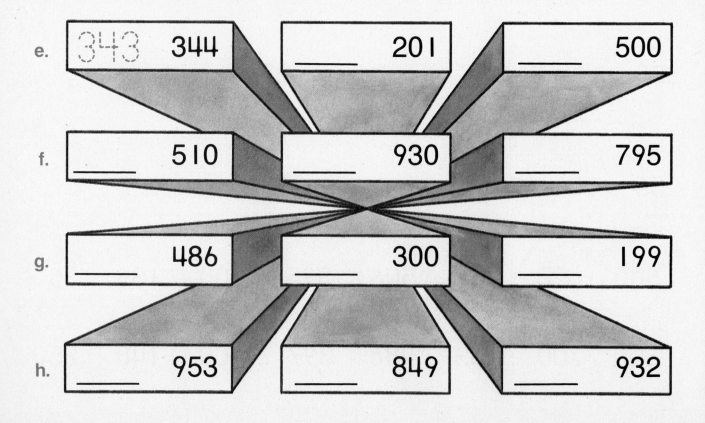

e. [343] 344   ____ 201   ____ 500

f. ____ 510   ____ 930   ____ 795

g. ____ 486   ____ 300   ____ 199

h. ____ 953   ____ 849   ____ 932

128

Comparing Numbers

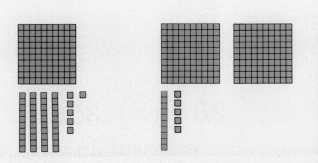

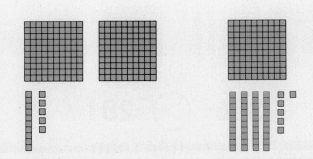

146 is less than **215**

146 < 215

215 is greater than **146**

215 > 146

Write the numbers.
Write > or <.

a.

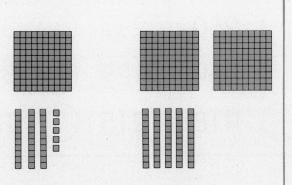

135 < 250

b.

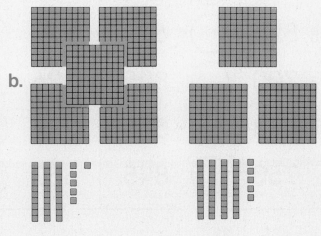

___ ◯ ___

c.

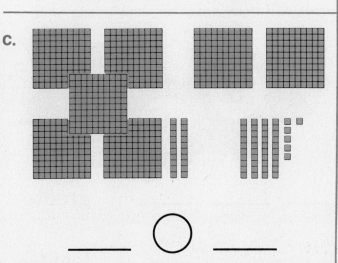

___ ◯ ___

d.

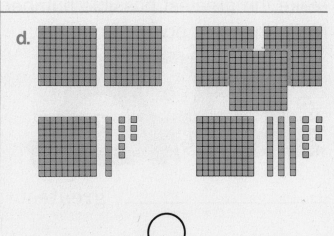

___ ◯ ___

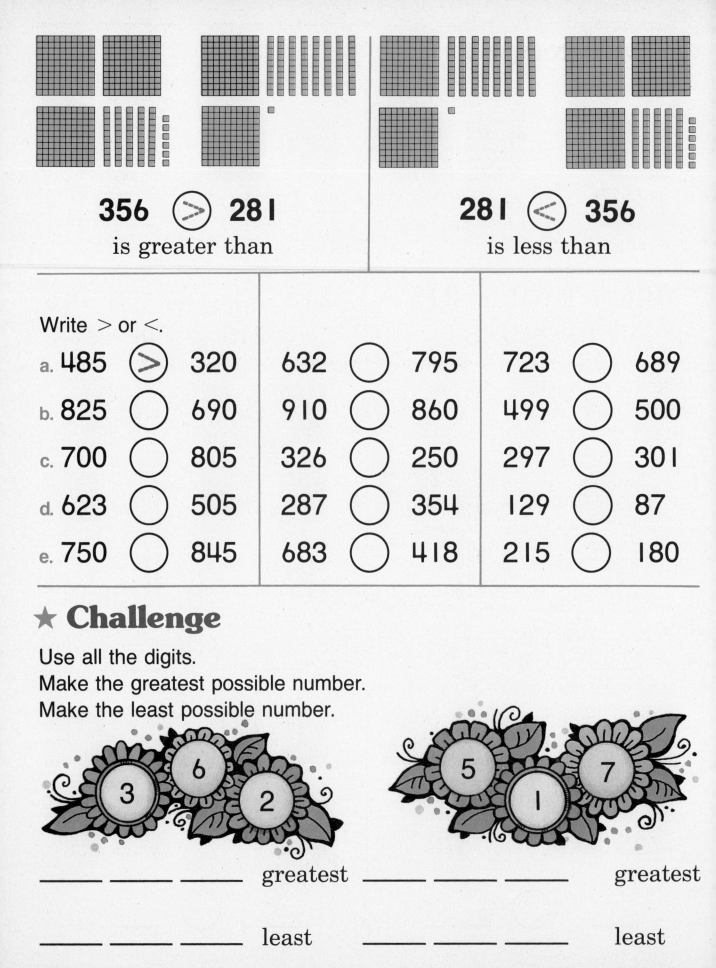

356 ⊃ 281
is greater than

281 ⊂ 356
is less than

Write > or <.

a. 485 ⟩ 320   632 ◯ 795   723 ◯ 689

b. 825 ◯ 690   910 ◯ 860   499 ◯ 500

c. 700 ◯ 805   326 ◯ 250   297 ◯ 301

d. 623 ◯ 505   287 ◯ 354   129 ◯ 87

e. 750 ◯ 845   683 ◯ 418   215 ◯ 180

★ Challenge

Use all the digits.
Make the greatest possible number.
Make the least possible number.

3 6 2

5 1 7

_____ _____ _____ greatest   _____ _____ _____ greatest

_____ _____ _____ least   _____ _____ _____ least

Write the numbers. (pages 115-120)

a. 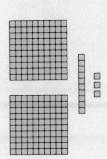 _____   _____

b. 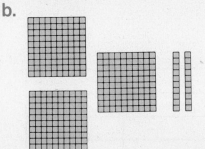 _____   _____

Write the missing numbers. (pages 121-122)

c. 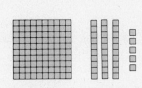 421 422 ___ ___ ___ ___ 428 ___ ___

d. 781 ___ ___ 784 ___ ___ ___ ___ ___

Count by fives. (pages 123-124)

e. 450   455   _____   _____   _____   475   _____

Write > or <. (pages 129-130)

f. 120 ◯ 200   235 ◯ 324   863 ◯ 683

g. 580 ◯ 524   450 ◯ 375   799 ◯ 800

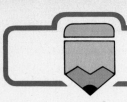

PROJECT

Making a Bar Graph

What is your favorite subject?

Ask each child in your class to choose his or her favorite subject.

Write how many children choose each subject. Complete the bar graph.

Reading
Math
Science
Social Studies

Number of Children

20

15

10

5

0

Reading   Math   Science   Social Studies

TEST

Write the numbers.

a.

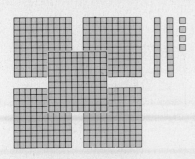

_____

_____

b.

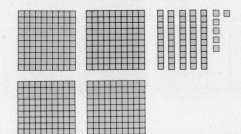

_____

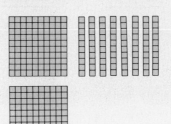

_____

Write the missing numbers.

c. | 881 | 882 | | | | 887 | | | |

d. | 651 | | 654 | | | | | |

Write > or <.

e. 880 ◯ 901   735 ◯ 550   800 ◯ 900

f. 642 ◯ 420   690 ◯ 790   401 ◯ 399

Count by fives.

g. 215 220 ____ ____ 235 ____ ____

ENRICHMENT

Ordering Numbers

Write these numbers in order from least to greatest.

| 405 | 219 | 350 | 286 |

219   286   350   ____

| 436 | 520 | 409 | 557 |

| 620 | 380 | 345 | 675 |

____ , ____ , ____ , ____

____ , ____ , ____ , ____

| 465 | 663 | 810 | 590 |

| 518 | 343 | 655 | 440 |

____ , ____ , ____ , ____

____ , ____ , ____ , ____

| 240 | 185 | 843 | 776 |

| 510 | 505 | 520 | 515 |

____ , ____ , ____ , ____

____ , ____ , ____ , ____

| 780 | 860 | 729 | 837 |

| 708 | 823 | 680 | 936 |

____ , ____ , ____ , ____

____ , ____ , ____ , ____

Time and Money

name

GETTING STARTED

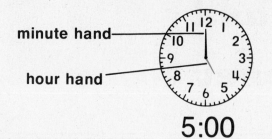

minute hand

hour hand

5 o'clock

five o'clock

5:00

5:00

What time is it?

a.

__3__ o'clock

3 : 00

_____ o'clock

____:____

_____ o'clock

____:____

b.

_____ o'clock

____:____

_____ o'clock

____:____

_____ o'clock

____:____

c.

_____ o'clock

____:____

_____ o'clock

____:____

_____ o'clock

____:____

136

name _____

Hour and Half Hour

One hour is **60** minutes.   One half hour is **30** minutes.

half past 4

four thirty

4:00   **4:30**

What time is it?

a.

8:00

8:30

___:___

b.

___:___

___:___

___:___

c.

___:___

___:___

___:___

What time is it?

a.

12:30

_____

_____

b.

_____

_____

_____

c.

_____

_____

_____

PROBLEM SOLVING

d. Alvin got on the bus at

.

He got off the bus
1 hour later.
What time did Alvin
get off the bus?

_____

e. Lily went shopping at

.

She finished shopping
2 hours later.
What time did Lily
finish shopping?

_____

138

Fifteen-Minute Intervals

One quarter hour is 15 minutes.

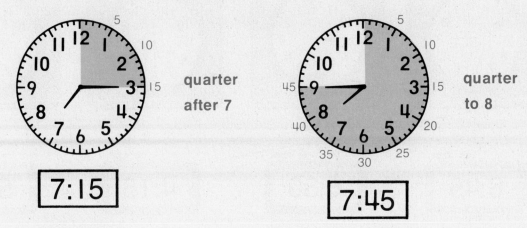

quarter
after 7

7:15

quarter
to 8

7:45

Ring the correct time.

a.

12:15

(1:15)

1:45

3:45

4:00

4:45

3:00

1:00

12:15

b.

6:00

8:30

9:30

5:00

6:00

7:00

11:45

12:45

1:00

c.

5:15

6:15

7:15

2:45

3:45

4:00

4:00

4:15

4:30

Match.

a.

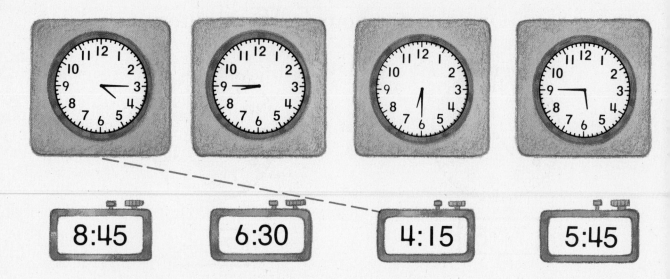

b.

Skills Maintenance

Subtract.

$$8 - 6 \qquad 10 - 3 \qquad 7 - 0 \qquad 9 - 1 \qquad 10 - 9 \qquad 9 - 6 \qquad 8 - 3$$

Five-Minute Intervals

What time is it?

a.

9:00   9:05   9:10   9:

b.

9:    9:   9:   9:

c.

9:    9:   9:   9:

d.

10:    :   :   :

Match.

a.

4:10

4:25

4:45

b.

2:50

2:35

2:55

c.

10:05

10:40

10:20

d.

7:15

7:30

7:25

142

name _____

Practice in Telling Time

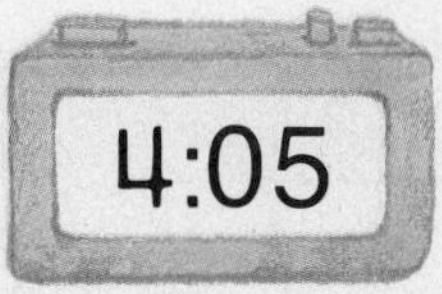

4:05

Ring the correct time.   4:05

a.

8:30
(8:45)
9:00

12:10
12:00
12:20

8:00
9:15
8:15

b.

3:30
4:00
3:55

5:30
5:20
6:00

5:40
5:20
5:50

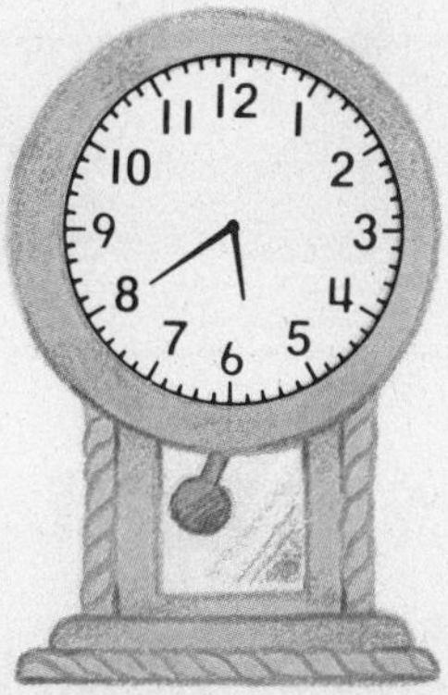

c.

7:50
8:00
7:30

7:30
6:30
8:00

10:15
10:45
10:25

Match.

a.

   7:00
8:15
9:00

   4:30
7:30
5:00

   12:30
2:00
2:25

b.

   6:30
6:15
7:00

   9:30
10:00
11:00

   12:30
1:30
12:45

c.

   6:00
11:00
12:00

   2:45
1:45
1:15

   7:50
7:30
7:10

★ Challenge

Draw the minute hands.

2:25   1:40   8:50   5:55

144

The Calendar

Sunday	Monday	Tuesday	Wednesday	Thursday	Friday	Saturday
				1	2	3
4	5	6	7	8	9	10
11	12	13	14	15	16	17
18	19	20	21	22	23	24
25	26	27	28	29	30	

Write the dates for each day of the week.

Mondays   5 , 12 , ____ , ____

Wednesdays ____ , ____ , ____ , ____

Thursdays ____ , ____ , ____ , ____ , ____

Saturdays ____ , ____ , ____ , ____

On what day does this month begin? _____

How many days are in this month? _____

How many days are in a week? _____

Complete the calendar for this month.

Month of _____

Sunday	Monday	Tuesday	Wednesday	Thursday	Friday	Saturday

a. Write the day of the week for each date.

7 _____   18 _____

13 _____   25 _____

3 _____   15 _____

b. Write the day that follows.

Sunday ___Monday___   Tuesday _____

Wednesday _____   Monday _____

Friday _____   Saturday _____

Penny, Nickel, and Dime

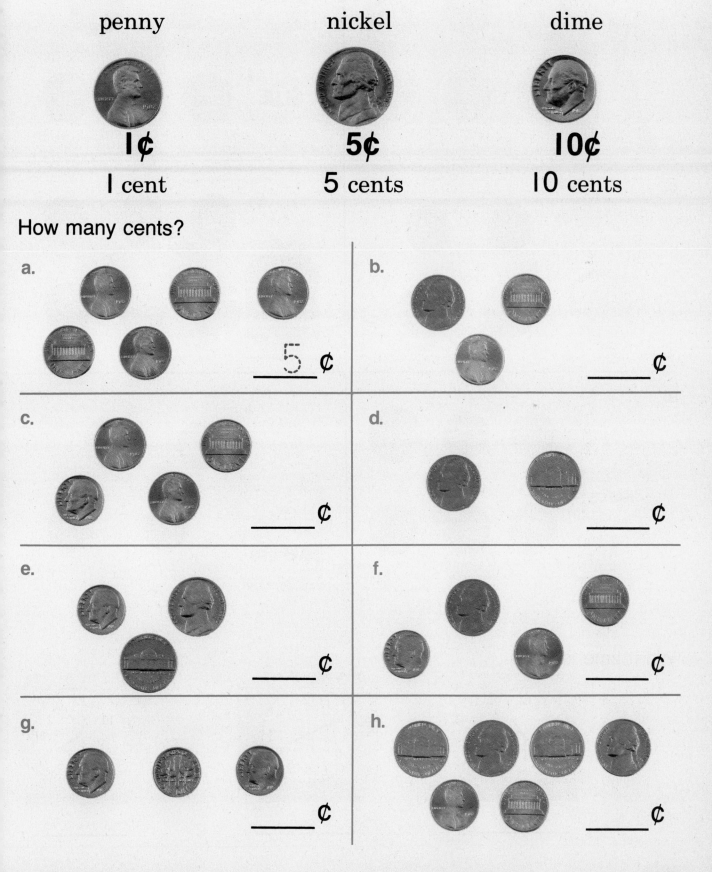

penny   nickel   dime

1¢   **5¢**   **10¢**

1 cent   5 cents   10 cents

How many cents?

a.   5 ¢

b.   ____ ¢

c.   ____ ¢

d.   ____ ¢

e.   ____ ¢

f.   ____ ¢

g.   ____ ¢

h.   ____ ¢

Ring how much money is needed.

a.

b.

c.

d.

e.

f.

Midchapter Review

What time is it?

_____   _____   _____

name _____

Quarter

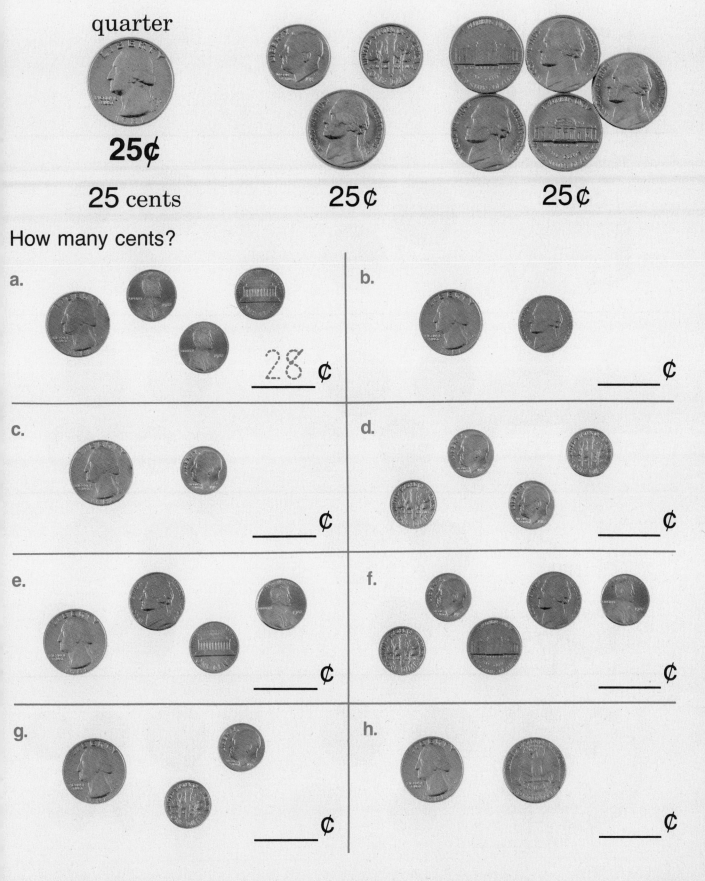

quarter

25¢

25 cents

25¢

25¢

How many cents?

a.

_28_ ¢

b.

_____ ¢

c.

_____ ¢

d.

_____ ¢

e.

_____ ¢

f.

_____ ¢

g.

_____ ¢

h.

_____ ¢

Ring the correct group of coins.

a.

b.

c.

d.

e.

PROBLEM SOLVING

Do You Have Enough Money?
Write how many cents.
Do you have enough?
Ring YES or NO.

a.

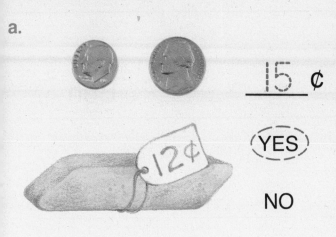

_15_ ¢

(YES)

NO

b.

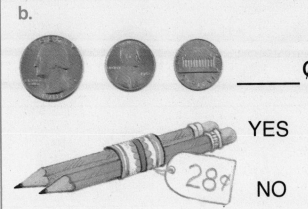

_____ ¢

YES

NO

c.

_____ ¢

YES

NO

d.

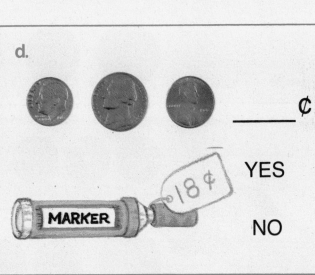

_____ ¢

YES

NO

e.

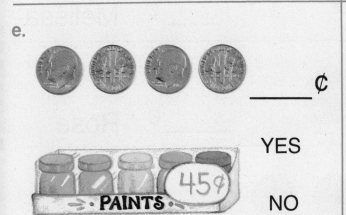

_____ ¢

YES

NO

f.

_____ ¢

YES

NO

Write how many cents.

Who has enough to buy?
Ring the name.

a.

28¢

_27_ ¢ Shawn

_30_ ¢ (Ben)

b.

34¢

____ ¢ Anna

____ ¢ Lucas

c.

43¢

____ ¢ Todd

____ ¢ Melissa

d.

55¢

____ ¢ Rose

____ ¢ Jennifer

Half-dollar

half-dollar

1¢　　**5¢**　　**10¢**　　**25¢**　　**50¢**

50 cents

How many cents?

a.

$\underline{50}$ ¢

b.

_____ ¢

c.

_____ ¢

d.

_____ ¢

e.

_____ ¢

f.

_____ ¢

g.

_____ ¢

h.

_____ ¢

Ring how much money is needed.

a.

b.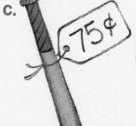

c.

d.

PROBLEM SOLVING

Write how many coins are needed to make 50¢.

e.

   |

_____   _____   _____

Dollar

1¢　　5¢　　10¢　　25¢　　50¢

$ .01　　$ .05　　$ .10　　$ .25　　$ .50

 $ is a dollar sign.

100¢ = $1.00

Write the amount in two ways.

a.

<u>　100　</u> ¢

$1.00

b.

_____ ¢

$ _____

---

c.

_____ ¢

$ _____

d.

_____ ¢

$ _____

Write the amount in two ways.

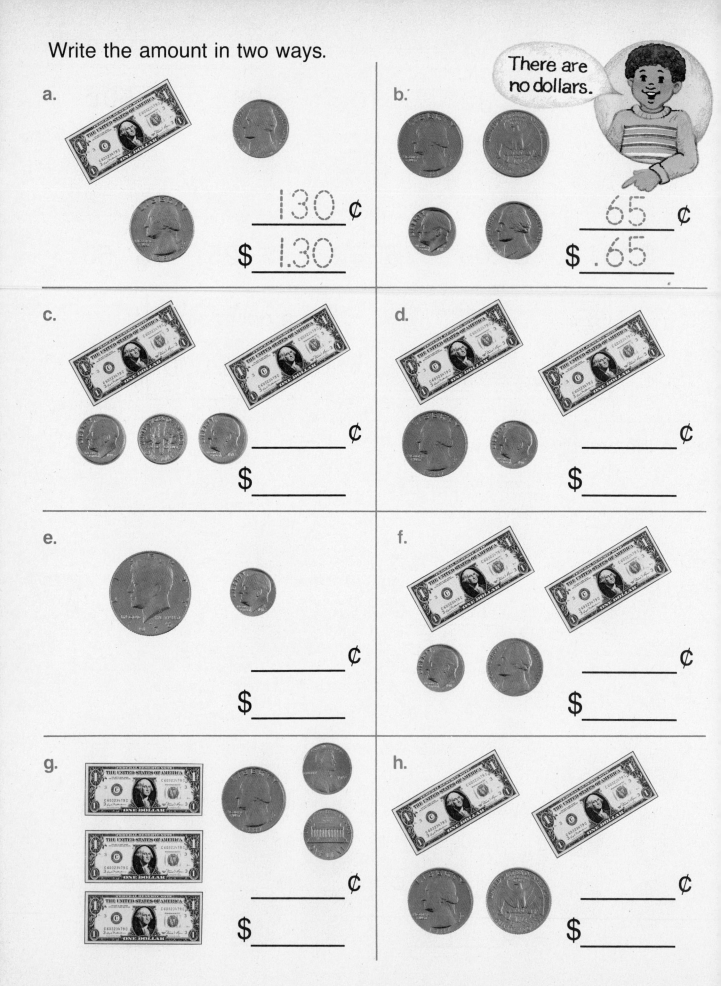

a.
_130_ ¢
$ _1.30_

b. There are no dollars.
_65_ ¢
$ _.65_

c.
_____ ¢
$ _____

d.
_____ ¢
$ _____

e.
_____ ¢
$ _____

f.
_____ ¢
$ _____

g.
_____ ¢
$ _____

h.
_____ ¢
$ _____

156

name

Money Practice

Write how much money.

a.

$ 1.75

b.

$ _____

c.

$ _____

d.

$ _____

e.

$ _____

f.

$ _____

g.

$ _____

h.

$ _____

Copyright © 1985 by Harcourt Brace Jovanovich, Inc.

157

Ring how much money is needed.

a.

b.

c.

d.

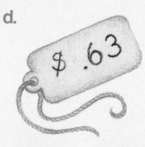

PROBLEM SOLVING

Write how many coins are needed to make the same amount.

e. 1 nickel = _____ pennies

f. 1 quarter = _____ nickels

g. 1 dime = _____ nickels

h. 1 dollar = _____ quarters

name

PROBLEM SOLVING

How Much Money Is Left?

Write how much money.
Cross out what is spent.
Write how much is left.

a.

Cora has __50__ ¢.

She buys ____ . 25¢

She has __25__ ¢ left.

b.

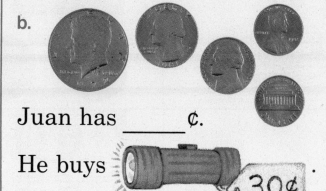

Juan has ____ ¢.

He buys ____ . 30¢

He has ____ ¢ left.

c.

Ed has ____ ¢.

He buys ____ . 16¢

He has ____ ¢ left.

d.

Jill has ____ ¢.

She buys ____ . 35¢

She has ____ ¢ left.

e.

Corey has ____ ¢.

He buys ____ . 13¢

He has ____ ¢ left.

f.

Flo has ____ ¢.

She buys ____ . 40¢

She has ____ ¢ left.

The Hardware Store

For Sale	Cross out what is spent.	Write how much is left.
a.  $4.35		$ __ .25
b.  $3.40		$ _____
c.  $3.50		$ _____
d.  $2.25		$ _____

What time is it? (pages 136-142)

a.

_____ _____ _____ _____

b.

_____ _____ _____ _____

How many cents? (pages 147, 149, 153)

c.

_____ ¢    _____ ¢

Ring how much is needed. (pages 148, 150, 154)

d.

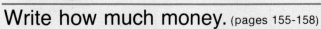  

Write how much money. (pages 155-158)

e.

  $ _____

  $ _____

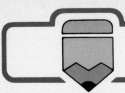

PROJECT

Earlier and Later

Start at now.
Draw the hands and write the time.

1 hour earlier	now	1 hour later

4:00

_____

_____

2 hours earlier	now	2 hours later

6:00

_____

_____

3 hours earlier	now	3 hours later

3:00

_____

_____

What time is it?

a.

_____ _____ _____ _____

b.

_____ _____ _____ _____

---

c. How many cents?

_____ ¢   _____ ¢

---

d. Ring how much is needed.

CRAFTS

32¢

---

e. Write how much money.

    $ _____     $ _____

ENRICHMENT

Making Change

Write how many of each coin is needed for the change.

Buy	Pay	Change

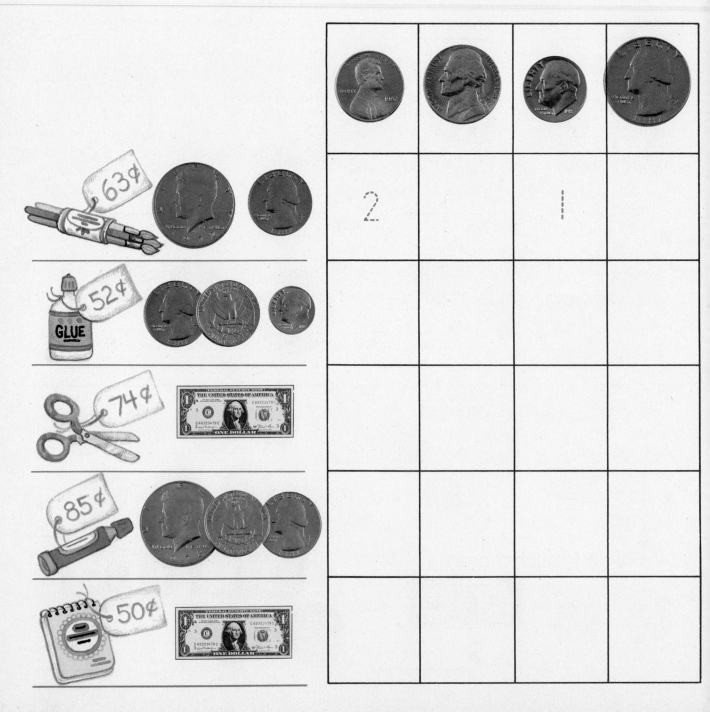

SKILLS MAINTENANCE

Choose the correct answers.

1. $9 + 8 =$ ___
   - (A) 9
   - **(B) 17**
   - (C) 16
   - (D) not here

2.
$$\begin{array}{r} 7 \\ +7 \\ \hline \end{array}$$
   - (A) 13
   - (B) 15
   - (C) 12
   - (D) not here

3.
$$\begin{array}{r} 9 \\ +9 \\ \hline \end{array}$$
   - (A) 18
   - (B) 17
   - (C) 15
   - (D) not here

4. $7 + 8 =$ ___
   - (A) 10
   - (B) 14
   - (C) 15
   - (D) not here

5.
$$\begin{array}{r} 3 \\ 4 \\ +4 \\ \hline \end{array}$$
   - (A) 10
   - (B) 11
   - (C) 12
   - (D) not here

6.
$$\begin{array}{r} 5 \\ 3 \\ +8 \\ \hline \end{array}$$
   - (A) 8
   - (B) 11
   - (C) 16
   - (D) not here

7. $16 - 7 =$ ___
   - (A) 9
   - (B) 7
   - (C) 10
   - (D) not here

8.
$$\begin{array}{r} 12 \\ - 8 \\ \hline \end{array}$$
   - (A) 8
   - (B) 5
   - (C) 4
   - (D) not here

9.
$$\begin{array}{r} 14 \\ - 6 \\ \hline \end{array}$$
   - (A) 8
   - (B) 6
   - (C) 10
   - (D) not here

10. $18 - 9 =$ ___
   - (A) 10
   - (B) 8
   - (C) 7
   - (D) not here

11.
$$\begin{array}{r} 9 \\ -2 \\ \hline \end{array}$$
   - (A) 6
   - (B) 5
   - (C) 8
   - (D) not here

12.
$$\begin{array}{r} 15 \\ - 9 \\ \hline \end{array}$$
   - (A) 6
   - (B) 9
   - (C) 7
   - (D) not here

Choose the correct answers.

13.

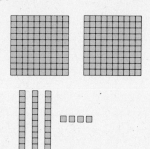

- (A) 432
- (B) 243
- (C) 234
- (D) not here

14.

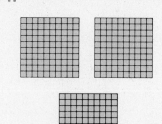

- (A) 300
- (B) 30
- (C) 130
- (D) not here

15.

There are 8 pens. Carl buys 6 more. How many pens in all?

- (A) 2
- (B) 14
- (C) 16
- (D) not here

16.

There are 15 pots. There are 7 plants. How many more pots than plants?

- (A) 7
- (B) 10
- (C) 8
- (D) not here

17.

- (A) 1:00
- (B) 12:45
- (C) 12:15
- (D) not here

18.

- (A) 9:20
- (B) 8:20
- (C) 9:40
- (D) not here

19.

- (A) 75¢
- (B) 85¢
- (C) 80¢
- (D) not here

20.

- (A) $1.45
- (B) $1.65
- (C) $1.40
- (D) not here

166

Addition of Two-Digit Numbers

CHAPTER 7

GETTING STARTED

Add.

a.
$$\begin{array}{r} 7 \\ +6 \\ \hline 13 \end{array}$$
$$\begin{array}{r} 5 \\ +9 \\ \hline \end{array}$$
$$\begin{array}{r} 9 \\ +9 \\ \hline \end{array}$$
$$\begin{array}{r} 4 \\ +7 \\ \hline \end{array}$$
$$\begin{array}{r} 6 \\ +2 \\ \hline \end{array}$$
$$\begin{array}{r} 4 \\ +3 \\ \hline \end{array}$$
$$\begin{array}{r} 8 \\ +8 \\ \hline \end{array}$$

b.
$$\begin{array}{r} 5 \\ +5 \\ \hline \end{array}$$
$$\begin{array}{r} 3 \\ +3 \\ \hline \end{array}$$
$$\begin{array}{r} 7 \\ +9 \\ \hline \end{array}$$
$$\begin{array}{r} 5 \\ +8 \\ \hline \end{array}$$
$$\begin{array}{r} 8 \\ +9 \\ \hline \end{array}$$
$$\begin{array}{r} 5 \\ +6 \\ \hline \end{array}$$
$$\begin{array}{r} 6 \\ +8 \\ \hline \end{array}$$

c.
$$\begin{array}{r} 8 \\ +7 \\ \hline \end{array}$$
$$\begin{array}{r} 3 \\ +7 \\ \hline \end{array}$$
$$\begin{array}{r} 6 \\ +9 \\ \hline \end{array}$$
$$\begin{array}{r} 1 \\ +9 \\ \hline \end{array}$$
$$\begin{array}{r} 3 \\ +5 \\ \hline \end{array}$$
$$\begin{array}{r} 7 \\ +7 \\ \hline \end{array}$$
$$\begin{array}{r} 8 \\ +2 \\ \hline \end{array}$$

d.
$$\begin{array}{r} 9 \\ +8 \\ \hline \end{array}$$
$$\begin{array}{r} 1 \\ +6 \\ \hline \end{array}$$
$$\begin{array}{r} 4 \\ +9 \\ \hline \end{array}$$
$$\begin{array}{r} 6 \\ +6 \\ \hline \end{array}$$
$$\begin{array}{r} 9 \\ +5 \\ \hline \end{array}$$
$$\begin{array}{r} 0 \\ +9 \\ \hline \end{array}$$
$$\begin{array}{r} 6 \\ +4 \\ \hline \end{array}$$

e.
$$\begin{array}{r} 6 \\ +3 \\ \hline \end{array}$$
$$\begin{array}{r} 8 \\ +6 \\ \hline \end{array}$$
$$\begin{array}{r} 1 \\ +7 \\ \hline \end{array}$$
$$\begin{array}{r} 8 \\ +3 \\ \hline \end{array}$$
$$\begin{array}{r} 9 \\ +7 \\ \hline \end{array}$$
$$\begin{array}{r} 2 \\ +7 \\ \hline \end{array}$$
$$\begin{array}{r} 4 \\ +8 \\ \hline \end{array}$$

f.
$$\begin{array}{r} 7 \\ +5 \\ \hline \end{array}$$
$$\begin{array}{r} 9 \\ +3 \\ \hline \end{array}$$
$$\begin{array}{r} 6 \\ +0 \\ \hline \end{array}$$
$$\begin{array}{r} 2 \\ +9 \\ \hline \end{array}$$
$$\begin{array}{r} 7 \\ +8 \\ \hline \end{array}$$
$$\begin{array}{r} 4 \\ +4 \\ \hline \end{array}$$
$$\begin{array}{r} 9 \\ +6 \\ \hline \end{array}$$

Adding Two-Digit Numbers

Step 1
Add the ones.
start
↓

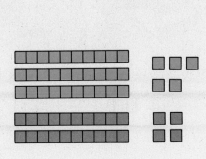

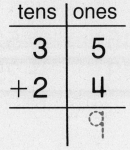

tens	ones
3	5
+2	4
	9

Step 2
Add the tens.

tens	ones
3	5
+2	4
5	9

Add.

a.

tens	ones
2	7
+4	1
6	8

tens	ones
5	1
+2	3

tens	ones
3	6
+	2

tens	ones
3	2
+2	7

b.

tens	ones
3	4
+	3

tens	ones
2	0
+1	5

tens	ones
2	2
+2	4

tens	ones
	8
+4	0

c.

tens	ones
1	2
+5	3

tens	ones
4	2
+	6

tens	ones
	5
+7	4

tens	ones
6	3
+1	5

	start
tens	ones
2	4
+5	2
7	6

start
↓
24
+52
76

Add.

a.
```
  64      45      52       8      61      32
+ 35    + 43    + 25    + 41    + 12    +  5
```

b.
```
  80      33      24      30      14      41
+ 10    +  6    + 35    + 40    + 52    + 18
```

c.
```
  54      19      37       5      13      23
+  3    + 70    + 61    + 34    + 50    + 23
```

d.
```
  60      25      18      32      52      75
+ 20    + 74    + 50    + 41    +  6    + 12
```

e.
```
  34       7      26      43      66      84
+ 51    + 82    + 31    + 52    + 20    + 14
```

170

Regrouping Ones as Tens

Jan regrouped ten ones
to make one more ten.

16 ones is
1 ten and 6 ones.

tens	ones
4	6

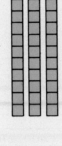

46

Write how many tens and ones.
Write the numbers.

a.

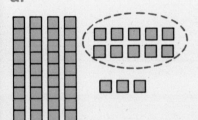

tens	ones
5	3

53

b.

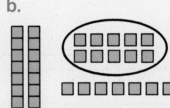

tens	ones

_____

c.

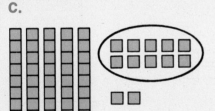

tens	ones

_____

d.

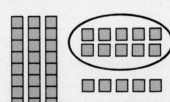

tens	ones

_____

e.

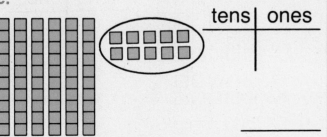

tens	ones

_____

f.

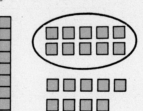

tens	ones

_____

Regroup ten ones to make one more ten.
Write the numbers.

a.

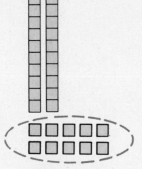

tens	ones
3	5

35

b.

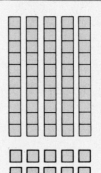

tens	ones

_____

c.

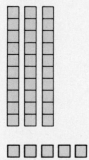

tens	ones

_____

d.

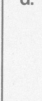

tens	ones

_____

e.

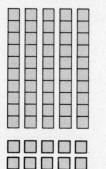

tens	ones

_____

f.

tens	ones

_____

g.

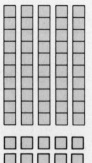

tens	ones

_____

h.

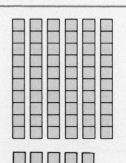

tens	ones

_____

172

Addition with Regrouping

Step 1
Add the ones.
Regroup.

start
↓

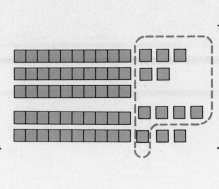

tens	ones
3	5
+2	7
	2

Step 2
Add the tens.

tens	ones
1	
3	5
+2	7
6	2

Add.

a.

tens	ones
4	3
+2	9
7	2

tens	ones
5	7
+	8
6	5

tens	ones
6	4
+1	8

tens	ones
2	6
+	7

b.

tens	ones
3	7
+1	8

tens	ones
4	4
+4	8

tens	ones
9	
+5	6

tens	ones
6	8
+1	2

tens	ones
4	5
+3	8
8	3

```
  45
+ 38
  83
```

Add.

a.
```
  29        77        49        45        36        25
+ 13      + 14      + 18      + 25      +  7      + 65
```

b.
```
  15        29        68        64        48        15
+  9      + 57      + 13      + 19      + 14      + 18
```

c.
```
   4        47        45        39        28        75
+ 29      + 26      +  8      + 21      + 26      +  9
```

★ Challenge

Find the missing numbers.

```
  3        7         6      7 6      4 9
+  5    + 3 0     + 5     + 1 8    + 3
  5 9     7        7 9
```

More Addition with Regrouping

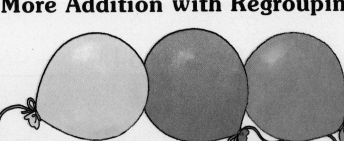

Stacey has **47** green balloons.
She has **28** red balloons.
How many balloons does she have?

Stacey has **75** balloons.

Step 1
Add the ones. Regroup.

start
↓

$$\begin{array}{r} 4\!\!7 \\ +28 \\ \hline 5 \end{array}$$

Step 2
Add the tens.

$$\begin{array}{r} \overset{1}{4}7 \\ +28 \\ \hline 75 \end{array}$$

Add.

a.
$$\begin{array}{r} 76 \\ +\ 9 \\ \hline 85 \end{array}$$
$$\begin{array}{r} 39 \\ +25 \\ \hline \end{array}$$
$$\begin{array}{r} 28 \\ +\ 5 \\ \hline \end{array}$$
$$\begin{array}{r} 45 \\ +37 \\ \hline \end{array}$$
$$\begin{array}{r} 17 \\ +34 \\ \hline \end{array}$$
$$\begin{array}{r} 52 \\ +38 \\ \hline \end{array}$$

b.
$$\begin{array}{r} 48 \\ +24 \\ \hline \end{array}$$
$$\begin{array}{r} 35 \\ +58 \\ \hline \end{array}$$
$$\begin{array}{r} 47 \\ +\ 8 \\ \hline \end{array}$$
$$\begin{array}{r} 59 \\ +11 \\ \hline \end{array}$$
$$\begin{array}{r} 4 \\ +18 \\ \hline \end{array}$$
$$\begin{array}{r} 29 \\ +36 \\ \hline \end{array}$$

c.
$$\begin{array}{r} 14 \\ +57 \\ \hline \end{array}$$
$$\begin{array}{r} 77 \\ +16 \\ \hline \end{array}$$
$$\begin{array}{r} 55 \\ +\ 9 \\ \hline \end{array}$$
$$\begin{array}{r} 18 \\ +45 \\ \hline \end{array}$$
$$\begin{array}{r} 68 \\ +13 \\ \hline \end{array}$$
$$\begin{array}{r} 43 \\ +27 \\ \hline \end{array}$$

d.
$$\begin{array}{r} 58 \\ +19 \\ \hline \end{array}$$
$$\begin{array}{r} 23 \\ +\ 7 \\ \hline \end{array}$$
$$\begin{array}{r} 64 \\ +19 \\ \hline \end{array}$$
$$\begin{array}{r} 56 \\ +\ 8 \\ \hline \end{array}$$
$$\begin{array}{r} 48 \\ +43 \\ \hline \end{array}$$
$$\begin{array}{r} 18 \\ +56 \\ \hline \end{array}$$

Add.

a.
$$\begin{array}{r} 68 \\ +22 \\ \hline 90 \end{array}$$
$$\begin{array}{r} 2 \\ +49 \\ \hline 51 \end{array}$$
$$\begin{array}{r} 67 \\ +16 \\ \hline \end{array}$$
$$\begin{array}{r} 87 \\ + 8 \\ \hline \end{array}$$
$$\begin{array}{r} 36 \\ +54 \\ \hline \end{array}$$
$$\begin{array}{r} 5 \\ +46 \\ \hline \end{array}$$

b.
$$\begin{array}{r} 66 \\ +15 \\ \hline \end{array}$$
$$\begin{array}{r} 21 \\ +69 \\ \hline \end{array}$$
$$\begin{array}{r} 74 \\ + 8 \\ \hline \end{array}$$
$$\begin{array}{r} 35 \\ +38 \\ \hline \end{array}$$
$$\begin{array}{r} 28 \\ +43 \\ \hline \end{array}$$
$$\begin{array}{r} 56 \\ +19 \\ \hline \end{array}$$

c.
$$\begin{array}{r} 65 \\ + 5 \\ \hline \end{array}$$
$$\begin{array}{r} 7 \\ +67 \\ \hline \end{array}$$
$$\begin{array}{r} 76 \\ +15 \\ \hline \end{array}$$
$$\begin{array}{r} 58 \\ +34 \\ \hline \end{array}$$
$$\begin{array}{r} 24 \\ +18 \\ \hline \end{array}$$
$$\begin{array}{r} 34 \\ +47 \\ \hline \end{array}$$

d.
$$\begin{array}{r} 53 \\ +37 \\ \hline \end{array}$$
$$\begin{array}{r} 54 \\ +38 \\ \hline \end{array}$$
$$\begin{array}{r} 75 \\ +17 \\ \hline \end{array}$$
$$\begin{array}{r} 36 \\ +36 \\ \hline \end{array}$$
$$\begin{array}{r} 83 \\ + 9 \\ \hline \end{array}$$
$$\begin{array}{r} 5 \\ +38 \\ \hline \end{array}$$

PROBLEM SOLVING

Solve.

e. Paul has **28** party hats.
He buys **7** more.
How many party
hats in all?

f. Mother buys **18** prizes.
Lisa buys **19** more.
How many prizes
are there?

176

Addition Practice

Sometimes we need to regroup . . .

. . . and sometimes we don't.

$$\begin{array}{r} 35 \\ +48 \\ \hline 83 \end{array}$$

$$\begin{array}{r} 41 \\ +26 \\ \hline 67 \end{array}$$

Add.

a.
$$\begin{array}{r} 37 \\ +24 \\ \hline 61 \end{array}$$
$$\begin{array}{r} 22 \\ +56 \\ \hline \end{array}$$
$$\begin{array}{r} 41 \\ +27 \\ \hline \end{array}$$
$$\begin{array}{r} 35 \\ +49 \\ \hline \end{array}$$
$$\begin{array}{r} 58 \\ +12 \\ \hline \end{array}$$
$$\begin{array}{r} 67 \\ +6 \\ \hline \end{array}$$

b.
$$\begin{array}{r} 54 \\ +36 \\ \hline \end{array}$$
$$\begin{array}{r} 45 \\ +25 \\ \hline \end{array}$$
$$\begin{array}{r} 23 \\ +16 \\ \hline \end{array}$$
$$\begin{array}{r} 83 \\ +5 \\ \hline \end{array}$$
$$\begin{array}{r} 21 \\ +70 \\ \hline \end{array}$$
$$\begin{array}{r} 47 \\ +26 \\ \hline \end{array}$$

c.
$$\begin{array}{r} 17 \\ +34 \\ \hline \end{array}$$
$$\begin{array}{r} 38 \\ +53 \\ \hline \end{array}$$
$$\begin{array}{r} 14 \\ +59 \\ \hline \end{array}$$
$$\begin{array}{r} 7 \\ +65 \\ \hline \end{array}$$
$$\begin{array}{r} 66 \\ +15 \\ \hline \end{array}$$
$$\begin{array}{r} 28 \\ +32 \\ \hline \end{array}$$

d.
$$\begin{array}{r} 8 \\ +46 \\ \hline \end{array}$$
$$\begin{array}{r} 29 \\ +61 \\ \hline \end{array}$$
$$\begin{array}{r} 33 \\ +44 \\ \hline \end{array}$$
$$\begin{array}{r} 20 \\ +57 \\ \hline \end{array}$$
$$\begin{array}{r} 45 \\ +4 \\ \hline \end{array}$$
$$\begin{array}{r} 39 \\ +43 \\ \hline \end{array}$$

e.
$$\begin{array}{r} 68 \\ +15 \\ \hline \end{array}$$
$$\begin{array}{r} 35 \\ +50 \\ \hline \end{array}$$
$$\begin{array}{r} 75 \\ +5 \\ \hline \end{array}$$
$$\begin{array}{r} 63 \\ +28 \\ \hline \end{array}$$
$$\begin{array}{r} 18 \\ +54 \\ \hline \end{array}$$
$$\begin{array}{r} 15 \\ +26 \\ \hline \end{array}$$

Add.

a.
$$43 + 39 = 82$$ $$62 + 37$$ $$18 + 2$$ $$46 + 35$$ $$25 + 55$$ $$61 + 14$$

b.
$$73 + 17$$ $$56 + 38$$ $$22 + 49$$ $$67 + 16$$ $$7 + 34$$ $$12 + 48$$

c.
$$26 + 52$$ $$36 + 4$$ $$41 + 28$$ $$29 + 32$$ $$61 + 19$$ $$58 + 13$$

d.
$$21 + 69$$ $$57 + 10$$ $$23 + 59$$ $$5 + 66$$ $$72 + 14$$ $$54 + 26$$

PROBLEM SOLVING

Solve.

e.

Melba has **35** seashells.
She finds **48** more.
How many seashells
does she have?

f.

Todd has **45** pebbles.
Ann gives him **14** more.
How many pebbles does
Todd have?

Three Addends

We can add three numbers.

Step 1 Add the ones.	**Step 2** Add the tens.	**Step 1** Add the ones. Regroup.	**Step 2** Add the tens.
21 34 +12 ___ 7	21 34 +12 ___ 67	23 16 +35 ___ 4	23 16 +35 ___ 74

Add.

a.

```
  18      36      21      32      21      23
  31      42      18      13       5      10
+ 10    +  7    + 41    + 26    + 11    + 34
-----   -----   -----   -----   -----   -----
  59
```

b.

```
  33      43      25      36      32      20
  12      15      12      31      56      32
+ 48    +  4    + 12    + 27    +  9    + 36
-----   -----   -----   -----   -----   -----
```

c.

```
   1      23      25      11      16      73
  46      36      40      46      21       3
+ 42    + 14    + 28    + 42    + 40    + 17
-----   -----   -----   -----   -----   -----
```

Add. Then color.

sums **50** to **59** 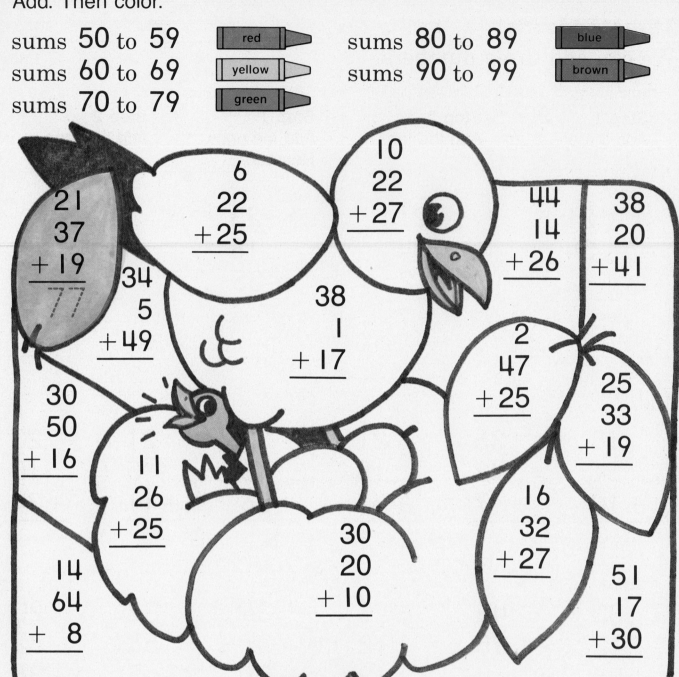 red

sums **60** to **69** yellow

sums **70** to **79** green

sums **80** to **89** blue

sums **90** to **99** brown

$$\begin{array}{r} 21 \\ 37 \\ +19 \\ \hline 77 \end{array}$$

$$\begin{array}{r} 6 \\ 22 \\ +25 \\ \hline \end{array}$$

$$\begin{array}{r} 10 \\ 22 \\ +27 \\ \hline \end{array}$$

$$\begin{array}{r} 44 \\ 14 \\ +26 \\ \hline \end{array}$$

$$\begin{array}{r} 38 \\ 20 \\ +41 \\ \hline \end{array}$$

$$\begin{array}{r} 34 \\ 5 \\ +49 \\ \hline \end{array}$$

$$\begin{array}{r} 38 \\ 1 \\ +17 \\ \hline \end{array}$$

$$\begin{array}{r} 2 \\ 47 \\ +25 \\ \hline \end{array}$$

$$\begin{array}{r} 25 \\ 33 \\ +19 \\ \hline \end{array}$$

$$\begin{array}{r} 30 \\ 50 \\ +16 \\ \hline \end{array}$$

$$\begin{array}{r} 11 \\ 26 \\ +25 \\ \hline \end{array}$$

$$\begin{array}{r} 16 \\ 32 \\ +27 \\ \hline \end{array}$$

$$\begin{array}{r} 14 \\ 64 \\ +8 \\ \hline \end{array}$$

$$\begin{array}{r} 30 \\ 20 \\ +10 \\ \hline \end{array}$$

$$\begin{array}{r} 51 \\ 17 \\ +30 \\ \hline \end{array}$$

Midchapter Review

Add.

$$\begin{array}{r} 36 \\ +42 \\ \hline \end{array}$$
$$\begin{array}{r} 50 \\ +39 \\ \hline \end{array}$$
$$\begin{array}{r} 27 \\ +64 \\ \hline \end{array}$$
$$\begin{array}{r} 19 \\ +75 \\ \hline \end{array}$$
$$\begin{array}{r} 35 \\ +8 \\ \hline \end{array}$$
$$\begin{array}{r} 43 \\ +27 \\ \hline \end{array}$$

Regrouping Ones and Tens

Step 1
Add the ones.

$$\begin{array}{r} 42 \\ +70 \\ \hline 2 \end{array}$$

Step 2
Add the tens. Regroup.

$$\begin{array}{r} 42 \\ +70 \\ \hline 112 \end{array}$$

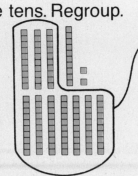

11 tens is
1 hundred and 1 ten.

Add.

a.
$$\begin{array}{r} 35 \\ +82 \\ \hline 117 \end{array}$$
$$\begin{array}{r} 83 \\ +45 \\ \hline \end{array}$$
$$\begin{array}{r} 67 \\ +42 \\ \hline \end{array}$$
$$\begin{array}{r} 50 \\ +70 \\ \hline \end{array}$$
$$\begin{array}{r} 33 \\ +86 \\ \hline \end{array}$$
$$\begin{array}{r} 44 \\ +72 \\ \hline \end{array}$$

b.
$$\begin{array}{r} 52 \\ +93 \\ \hline \end{array}$$
$$\begin{array}{r} 65 \\ +51 \\ \hline \end{array}$$
$$\begin{array}{r} 84 \\ +84 \\ \hline \end{array}$$
$$\begin{array}{r} 37 \\ +71 \\ \hline \end{array}$$
$$\begin{array}{r} 46 \\ +92 \\ \hline \end{array}$$
$$\begin{array}{r} 73 \\ +75 \\ \hline \end{array}$$

c.
$$\begin{array}{r} 40 \\ +85 \\ \hline \end{array}$$
$$\begin{array}{r} 72 \\ +64 \\ \hline \end{array}$$
$$\begin{array}{r} 53 \\ +76 \\ \hline \end{array}$$
$$\begin{array}{r} 90 \\ +60 \\ \hline \end{array}$$
$$\begin{array}{r} 24 \\ +83 \\ \hline \end{array}$$
$$\begin{array}{r} 81 \\ +52 \\ \hline \end{array}$$

d.
$$\begin{array}{r} 64 \\ +83 \\ \hline \end{array}$$
$$\begin{array}{r} 31 \\ +95 \\ \hline \end{array}$$
$$\begin{array}{r} 82 \\ +72 \\ \hline \end{array}$$
$$\begin{array}{r} 54 \\ +95 \\ \hline \end{array}$$
$$\begin{array}{r} 63 \\ +63 \\ \hline \end{array}$$
$$\begin{array}{r} 90 \\ +81 \\ \hline \end{array}$$

e.
$$\begin{array}{r} 75 \\ +92 \\ \hline \end{array}$$
$$\begin{array}{r} 62 \\ +44 \\ \hline \end{array}$$
$$\begin{array}{r} 41 \\ +73 \\ \hline \end{array}$$
$$\begin{array}{r} 96 \\ +91 \\ \hline \end{array}$$
$$\begin{array}{r} 50 \\ +80 \\ \hline \end{array}$$
$$\begin{array}{r} 62 \\ +86 \\ \hline \end{array}$$

Step 1
Add the ones.
Regroup.

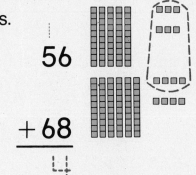

$$56$$
$$+68$$
$$4$$

Step 2
Add the tens.
Regroup.

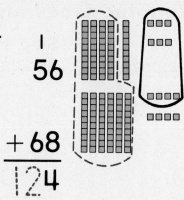

$$56$$
$$+68$$
$$124$$

a.

45	56	73	67	46	82
+78	+89	+68	+58	+64	+39
123					

b.

58	74	49	96	76	93
+58	+89	+85	+17	+48	+27

c.

65	56	78	84	25	66
+87	+44	+94	+57	+98	+78

★ Challenge

Find the missing numbers.

$$6$$
$$+9$$
$$139$$

$$3\,7$$
$$+5$$
$$1\,2$$

$$6\,8$$
$$+3$$
$$5$$

$$5$$
$$+1$$
$$130$$

$$4$$
$$+8$$
$$100$$

Addition Sentences

46 + 29 = _____   38 + 5 = _____

46 + 29 = __75__   38 + 5 = __43__

Add.

a. 56 + 27 = __83__   b. 37 + 25 = _____

c. 32 + 8 = _____   d. 43 + 27 = _____

e. 24 + 55 = _____   f. 7 + 48 = _____

g. 38 + 15 = _____   h. 80 + 36 = _____

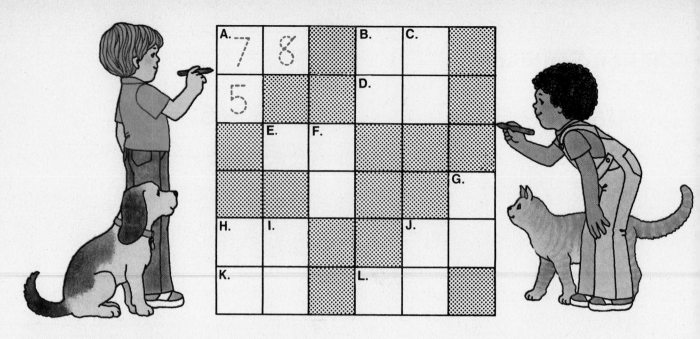

Add. Write each sum in the puzzle.

Across		Down	
A. 39 + 39 = 76	$\begin{array}{r}39\\+39\\\hline 78\end{array}$	A. 50 + 25 = 75	$\begin{array}{r}50\\+25\\\hline 75\end{array}$
B. 27 + 65 = ___		B. 64 + 29 = ___	
D. 23 + 14 = ___		C. 13 + 14 = ___	
E. 35 + 22 = ___		F. 36 + 38 = ___	
H. 7 + 35 = ___		G. 28 + 34 = ___	
J. 16 + 16 = ___		H. 39 + 9 = ___	
K. 58 + 26 = ___		I. 12 + 12 = ___	
L. 20 + 37 = ___		J. 18 + 19 = ___	

184

Checking Addition

Add.

$$\begin{array}{r} 43 \\ +29 \\ \hline 72 \end{array}$$

Check.

$$\begin{array}{r} 29 \\ +43 \\ \hline 72 \end{array}$$

Change the order of the addends to check your answer.

The sums are the same.

Add. Check your answers.

a.
$$\begin{array}{r} 14 \\ +59 \\ \hline 73 \end{array} \qquad \begin{array}{r} 59 \\ +14 \\ \hline 73 \end{array}$$

$$\begin{array}{r} 58 \\ + 7 \\ \hline \end{array} \qquad \begin{array}{r} 7 \\ +58 \\ \hline \end{array}$$

$$\begin{array}{r} 28 \\ +32 \\ \hline \end{array}$$

b.
$$\begin{array}{r} 35 \\ +49 \\ \hline \end{array} \qquad \begin{array}{r} 4 \\ +36 \\ \hline \end{array} \qquad \begin{array}{r} 21 \\ +43 \\ \hline \end{array}$$

c.
$$\begin{array}{r} 22 \\ +56 \\ \hline \end{array} \qquad \begin{array}{r} 63 \\ +28 \\ \hline \end{array} \qquad \begin{array}{r} 32 \\ +20 \\ \hline \end{array}$$

d.
$$\begin{array}{r} 37 \\ + 5 \\ \hline \end{array} \qquad \begin{array}{r} 29 \\ +28 \\ \hline \end{array} \qquad \begin{array}{r} 16 \\ +19 \\ \hline \end{array}$$

Add. Check your answers.

a.

$$\begin{array}{r} 18 \\ +27 \\ \hline 45 \end{array} \qquad \begin{array}{r} 27 \\ +18 \\ \hline 45 \end{array}$$

$$\begin{array}{r} 66 \\ +28 \\ \hline \end{array} \qquad \begin{array}{r} 83 \\ +9 \\ \hline \end{array}$$

b.

$$\begin{array}{r} 59 \\ +25 \\ \hline \end{array} \qquad \begin{array}{r} 33 \\ +61 \\ \hline \end{array} \qquad \begin{array}{r} 73 \\ +14 \\ \hline \end{array}$$

c.

$$\begin{array}{r} 47 \\ +30 \\ \hline \end{array} \qquad \begin{array}{r} 8 \\ +54 \\ \hline \end{array} \qquad \begin{array}{r} 58 \\ +12 \\ \hline \end{array}$$

d.

$$\begin{array}{r} 39 \\ +15 \\ \hline \end{array} \qquad \begin{array}{r} 50 \\ +23 \\ \hline \end{array} \qquad \begin{array}{r} 62 \\ +7 \\ \hline \end{array}$$

Skills Maintenance

How many cents?

_____ ¢   _____ ¢   _____ ¢

PROBLEM SOLVING

Addition
Solve.

a. There are **22** girls and **19** boys in the art class. How many children in all?

b. There are **37** jars of paint. There are **9** jars of water. How many jars are there?

c. José has **46** pieces of red paper. Bill has **16** pieces of blue paper. How many pieces of paper in all?

d. Mark cuts out **18** pictures. He cuts out **9** more. How many pictures does he cut?

e. Alice pastes **24** pictures. George pastes **37** pictures. How many pictures in all?

f. There are **36** boxes of crayons. Lulu finds **14** more. How many boxes in all?

Solve.

a. There are **28** shoppers. **34** more shoppers come. How many shoppers in all?

$$\overset{1}{28} \\ +34 \\ \hline 62$$

b. **45** cars are in the parking lot. **29** more cars come. How many cars in all?

c. The shoppers use **16** carts. They use **33** more carts. How many carts are used?

d. Hector buys **14** apples. Ellen buys **9** apples. How many apples do they buy?

e. Darnell buys **12** eggs. Keith buys **18** eggs. How many eggs in all?

f. Nancy counts **33** cans of bean soup. Richard counts **24** cans of cream soup. Julia counts **37** cans of tomato soup. How many cans of soup in all?

Adding Money

Dave buys a sandwich for 46¢.
He buys a drink for 37¢.
How much does he spend?

$$
\begin{array}{r}
46¢ \\
+\,37¢ \\
\hline
83¢
\end{array}
$$

Dave spends 83¢.

Add.

a.
$$
\begin{array}{r} 39¢ \\ +\,36¢ \\ \hline 75¢ \end{array}
\quad
\begin{array}{r} 53¢ \\ +\,24¢ \\ \hline \end{array}
\quad
\begin{array}{r} 47¢ \\ +\,29¢ \\ \hline \end{array}
\quad
\begin{array}{r} 49¢ \\ +\,24¢ \\ \hline \end{array}
\quad
\begin{array}{r} 19¢ \\ +\,57¢ \\ \hline \end{array}
\quad
\begin{array}{r} 46¢ \\ +\,39¢ \\ \hline \end{array}
$$

b.
$$
\begin{array}{r} 25¢ \\ +\,56¢ \\ \hline \end{array}
\quad
\begin{array}{r} 19¢ \\ +\,79¢ \\ \hline \end{array}
\quad
\begin{array}{r} 30¢ \\ +\,25¢ \\ \hline \end{array}
\quad
\begin{array}{r} 56¢ \\ +\,\ 8¢ \\ \hline \end{array}
\quad
\begin{array}{r} 24¢ \\ +\,38¢ \\ \hline \end{array}
\quad
\begin{array}{r} 28¢ \\ +\,\ 6¢ \\ \hline \end{array}
$$

c.
$$
\begin{array}{r} 36¢ \\ +\,46¢ \\ \hline \end{array}
\quad
\begin{array}{r} 29¢ \\ +\,59¢ \\ \hline \end{array}
\quad
\begin{array}{r} 27¢ \\ +\,65¢ \\ \hline \end{array}
\quad
\begin{array}{r} 18¢ \\ +\,42¢ \\ \hline \end{array}
\quad
\begin{array}{r} 25¢ \\ +\,14¢ \\ \hline \end{array}
\quad
\begin{array}{r} 63¢ \\ +\,19¢ \\ \hline \end{array}
$$

d.
$$
\begin{array}{r} 50¢ \\ +\,25¢ \\ \hline \end{array}
\quad
\begin{array}{r} 20¢ \\ +\,66¢ \\ \hline \end{array}
\quad
\begin{array}{r} 45¢ \\ +\,29¢ \\ \hline \end{array}
\quad
\begin{array}{r} 61¢ \\ +\,19¢ \\ \hline \end{array}
\quad
\begin{array}{r} 5¢ \\ +\,35¢ \\ \hline \end{array}
\quad
\begin{array}{r} 78¢ \\ +\,14¢ \\ \hline \end{array}
$$

PROBLEM SOLVING

55¢ TOOTHPASTE

38¢

39¢

53¢ SHAMPOO

27¢

25¢ SOAP

46¢

Find the total cost.

a.

```
 1
39¢
+53¢
92¢
```

b.

c.

d.

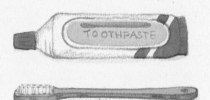

e.

f.

g.

h.

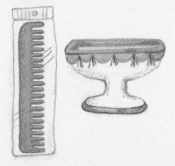

190

REVIEW

Add. (pages 169-170, 173-178, 189-190)

a.
```
  56      42      37      26      64      76
+ 39    + 36    + 53    +  8    + 58    + 87
```

b.
```
  50¢     44¢     67¢     52¢     25¢     84¢
+ 46¢   + 41¢   + 24¢   +  9¢   + 25¢   +  6¢
```

Add. (pages 179-180)

c.
```
  13      25      34      26      55      17
  25      10       3      41      24      32
+ 54    + 43    + 47    +  8    + 11    + 25
```

Add. (pages 183-184)

d.   42 + 26 = _____   59 + 13 = _____

e.   58 + 34 = _____   74 + 12 = _____

Solve. (pages 187-188)

f.

There are **38** animal floats in the parade. There are **26** clown floats. How many floats in all?

g.

There are **56** girls and **42** boys watching the parade. How many children are watching the parade?

PROJECT

Nomograph

This is a nomograph.

The middle line on the nomograph shows $\begin{array}{r} 42 \\ +39 \\ \hline 81 \end{array}$.

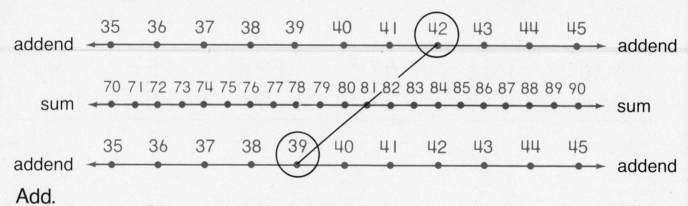

Add.

Use the nomograph to check your answers.

a.
$\begin{array}{r} 35 \\ +38 \\ \hline \end{array}$
$\begin{array}{r} 43 \\ +39 \\ \hline \end{array}$
$\begin{array}{r} 40 \\ +35 \\ \hline \end{array}$
$\begin{array}{r} 42 \\ +42 \\ \hline \end{array}$
$\begin{array}{r} 36 \\ +45 \\ \hline \end{array}$
$\begin{array}{r} 37 \\ +41 \\ \hline \end{array}$

b.
$\begin{array}{r} 36 \\ +36 \\ \hline \end{array}$
$\begin{array}{r} 37 \\ +42 \\ \hline \end{array}$
$\begin{array}{r} 35 \\ +43 \\ \hline \end{array}$
$\begin{array}{r} 41 \\ +39 \\ \hline \end{array}$
$\begin{array}{r} 37 \\ +37 \\ \hline \end{array}$
$\begin{array}{r} 42 \\ +38 \\ \hline \end{array}$

c.
$\begin{array}{r} 38 \\ +40 \\ \hline \end{array}$
$\begin{array}{r} 40 \\ +40 \\ \hline \end{array}$
$\begin{array}{r} 45 \\ +45 \\ \hline \end{array}$
$\begin{array}{r} 40 \\ +43 \\ \hline \end{array}$
$\begin{array}{r} 45 \\ +35 \\ \hline \end{array}$
$\begin{array}{r} 39 \\ +42 \\ \hline \end{array}$

d.
$\begin{array}{r} 42 \\ +35 \\ \hline \end{array}$
$\begin{array}{r} 44 \\ +37 \\ \hline \end{array}$
$\begin{array}{r} 41 \\ +43 \\ \hline \end{array}$
$\begin{array}{r} 36 \\ +38 \\ \hline \end{array}$
$\begin{array}{r} 39 \\ +45 \\ \hline \end{array}$
$\begin{array}{r} 36 \\ +41 \\ \hline \end{array}$

Add.

a.
76	25	6	66	73	43
+14	+58	+82	+27	+48	+75

b.
42¢	53¢	35¢	50¢	27¢	18¢
+35¢	+28¢	+35¢	+25¢	+ 6¢	+48¢

c.
56	23	30	15	34	3
13	43	25	34	54	15
+28	+16	+41	+29	+ 8	+42

d. $39 + 25 =$ _____ $57 + 26 =$ _____

e. $46 + 14 =$ _____ $72 + 72 =$ _____

f. $36 + 41 =$ _____ $15 + 75 =$ _____

Solve.

g.
Laura has **18** crayons.
She is given **27** more.
How many crayons
does she have?

h.
Larry buys a book
for **45¢** and pencils
for **49¢** . What is the
total cost?

Magic Triangles

This is a magic triangle.
When you add the numbers
along each side you get
the same sum.

Each side adds to 15.

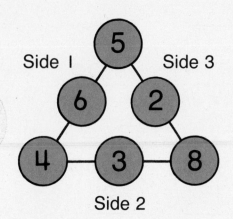

Side 1 _____15_____

Side 2 _____

Side 3 _____

Find the sums for each side.
Is it a magic triangle?
Ring YES or NO.

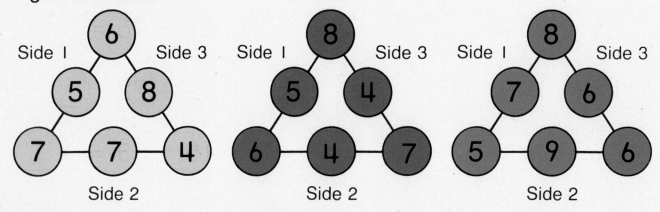

Side 1 _____

Side 2 _____

Side 3 _____

YES   NO

Side 1 _____

Side 2 _____

Side 3 _____

YES   NO

Side 1 _____

Side 2 _____

Side 3 _____

YES   NO

Subtraction of Two-Digit Numbers

CHAPTER 8

CABBAGE $1.50
SPECIAL 30¢ OFF!

GETTING STARTED

Subtract.

a.
$$16 - 7 = 9$$ $$11 - 3$$ $$15 - 8$$ $$17 - 9$$ $$14 - 6$$ $$9 - 8$$ $$6 - 1$$

b.
$$18 - 9$$ $$15 - 6$$ $$13 - 7$$ $$6 - 4$$ $$8 - 4$$ $$16 - 8$$ $$13 - 9$$

c.
$$14 - 8$$ $$12 - 4$$ $$9 - 0$$ $$7 - 3$$ $$10 - 3$$ $$14 - 9$$ $$10 - 1$$

d.
$$11 - 7$$ $$13 - 8$$ $$17 - 8$$ $$12 - 6$$ $$13 - 5$$ $$15 - 9$$ $$10 - 8$$

e.
$$12 - 9$$ $$16 - 9$$ $$7 - 5$$ $$14 - 5$$ $$11 - 5$$ $$12 - 5$$ $$13 - 4$$

f.
$$15 - 7$$ $$8 - 6$$ $$13 - 6$$ $$10 - 5$$ $$9 - 5$$ $$14 - 7$$ $$7 - 7$$

196

Subtracting Two-Digit Numbers

Step 1
Subtract the ones.

Step 2
Subtract the tens.

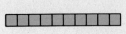

start
↓

tens	ones
4	6
−3	2
	4

tens	ones
4	6
−3	2
1	4

Subtract.

a.

tens	ones
3	7
−1	4
2	3

tens	ones
3	5
−1	2

tens	ones
5	6
−2	4

tens	ones
5	8
−	7

b.

tens	ones
6	9
−6	2

tens	ones
9	4
−8	0

tens	ones
5	9
−3	1

tens	ones
4	6
−2	5

c.

tens	ones
9	6
−2	6

tens	ones
6	5
−	5

tens	ones
8	5
−4	3

tens	ones
7	8
−7	6

197

start
↓

tens	ones
6	2
− 4	1
2	1

62
−41
21

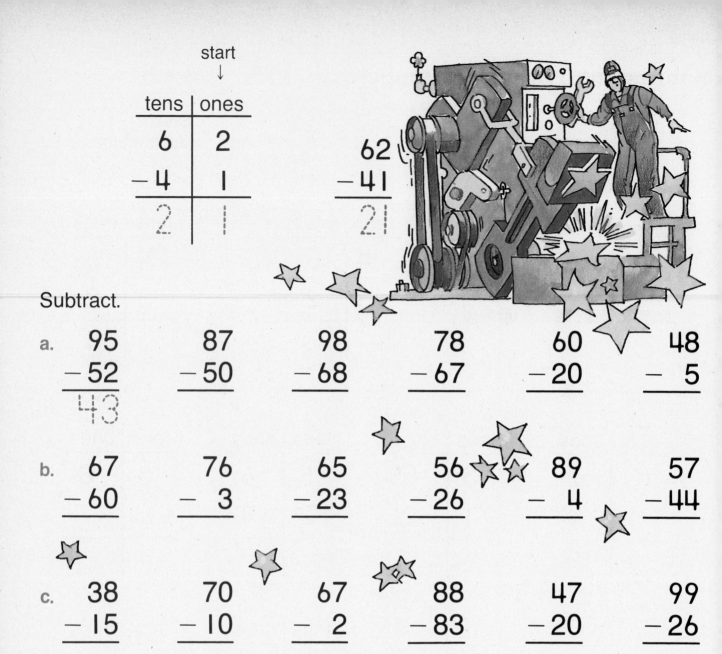

Subtract.

a.
```
  95        87        98        78        60        48
− 52      − 50      − 68      − 67      − 20      −  5
  43
```

b.
```
  67        76        65        56        89        57
− 60      −  3      − 23      − 26      −  4      − 44
```

c.
```
  38        70        67        88        47        99
− 15      − 10      −  2      − 83      − 20      − 26
```

PROBLEM SOLVING

Solve.

d. There are 55 gold stars in a box. The teacher gives out 21 gold stars. How many gold stars are left in the box?

e. There are 40 red stars. There are 30 blue stars. How many more red stars than blue stars?

198

name

Regrouping Tens as Ones

Show one fewer ten and ten more ones.

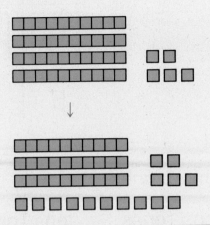

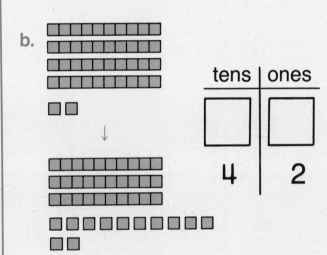

Regroup to show one fewer ten
and ten more ones.

a.

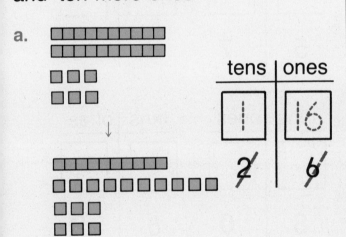

b.

c.

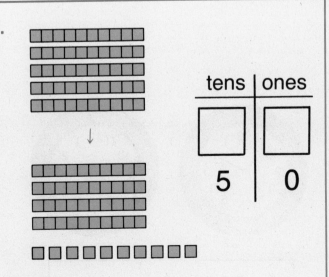

d.

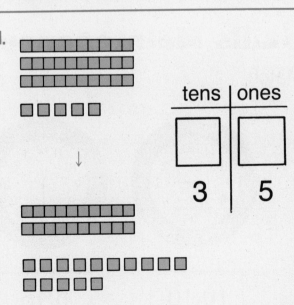

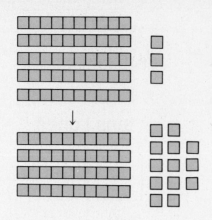

	tens	ones
	4 ~~5~~	13 ~~3~~

Regroup to show one fewer ten and ten more ones.

a.

tens	ones		tens	ones		tens	ones		tens	ones
3	10									
~~4~~	~~0~~		3	6		5	7		8	3

b.

tens	ones		tens	ones		tens	ones		tens	ones
5	9		9	8		8	0		6	2

Skills Maintenance

Match.

10:10	8:15	11:30	7:45

Subtraction with Regrouping

Step 1
You need more ones.
Regroup to show one fewer
ten and ten more ones.

Step 2
Subtract the ones.

Step 3
Subtract the tens.

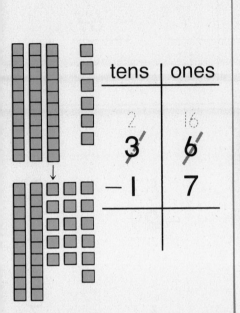

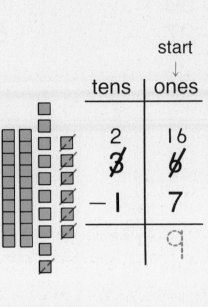

	tens	ones
	2	16
	3̷	6̷
	− 1	7

start ↓

	tens	ones
	2	16
	3̷	6̷
	− 1	7
		9

	tens	ones
	2	16
	3̷	6̷
	− 1	7
	1	9

Subtract.

a.

tens	ones
6 7̷	14 4̷
− 3	6
3	8

tens	ones
7 8̷	16 6̷
−	7
7	9

tens	ones
6	2
− 2	4

tens	ones
9	1
−	7

b.

tens	ones
9	5
−	8

tens	ones
8	1
− 6	5

tens	ones
9	3
− 3	7

tens	ones
7	4
− 2	5

	tens	ones				tens	ones	

$$
\begin{array}{c|c}
 & \downarrow \\
\text{tens} & \text{ones}
\end{array}
\qquad
\begin{array}{c|c}
 & \downarrow \\
\text{tens} & \text{ones}
\end{array}
$$

$$
\begin{array}{r}
\overset{4}{\cancel{5}}\ \overset{10}{\cancel{0}} \\
-2\ \ 7 \\
\hline
2\ \ 3
\end{array}
\qquad
\begin{array}{r}
\overset{410}{\cancel{50}} \\
-27 \\
\hline
23
\end{array}
\qquad
\begin{array}{r}
\overset{6}{\cancel{7}}\ \overset{12}{\cancel{2}} \\
-6\ \ 7 \\
\hline
5
\end{array}
\qquad
\begin{array}{r}
\overset{612}{\cancel{72}} \\
-67 \\
\hline
5
\end{array}
$$

Subtract.

a.
$$
\begin{array}{r}
\overset{3\,16}{\cancel{46}} \\
-28 \\
\hline
18
\end{array}
\quad
\begin{array}{r}
\overset{7\,11}{\cancel{81}} \\
-\ 6 \\
\hline
75
\end{array}
\quad
\begin{array}{r}
\overset{5\,12}{\cancel{62}} \\
-59 \\
\hline
3
\end{array}
\quad
\begin{array}{r}
45 \\
-\ 6 \\
\hline
\end{array}
\quad
\begin{array}{r}
57 \\
-29 \\
\hline
\end{array}
\quad
\begin{array}{r}
27 \\
-\ 8 \\
\hline
\end{array}
$$

b.
$$
\begin{array}{r}
90 \\
-36 \\
\hline
\end{array}
\quad
\begin{array}{r}
51 \\
-14 \\
\hline
\end{array}
\quad
\begin{array}{r}
98 \\
-89 \\
\hline
\end{array}
\quad
\begin{array}{r}
80 \\
-48 \\
\hline
\end{array}
\quad
\begin{array}{r}
61 \\
-\ 4 \\
\hline
\end{array}
\quad
\begin{array}{r}
71 \\
-39 \\
\hline
\end{array}
$$

c.
$$
\begin{array}{r}
43 \\
-19 \\
\hline
\end{array}
\quad
\begin{array}{r}
35 \\
-\ 7 \\
\hline
\end{array}
\quad
\begin{array}{r}
33 \\
-15 \\
\hline
\end{array}
\quad
\begin{array}{r}
66 \\
-47 \\
\hline
\end{array}
\quad
\begin{array}{r}
90 \\
-74 \\
\hline
\end{array}
\quad
\begin{array}{r}
82 \\
-79 \\
\hline
\end{array}
$$

★ Challenge

Find the missing numbers.

$$
\begin{array}{r}
6\ 7 \\
-2\ \Box \\
\hline
\Box\ 2
\end{array}
\quad
\begin{array}{r}
\Box\ 9 \\
-6\ \Box \\
\hline
2\ 6
\end{array}
\quad
\begin{array}{r}
4\ \Box \\
-\Box\ 1 \\
\hline
2\ 4
\end{array}
\quad
\begin{array}{r}
7\ 3 \\
-3\ \Box \\
\hline
\Box\ 8
\end{array}
\quad
\begin{array}{r}
5\ 6 \\
-\Box\ 8 \\
\hline
3\ \Box
\end{array}
\quad
\begin{array}{r}
\Box\ 2 \\
-2\ \Box \\
\hline
1\ 5
\end{array}
$$

More Subtraction with Regrouping

The pet shop has 63 rabbits.
18 rabbits are sold.
How many rabbits are left?

Step 1
You need more ones.
Regroup.

$$\begin{array}{r} {\scriptstyle 5\,13} \\ \cancel{63} \\ -\ 18 \\ \hline \end{array}$$

Step 2
Subtract the ones.

$$\begin{array}{r} {\scriptstyle 5\,13} \\ \cancel{63} \\ -\ 18 \\ \hline 5 \end{array}$$

Step 3
Subtract the tens.

$$\begin{array}{r} {\scriptstyle 5\,13} \\ \cancel{63} \\ -\ 18 \\ \hline 4\,5 \end{array}$$

45 rabbits are left.

Subtract.

a.
$$\begin{array}{r} {\scriptstyle 8\,11} \\ \cancel{91} \\ -\ 5 \\ \hline 86 \end{array}$$
$$\begin{array}{r} 73 \\ -59 \\ \hline \end{array}$$
$$\begin{array}{r} 53 \\ -\ 7 \\ \hline \end{array}$$
$$\begin{array}{r} 81 \\ -56 \\ \hline \end{array}$$
$$\begin{array}{r} 80 \\ -79 \\ \hline \end{array}$$
$$\begin{array}{r} 97 \\ -59 \\ \hline \end{array}$$

b.
$$\begin{array}{r} 71 \\ -48 \\ \hline \end{array}$$
$$\begin{array}{r} 42 \\ -\ 8 \\ \hline \end{array}$$
$$\begin{array}{r} 82 \\ -34 \\ \hline \end{array}$$
$$\begin{array}{r} 43 \\ -15 \\ \hline \end{array}$$
$$\begin{array}{r} 50 \\ -\ 5 \\ \hline \end{array}$$
$$\begin{array}{r} 62 \\ -\ 5 \\ \hline \end{array}$$

c.
$$\begin{array}{r} 93 \\ -28 \\ \hline \end{array}$$
$$\begin{array}{r} 54 \\ -48 \\ \hline \end{array}$$
$$\begin{array}{r} 60 \\ -14 \\ \hline \end{array}$$
$$\begin{array}{r} 31 \\ -\ 2 \\ \hline \end{array}$$
$$\begin{array}{r} 74 \\ -29 \\ \hline \end{array}$$
$$\begin{array}{r} 87 \\ -28 \\ \hline \end{array}$$

Subtract.

a.
$$\begin{array}{r} 3\ 16 \\ \cancel{4}\cancel{6} \\ -37 \\ \hline 9 \end{array}$$
$$\begin{array}{r} 54 \\ -16 \\ \hline \end{array}$$
$$\begin{array}{r} 62 \\ -26 \\ \hline \end{array}$$
$$\begin{array}{r} 80 \\ -13 \\ \hline \end{array}$$
$$\begin{array}{r} 78 \\ -\ 9 \\ \hline \end{array}$$
$$\begin{array}{r} 43 \\ -37 \\ \hline \end{array}$$

b.
$$\begin{array}{r} 34 \\ -17 \\ \hline \end{array}$$
$$\begin{array}{r} 73 \\ -58 \\ \hline \end{array}$$
$$\begin{array}{r} 60 \\ -24 \\ \hline \end{array}$$
$$\begin{array}{r} 91 \\ -43 \\ \hline \end{array}$$
$$\begin{array}{r} 35 \\ -\ 7 \\ \hline \end{array}$$
$$\begin{array}{r} 55 \\ -18 \\ \hline \end{array}$$

c.
$$\begin{array}{r} 63 \\ -57 \\ \hline \end{array}$$
$$\begin{array}{r} 90 \\ -35 \\ \hline \end{array}$$
$$\begin{array}{r} 58 \\ -\ 9 \\ \hline \end{array}$$
$$\begin{array}{r} 43 \\ -17 \\ \hline \end{array}$$
$$\begin{array}{r} 76 \\ -67 \\ \hline \end{array}$$
$$\begin{array}{r} 50 \\ -38 \\ \hline \end{array}$$

d.
$$\begin{array}{r} 54 \\ -\ 6 \\ \hline \end{array}$$
$$\begin{array}{r} 38 \\ -19 \\ \hline \end{array}$$
$$\begin{array}{r} 66 \\ -58 \\ \hline \end{array}$$
$$\begin{array}{r} 33 \\ -\ 5 \\ \hline \end{array}$$
$$\begin{array}{r} 40 \\ -25 \\ \hline \end{array}$$
$$\begin{array}{r} 55 \\ -38 \\ \hline \end{array}$$

PROBLEM SOLVING

Solve.

e. There are **73** goldfish.
There are **27** angelfish.
How many more goldfish
than angelfish?

f. Mr. Stein has **37** dog collars.
He sells **19**.
How many dog collars are left?

Subtraction Practice

$$\begin{array}{r} 47 \\ -15 \\ \hline 32 \end{array}$$

There are enough ones. Subtract.

There are not enough ones. Regroup and subtract.

$$\begin{array}{r} {\scriptstyle 4\ 16} \\ 5\!\!\!/6 \\ -38 \\ \hline 18 \end{array}$$

Subtract.

a.
$$\begin{array}{r} {\scriptstyle 4\ 17} \\ 5\!\!\!/7 \\ -28 \\ \hline 29 \end{array}$$
$$\begin{array}{r} 46 \\ -23 \\ \hline \end{array}$$
$$\begin{array}{r} 85 \\ -38 \\ \hline \end{array}$$
$$\begin{array}{r} 96 \\ -32 \\ \hline \end{array}$$
$$\begin{array}{r} 36 \\ -\ 9 \\ \hline \end{array}$$
$$\begin{array}{r} 42 \\ -37 \\ \hline \end{array}$$

b.
$$\begin{array}{r} 39 \\ -16 \\ \hline \end{array}$$
$$\begin{array}{r} 80 \\ -42 \\ \hline \end{array}$$
$$\begin{array}{r} 77 \\ -29 \\ \hline \end{array}$$
$$\begin{array}{r} 52 \\ -21 \\ \hline \end{array}$$
$$\begin{array}{r} 43 \\ -18 \\ \hline \end{array}$$
$$\begin{array}{r} 57 \\ -\ 6 \\ \hline \end{array}$$

c.
$$\begin{array}{r} 92 \\ -47 \\ \hline \end{array}$$
$$\begin{array}{r} 88 \\ -44 \\ \hline \end{array}$$
$$\begin{array}{r} 63 \\ -56 \\ \hline \end{array}$$
$$\begin{array}{r} 27 \\ -18 \\ \hline \end{array}$$
$$\begin{array}{r} 90 \\ -40 \\ \hline \end{array}$$
$$\begin{array}{r} 42 \\ -15 \\ \hline \end{array}$$

d.
$$\begin{array}{r} 36 \\ -\ 8 \\ \hline \end{array}$$
$$\begin{array}{r} 24 \\ -12 \\ \hline \end{array}$$
$$\begin{array}{r} 50 \\ -26 \\ \hline \end{array}$$
$$\begin{array}{r} 34 \\ -18 \\ \hline \end{array}$$
$$\begin{array}{r} 75 \\ -50 \\ \hline \end{array}$$
$$\begin{array}{r} 84 \\ -27 \\ \hline \end{array}$$

e.
$$\begin{array}{r} 40 \\ -31 \\ \hline \end{array}$$
$$\begin{array}{r} 76 \\ -59 \\ \hline \end{array}$$
$$\begin{array}{r} 63 \\ -23 \\ \hline \end{array}$$
$$\begin{array}{r} 33 \\ -18 \\ \hline \end{array}$$
$$\begin{array}{r} 43 \\ -\ 9 \\ \hline \end{array}$$
$$\begin{array}{r} 46 \\ -20 \\ \hline \end{array}$$

Subtract.
Use the code to solve.

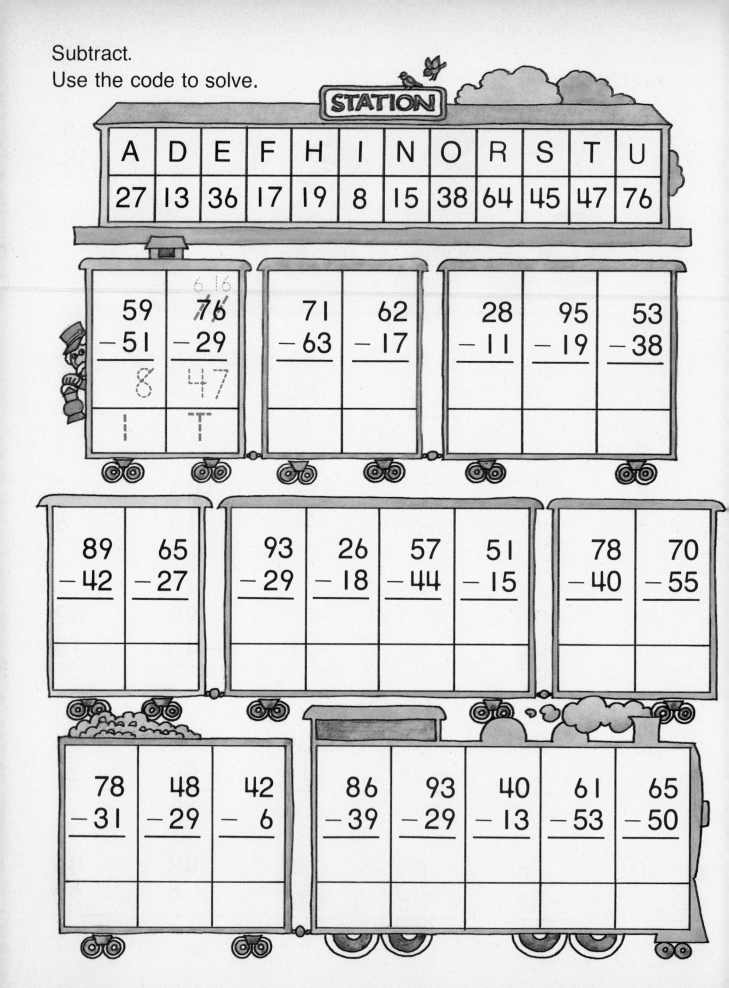

STATION

A	D	E	F	H	I	N	O	R	S	T	U
27	13	36	17	19	8	15	38	64	45	47	76

Car 1:

```
  59      76
- 51    - 29
 ----    ----
   8      47

   I       T
```

Car 2:

```
  71      62
- 63    - 17
 ----    ----
```

Car 3:

```
  28      95      53
- 11    - 19    - 38
 ----    ----    ----
```

Car 4:

```
  89      65
- 42    - 27
 ----    ----
```

Car 5:

```
  93      26      57      51
- 29    - 18    - 44    - 15
 ----    ----    ----    ----
```

Car 6:

```
  78      70
- 40    - 55
 ----    ----
```

Car 7:

```
  78      48      42
- 31    - 29    -  6
 ----    ----    ----
```

Car 8:

```
  86      93      40      61      65
- 39    - 29    - 13    - 53    - 50
 ----    ----    ----    ----    ----
```

206

Subtraction Sentences

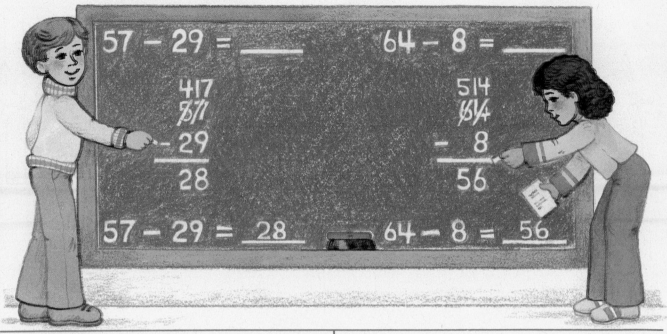

57 − 29 = _____   64 − 8 = _____

```
 417
 5̶7̶
−29
────
 28
```

```
 514
 6̶4̶
−  8
────
  56
```

57 − 29 = __28__   64 − 8 = __56__

Subtract.

a. 84 − 37 = __47__

```
 7 14
 8̶4̶
−37
────
 47
```

b. 58 − 35 = ____

c. 53 − 6 = ____

d. 78 − 29 = ____

e. 80 − 56 = ____

f. 46 − 9 = ____

g. 49 − 23 = ____

h. 34 − 26 = ____

Subtract. Write each difference in the puzzle.

Across

A. $43 - 17 = \underline{26}$

B. $72 - 19 = \underline{}$

D. $80 - 33 = \underline{}$

E. $92 - 28 = \underline{}$

H. $89 - 34 = \underline{}$

J. $70 - 25 = \underline{}$

K. $95 - 33 = \underline{}$

L. $68 - 50 = \underline{}$

$$
\begin{array}{r}
{\scriptstyle 3\ \ 13} \\
\cancel{4\cancel{3}} \\
-\ 17 \\
\hline
2\ 6
\end{array}
$$

Down

A. $48 - 24 = \underline{24}$

B. $62 - 8\ \ = \underline{}$

C. $64 - 27 = \underline{}$

F. $70 - 30 = \underline{}$

G. $50 - 25 = \underline{}$

H. $79 - 23 = \underline{}$

I. $61 - 9\ \ = \underline{}$

J. $85 - 37 = \underline{}$

$$
\begin{array}{r}
48 \\
-\ 24 \\
\hline
24
\end{array}
$$

Checking Subtraction

Subtract. Check.

Add to check your answers.

$$
\begin{array}{r} \overset{5,15}{\cancel{65}} \\ -\,28 \\ \hline 37 \end{array}
$$

← These should be the same. →

$$
\begin{array}{r} 37 \\ +\,28 \\ \hline 65 \end{array}
$$

Subtract. Add to check your answers.

a.

$$
\begin{array}{r} \overset{310}{\cancel{40}} \\ -\,26 \\ \hline 14 \end{array}
\qquad
\begin{array}{r} 14 \\ +\,26 \\ \hline 40 \end{array}
\qquad
\begin{array}{r} 8\cancel{2} \\ -\,7 \\ \hline \end{array}
\qquad
\begin{array}{r} 75 \\ +\,7 \\ \hline \end{array}
\qquad
\begin{array}{r} 56 \\ -\,24 \\ \hline \end{array}
\qquad
\begin{array}{r} 32 \\ +\,24 \\ \hline \end{array}
$$

b.

$$
\begin{array}{r} 65 \\ -\,57 \\ \hline \end{array}
\qquad
\begin{array}{r} 73 \\ -\,38 \\ \hline \end{array}
\qquad
\begin{array}{r} 37 \\ -\,25 \\ \hline \end{array}
$$

c.

$$
\begin{array}{r} 60 \\ -\,35 \\ \hline \end{array}
\qquad
\begin{array}{r} 43 \\ -\,6 \\ \hline \end{array}
\qquad
\begin{array}{r} 50 \\ -\,25 \\ \hline \end{array}
$$

d.

$$
\begin{array}{r} 65 \\ -\,8 \\ \hline \end{array}
\qquad
\begin{array}{r} 56 \\ -\,16 \\ \hline \end{array}
\qquad
\begin{array}{r} 45 \\ -\,18 \\ \hline \end{array}
$$

Subtract. Add to check your answers.

a.
$$\begin{array}{r} {}^{6}\!\!\not 7^{13} \\ -45 \\ \hline 28 \end{array}$$
$$\begin{array}{r} {}^{1}28 \\ +45 \\ \hline 73 \end{array}$$
$$\begin{array}{r} 63 \\ -42 \\ \hline \end{array}$$
$$\begin{array}{r} 57 \\ -38 \\ \hline \end{array}$$

b.
$$\begin{array}{r} 46 \\ -18 \\ \hline \end{array}$$
$$\begin{array}{r} 44 \\ -16 \\ \hline \end{array}$$
$$\begin{array}{r} 70 \\ -12 \\ \hline \end{array}$$

c.
$$\begin{array}{r} 83 \\ -17 \\ \hline \end{array}$$
$$\begin{array}{r} 96 \\ -25 \\ \hline \end{array}$$
$$\begin{array}{r} 38 \\ -14 \\ \hline \end{array}$$

d.
$$\begin{array}{r} 50 \\ -25 \\ \hline \end{array}$$
$$\begin{array}{r} 82 \\ -56 \\ \hline \end{array}$$
$$\begin{array}{r} 75 \\ -20 \\ \hline \end{array}$$

Midchapter Review

Subtract.

$$\begin{array}{r} 68 \\ -23 \\ \hline \end{array}$$
$$\begin{array}{r} 54 \\ -31 \\ \hline \end{array}$$
$$\begin{array}{r} 82 \\ -65 \\ \hline \end{array}$$
$$\begin{array}{r} 41 \\ -9 \\ \hline \end{array}$$
$$\begin{array}{r} 73 \\ -64 \\ \hline \end{array}$$
$$\begin{array}{r} 90 \\ -36 \\ \hline \end{array}$$

PROBLEM SOLVING
Subtraction
Solve.

a. There are **36** puppies at the pet shop. **17** puppies are sold. How many puppies are left?

$$\begin{array}{r} {\scriptstyle 2\,16} \\ \cancel{36} \\ -17 \\ \hline 19 \end{array}$$

b. The pet shop has **27** dog collars. There are **12** dog bowls. How many more collars than bowls are there?

c. The pet shop has **26** fish tanks. **19** of the tanks have fish. How many do not have fish?

d. Mr. Ortega sells **50** goldfish. He sells **25** guppies. How many more goldfish than guppies does he sell?

e. Mrs. Ortega has **53** dog bones. She sells **27** dog bones. How many dog bones are left?

Solve.

a. **43** girls are in the school play. **28** boys are in the play. How many more girls than boys are in the play?

$$\begin{array}{r} 3\ 13 \\ \cancel{4}\cancel{3} \\ -28 \\ \hline 15 \end{array}$$

b. There are **85** seats. **49** seats are filled. How many seats are empty?

c. **78** tickets are sold on Monday. **59** tickets are sold on Tuesday. How many more tickets are sold on Monday than on Tuesday?

d. Rita pours **75** cups of juice. She sells **48** cups. How many cups of juice are left?

e. There are **95** cookies for sale. **67** cookies are sold. How many cookies are left?

f. Mr. Murphy's class has **39** children. **15** children go to see the play. How many children do not go to see the play?

212

Subtracting Money

Ricky has 42¢. He buys
a birthday card for 15¢.
How much does he have left?

312
42¢
− 15¢
27¢

Ricky has 27¢ left.

Subtract.

713
a. 83¢
− 16¢
67¢

90¢
− 45¢

75¢
− 30¢

46¢
− 38¢

83¢
− 64¢

47¢
− 15¢

b. 34¢
− 9¢

80¢
− 50¢

45¢
− 25¢

76¢
− 39¢

52¢
− 26¢

37¢
− 8¢

c. 47¢
− 25¢

60¢
− 35¢

82¢
− 42¢

56¢
− 8¢

49¢
− 7¢

81¢
− 26¢

d. 24¢
− 18¢

30¢
− 5¢

40¢
− 27¢

75¢
− 50¢

49¢
− 36¢

77¢
− 37¢

e. 89¢
− 57¢

55¢
− 38¢

34¢
− 7¢

46¢
− 19¢

69¢
− 49¢

85¢
− 47¢

Find how much is left.

	Had	Bought	Have left
a.	43¢	 18¢	3 13 ~~4 3~~ ¢ − 1 8 ¢ ――――― 2 5 ¢ ___25___ ¢
b.	50¢	 25¢	_____ ¢
c.	75¢	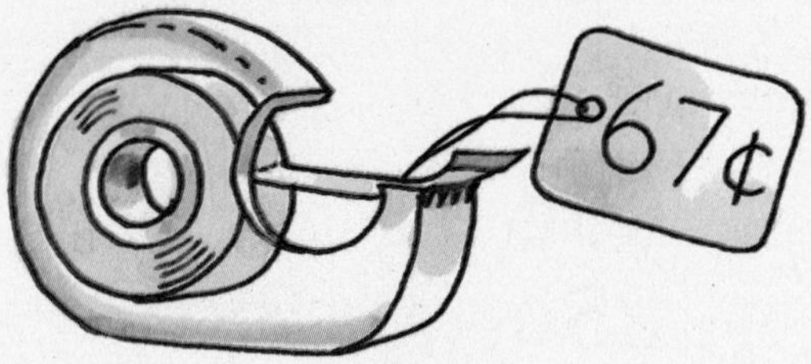 67¢	_____ ¢
d.	80¢	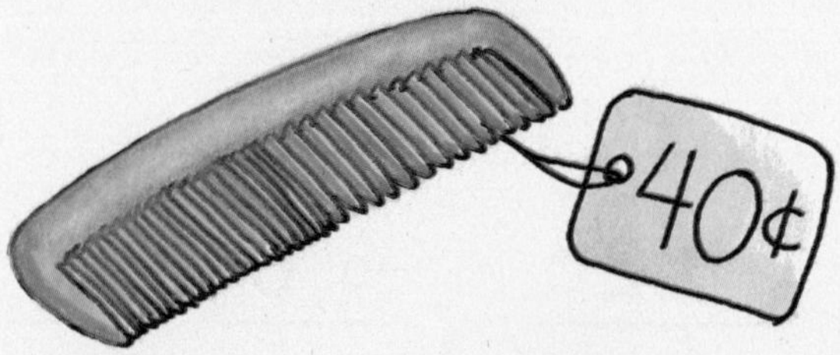 40¢	_____ ¢
e.	98¢	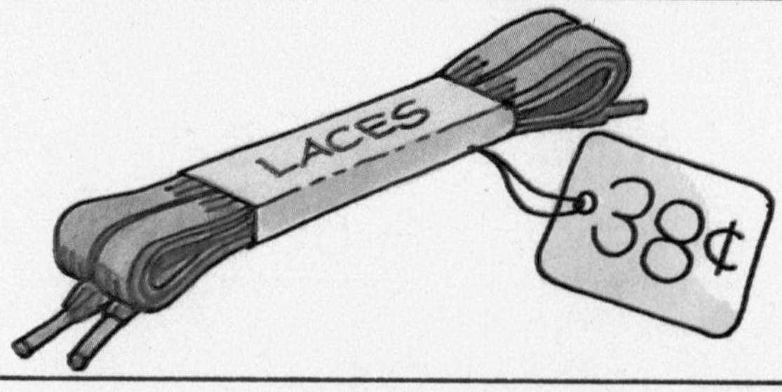 38¢	_____ ¢
f.	40¢	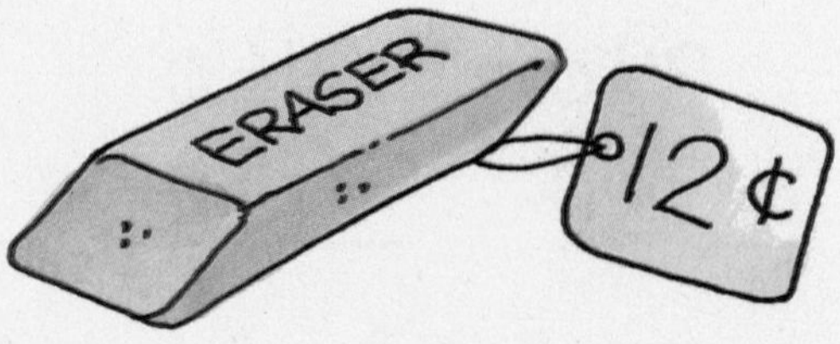 12¢	_____ ¢

214

Mixed Practice

Add.

$$\begin{array}{r} 26 \\ + 28 \\ \hline 54 \end{array}$$

Subtract.

$$\begin{array}{r} \overset{7\;14}{8\;4} \\ - 6\;5 \\ \hline 1\;9 \end{array}$$

Add or subtract. Watch the signs.

a.
$$\begin{array}{r} 36 \\ +25 \\ \hline 61 \end{array}$$
$$\begin{array}{r} 57 \\ -19 \\ \hline \end{array}$$
$$\begin{array}{r} 42 \\ +33 \\ \hline \end{array}$$
$$\begin{array}{r} 48 \\ + 7 \\ \hline \end{array}$$
$$\begin{array}{r} 65 \\ -12 \\ \hline \end{array}$$
$$\begin{array}{r} 80 \\ -34 \\ \hline \end{array}$$

b.
$$\begin{array}{r} 56 \\ +21 \\ \hline \end{array}$$
$$\begin{array}{r} 42 \\ -36 \\ \hline \end{array}$$
$$\begin{array}{r} 6 \\ +54 \\ \hline \end{array}$$
$$\begin{array}{r} 21 \\ -10 \\ \hline \end{array}$$
$$\begin{array}{r} 84 \\ -55 \\ \hline \end{array}$$
$$\begin{array}{r} 34 \\ +47 \\ \hline \end{array}$$

c.
$$\begin{array}{r} 29 \\ - 6 \\ \hline \end{array}$$
$$\begin{array}{r} 53 \\ -45 \\ \hline \end{array}$$
$$\begin{array}{r} 18 \\ +40 \\ \hline \end{array}$$
$$\begin{array}{r} 82 \\ -27 \\ \hline \end{array}$$
$$\begin{array}{r} 45 \\ +45 \\ \hline \end{array}$$
$$\begin{array}{r} 66 \\ - 9 \\ \hline \end{array}$$

d.
$$\begin{array}{r} 62 \\ + 8 \\ \hline \end{array}$$
$$\begin{array}{r} 45 \\ + 6 \\ \hline \end{array}$$
$$\begin{array}{r} 47 \\ -34 \\ \hline \end{array}$$
$$\begin{array}{r} 36 \\ -18 \\ \hline \end{array}$$
$$\begin{array}{r} 52 \\ +39 \\ \hline \end{array}$$

e.
$$\begin{array}{r} 7 \\ +38 \\ \hline \end{array}$$
$$\begin{array}{r} 50 \\ -45 \\ \hline \end{array}$$
$$\begin{array}{r} 28 \\ -14 \\ \hline \end{array}$$
$$\begin{array}{r} 19 \\ +26 \\ \hline \end{array}$$
$$\begin{array}{r} 58 \\ -17 \\ \hline \end{array}$$

PROBLEM SOLVING

Add or subtract to solve the problems.

a.
There are **36** girls and **47** boys in the park. How many children in all?

$$\begin{array}{r} 36 \\ +47 \\ \hline 83 \end{array}$$

b.
Bobby counts **46** oak trees in the park. He counts **18** elm trees. How many trees does he count in all?

c.
There are **29** boys on the swings. **17** boys leave to play ball. How many boys are left?

d.
50 flowers are in the park. **26** are roses. How many are not roses?

e.
Betty sees **38** children playing kickball. **12** more children join them. How many children in all?

f.
There are **57** sandwiches and **39** apples at the picnic. How many more sandwiches than apples are there?

216

PROBLEM SOLVING

Adding and Subtracting Money

a.

What is the total
cost?

$$\begin{array}{r} 1 \\ 43¢ \\ +38¢ \\ \hline 81¢ \end{array}$$

b. Which costs more?

How much more
does it cost?

$$\begin{array}{r} 8\;13 \\ 9\cancel{3}¢ \\ -65¢ \\ \hline 28¢ \end{array}$$

c. Which costs more?

How much more does
it cost?

d.

What is the total
cost?

e.

How much for
and   ?

f. Which costs more?

How much more
does it cost?

a.

$$
\begin{array}{r}
45\cent \\
-20\cent \\
\hline
25\cent
\end{array}
$$

How much more for 🔒 than 🔑 ?

b.

What is the cost for 🔨 and 🪛 ?

c.

What is the total cost?

d.

How much more for 🧢 than 🔔 ?

e.

How much more for 🧤 than ⚾ ?

f.

What is the total cost?

g.

What is the total cost?

h.

How much more for 👕 than 🩳 ?

218

Subtract. (pages 197-198, 201-208, 213-214)

a.
$$65 - 30$$ $$42 - 19$$ $$70 - 25$$ $$86 - 24$$ $$56 - 8$$ $$95 - 40$$

b.
$$82¢ - 15¢$$ $$90¢ - 45¢$$ $$32¢ - 18¢$$ $$50¢ - 37¢$$ $$69¢ - 40¢$$ $$75¢ - 45¢$$

c. $56 - 18 =$ _____ $92 - 50 =$ _____

d. $63 - 45 =$ _____ $80 - 34 =$ _____

Add or subtract. (pages 215-216)

e.
$$27 + 46$$ $$96 - 35$$ $$37 + 48$$ $$25 + 25$$ $$74 - 18$$ $$68 - 29$$

Solve.

f.

Chan finds 36 brown shells. He finds 17 white shells. How many more brown shells than white shells?

g.

Debby is watching 27 children. 9 children leave for home. How many children are left?

Secret Code

Find the number that is inside each shape.
Write the subtraction example.
Then solve.

50	75	46
34	82	97
29	63	38

```
  7 12
   82
 - 38
 ----
   44
```

Make up some of your own.
Give them to a friend to solve.

Subtract.

a.
| 85 | 73 | 56 | 40 | 62 | 88 |
| −43 | −36 | −15 | −25 | −15 | −39 |

b.
| 37¢ | 63¢ | 49¢ | 93¢ | 80¢ | 55¢ |
| −27¢ | − 9¢ | −25¢ | −48¢ | − 5¢ | −27¢ |

c. $95 - 50 =$ _____ $36 - 18 =$ _____

d. $46 - 29 =$ _____ $58 - 39 =$ _____

Add or subtract.

e.
| 75 | 18 | 57 | 65 | 7 | 83 |
| − 6 | +34 | +22 | −28 | +46 | −45 |

Solve.

f.

Kathy has 70¢.

She buys  57¢.

How much does she have left?

g.

Mr. Gilbert has 43 notebooks in his store. He sells 26 notebooks. How many does he have left?

ENRICHMENT

Saving With Coupons

Ring the store coupon that saves you more money.
Find how much you will spend.

Clam Stew **23¢ off**   Clam Stew **18¢ off**

```
   7 12
   8 2 ¢
 - 2 3 ¢
   5 9 ¢
```

Crackers **8¢ off**   Crackers **10¢ off**

Mustard **11¢ off**   Mustard **21¢ off**

Dog Food **12¢ off**   Dog Food **18¢ off**

Tissues **18¢ off**   Tissues **13¢ off**

Milk **35¢ off**   Milk **20¢ off**

SKILLS MAINTENANCE

Choose the correct answers.

1.

$$37 + 52$$

Ⓐ 90
Ⓑ 79
Ⓒ 89
Ⓓ not here

2.

$$46 + 28$$

Ⓐ 74
Ⓑ 64
Ⓒ 66
Ⓓ not here

3.

$$54 + 60$$

Ⓐ 104
Ⓑ 114
Ⓒ 100
Ⓓ not here

4.

$$17 + 23 = \underline{}$$

Ⓐ 30
Ⓑ 50
Ⓒ 40
Ⓓ not here

5.

$$15 \\ 34 \\ + 48$$

Ⓐ 87
Ⓑ 86
Ⓒ 97
Ⓓ not here

6.

$$39¢ + 25¢$$

Ⓐ 54¢
Ⓑ 64¢
Ⓒ 68¢
Ⓓ not here

7.

$$75 - 49 = \underline{}$$

Ⓐ 18
Ⓑ 26
Ⓒ 25
Ⓓ not here

8.

$$90 - 45$$

Ⓐ 35
Ⓑ 40
Ⓒ 45
Ⓓ not here

9.

$$42¢ - 29¢$$

Ⓐ 23¢
Ⓑ 71¢
Ⓒ 13¢
Ⓓ not here

10.

$$56 - 35 = \underline{}$$

Ⓐ 91
Ⓑ 80
Ⓒ 21
Ⓓ not here

11.

$$67 - 35$$

Ⓐ 32
Ⓑ 17
Ⓒ 22
Ⓓ not here

12.

$$86¢ - 38¢$$

Ⓐ 47¢
Ⓑ 50¢
Ⓒ 36¢
Ⓓ not here

Choose the correct answers.

13.

(A) 3:30
(B) 6:15
(C) 6:05
(D) not here

14.

(A) 10:30
(B) 8:50
(C) 11:40
(D) not here

15.

(A) 25¢
(B) 32¢
(C) 30¢
(D) not here

16.

(A) 25¢
(B) 28¢
(C) 30¢
(D) not here

17.

(A) $1.50
(B) $1.25
(C) $2.50
(D) not here

18.

(A) $1.00
(B) $1.35
(C) $2.35
(D) not here

19. Polly's Plant Store has 46 plants. 18 plants are sold. How many plants are left?

(A) 28
(B) 40
(C) 64
(D) not here

20. Polly has 39 clay pots. She has 22 white pots. How many pots does she have in all?

(A) 25
(B) 17
(C) 61
(D) not here

Geometry and Fractions

CHAPTER 9

GETTING STARTED

Ring the shape that fits.

a.
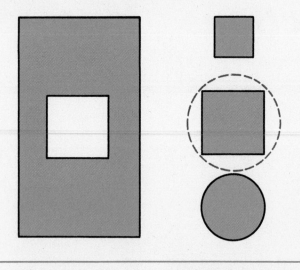

b.
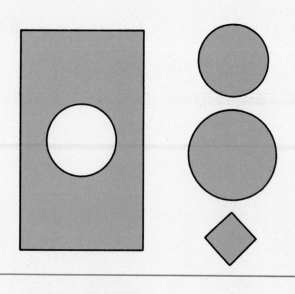

c.
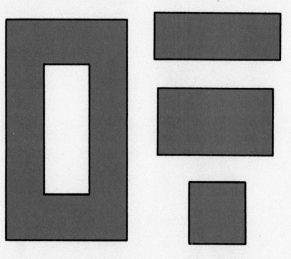

d.
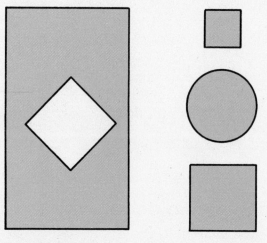

e.

f.
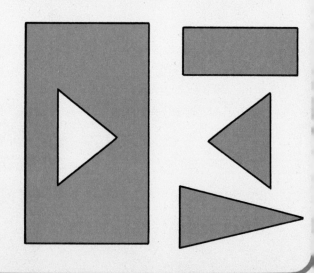

Solid Geometric Shapes

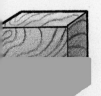

cube   sphere   cone   cylinder   rectangular prism

Ring the objects that are the same shape.

a.

b.

c.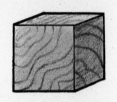

d.

e.

Count how many.

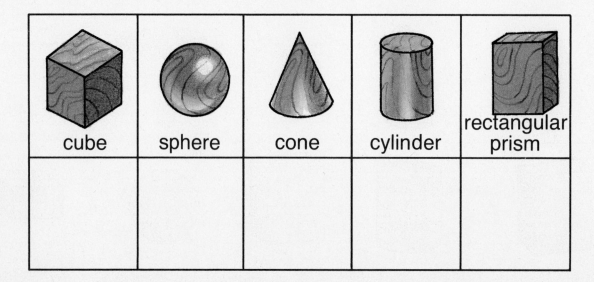

cube	sphere	cone	cylinder	rectangular prism

Circles, Squares, Triangles, and Rectangles

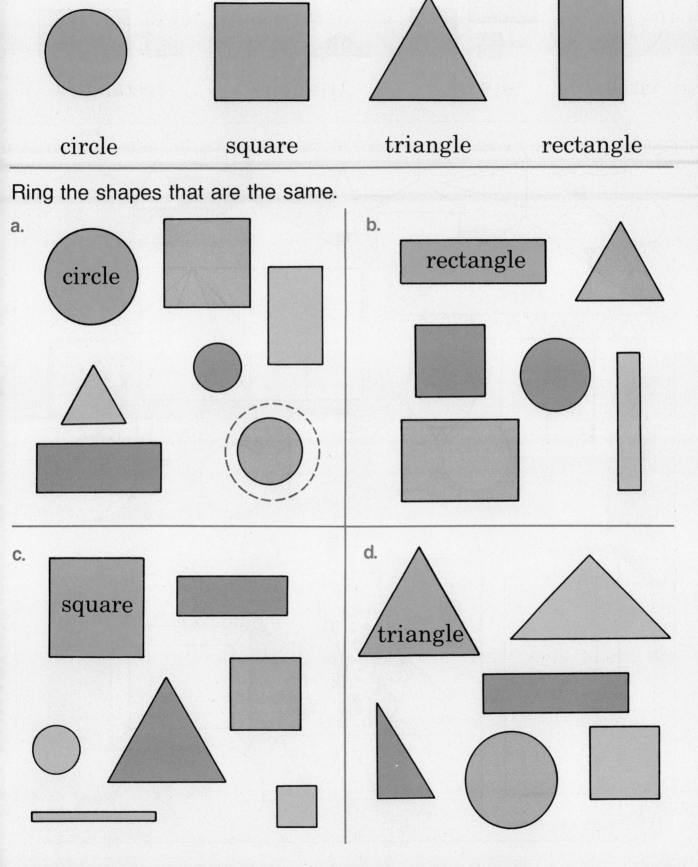

circle   square   triangle   rectangle

Ring the shapes that are the same.

a.

circle

b.

rectangle

c.

square

d.

triangle

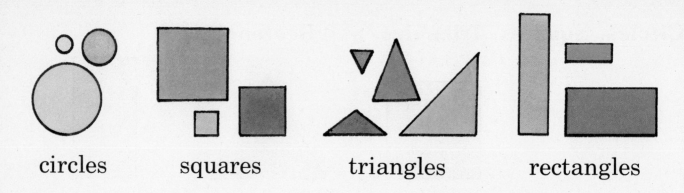

circles   squares   triangles   rectangles

Color.

Sides and Corners

side
↓

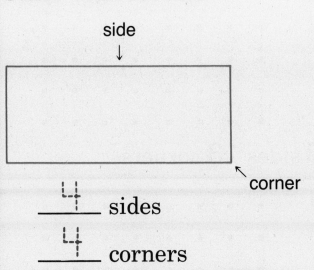

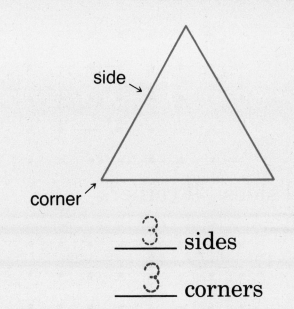

side →

corner

_**4**_ sides

_**4**_ corners

corner →

_**3**_ sides

_**3**_ corners

How many sides and corners?

a.

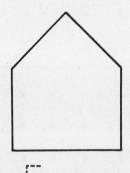

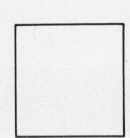

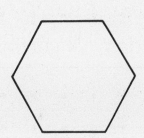

_**5**_ sides

_**5**_ corners

_____ sides

_____ corners

_____ sides

_____ corners

b.

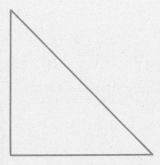

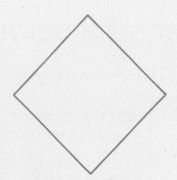

_____ sides

_____ corners

_____ sides

_____ corners

_____ sides

_____ corners

Draw each shape.

a.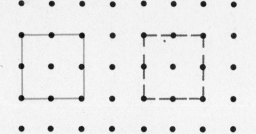

4 sides **4** corners

b.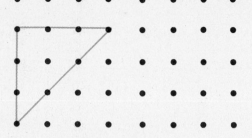

3 sides **3** corners

c.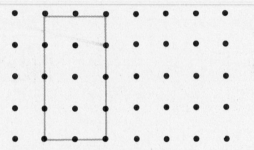

4 sides **4** corners

d.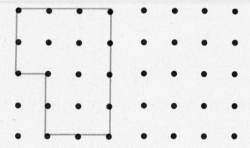

6 sides **6** corners

e.

5 sides **5** corners

f.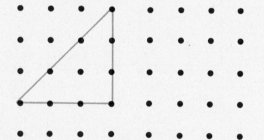

3 sides **3** corners

PROBLEM SOLVING

g. How many rectangles?

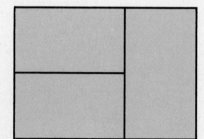

_____

h. How many triangles?

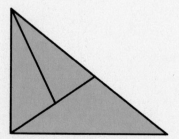

_____

PROBLEM SOLVING

Reading a Table

The children made a table to show how many books they read.

Name	Laura	Carlos	Joan	Hirro	Flora	Andrea	Benny	Dick
Books Read	4	7	9	5	6	2	3	1

a. Who read more books?

Benny   or   (Joan)

Laura   or   Carlos

Hirro   or   Benny

Andrea   or   Dick

Laura   or   Hirro

Flora   or   Andrea

b. Who read fewer books?

Hirro   or   (Dick)

Joan   or   Benny

Flora   or   Carlos

Benny   or   Andrea

Hirro   or   Flora

Laura   or   Joan

Name	Laura	Carlos	Joan	Hirro	Flora	Andrea	Benny	Dick
Books Read	4	7	9	5	6	2	3	1

Complete.

a. Laura read __4__ books.

Carlos read __7__ books.

How many books did Laura and Carlos read in all? __11__

b. Flora read ____ books.

Joan read ____ books.

How many books did Flora and Joan read in all? ____

c. How many books did Benny and Hirro read in all? ____

d. How many books did Hirro and Carlos read in all? ____

e. Andrea read ____ books.

Flora read ____ books.

Dick read ____ book.

How many books in all?

____

f. Benny read ____ books.

Joan read ____ books.

Carlos read ____ books.

How many books in all?

____

g. How many books did Laura, Hirro, and Carlos read in all? ____

h. How many books did Hirro, Joan, and Flora read in all? ____

234

Equal Parts

These two parts match.
They are equal.

These do not match.
They are <u>not</u> equal.

Are the parts equal?
Ring YES or NO.

a.

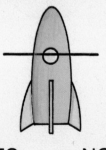

(YES)　　NO

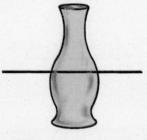

YES　　NO

YES　　NO

b.

YES　　NO

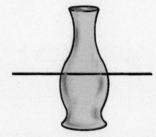

YES　　NO

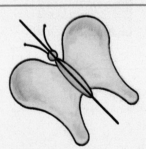

YES　　NO

c.

YES　　NO

YES　　NO

YES　　NO

Ring the shapes that show equal parts.

a.

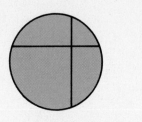 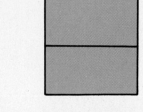 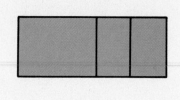

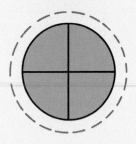 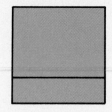 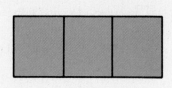

b.

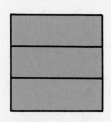 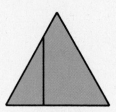 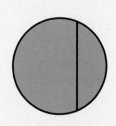

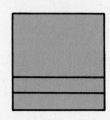 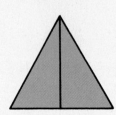 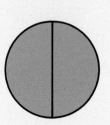

Midchapter Review

Match.

 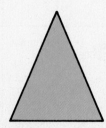 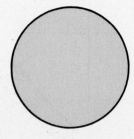

circle   rectangle   triangle

Fractions

Halves	Thirds	Fourths
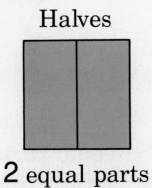	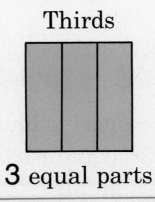	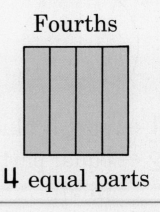
2 equal parts	**3** equal parts	**4** equal parts

Ring the shapes that show halves.

a.

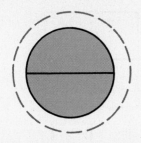  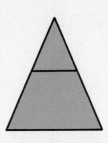 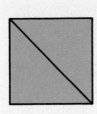 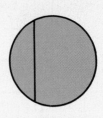

Ring the shapes that show thirds.

b.

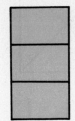 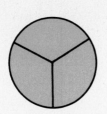 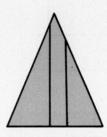  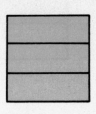

Ring the shapes that show fourths.

c.

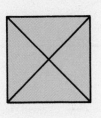 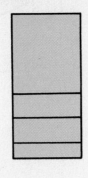 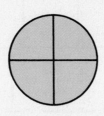 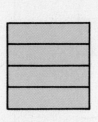 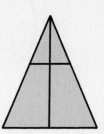

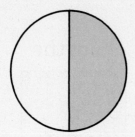 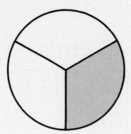 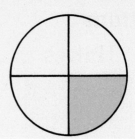

$\dfrac{1}{2}$ ← part is blue.
← equal parts in all

$\dfrac{1}{3}$ ← part is blue.
← equal parts in all

$\dfrac{1}{4}$ ← part is blue.
← equal parts in all

Ring the correct fractions.

a.

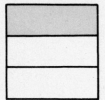

$\dfrac{1}{2}$ $\boxed{\dfrac{1}{3}}$ $\dfrac{1}{4}$

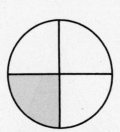

$\dfrac{1}{2}$ $\dfrac{1}{3}$ $\dfrac{1}{4}$

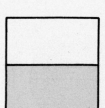

$\dfrac{1}{2}$ $\dfrac{1}{3}$ $\dfrac{1}{4}$

b.

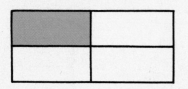

$\dfrac{1}{2}$ $\dfrac{1}{3}$ $\dfrac{1}{4}$

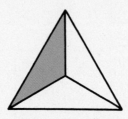

$\dfrac{1}{2}$ $\dfrac{1}{3}$ $\dfrac{1}{4}$

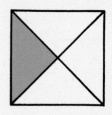

$\dfrac{1}{2}$ $\dfrac{1}{3}$ $\dfrac{1}{4}$

c.

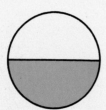

$\dfrac{1}{2}$ $\dfrac{1}{3}$ $\dfrac{1}{4}$

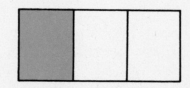

$\dfrac{1}{2}$ $\dfrac{1}{3}$ $\dfrac{1}{4}$

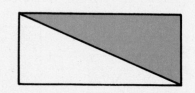

$\dfrac{1}{2}$ $\dfrac{1}{3}$ $\dfrac{1}{4}$

More About Fractions

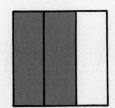  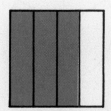

$\dfrac{2}{3}$ ← parts are brown.
← equal parts in all

$\dfrac{2}{4}$ ← parts are brown.
← equal parts in all

$\dfrac{3}{4}$ ← parts are brown.
← equal parts in all

Ring the correct fractions.

a.

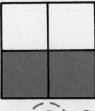

$\dfrac{1}{2}$ $\left(\dfrac{2}{4}\right)$ $\dfrac{3}{4}$

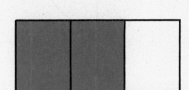

$\dfrac{2}{3}$ $\dfrac{1}{4}$ $\dfrac{2}{4}$

$\dfrac{1}{3}$ $\dfrac{2}{3}$ $\dfrac{3}{4}$

b.

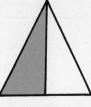

$\dfrac{1}{2}$ $\dfrac{1}{3}$ $\dfrac{1}{4}$

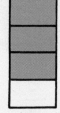

$\dfrac{1}{4}$ $\dfrac{2}{4}$ $\dfrac{3}{4}$

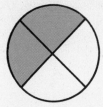

$\dfrac{1}{3}$ $\dfrac{2}{3}$ $\dfrac{2}{4}$

c.

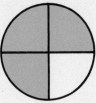

$\dfrac{2}{3}$ $\dfrac{2}{4}$ $\dfrac{3}{4}$

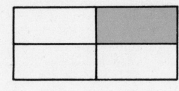

$\dfrac{1}{3}$ $\dfrac{1}{2}$ $\dfrac{1}{4}$

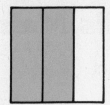

$\dfrac{1}{2}$ $\dfrac{2}{3}$ $\dfrac{3}{4}$

Color.

a.

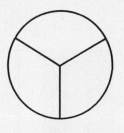

$\frac{2}{3}$

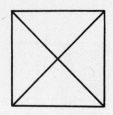

$\frac{1}{4}$

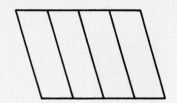

$\frac{3}{4}$

b.

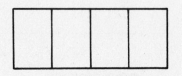

$\frac{2}{4}$

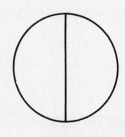

$\frac{1}{2}$

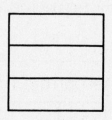

$\frac{1}{3}$

c.

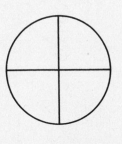

$\frac{3}{4}$

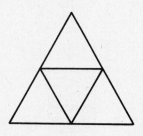

$\frac{2}{4}$

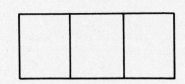

$\frac{2}{3}$

Skills Maintenance

Subtract.

74	80	66	78	53	96
−38	−25	−34	− 9	−10	−48

240

name

Writing Fractions

241

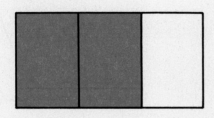

 parts are red.

 equal parts in all.

Write the fraction that tells what part is shaded.

a.
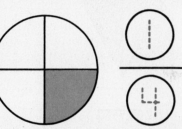
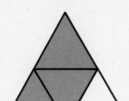
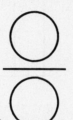
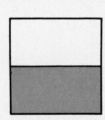

b.
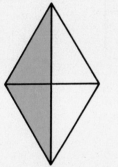
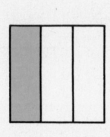
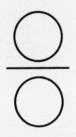
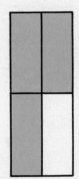

c.
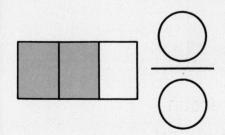

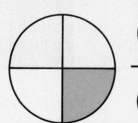

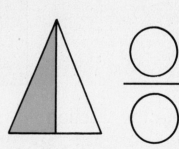

Copyright © 1985 by Harcourt Brace Jovanovich, Inc.

241

Write the fraction that tells
what part is shaded.

a.

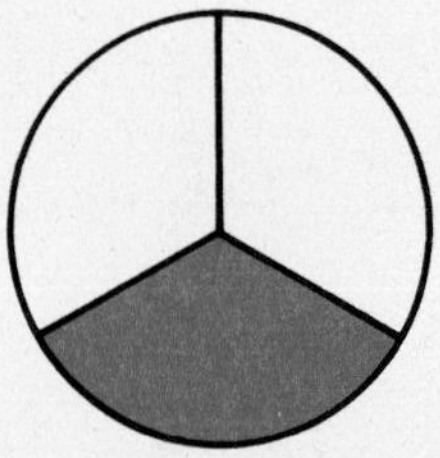

$\frac{1}{3}$

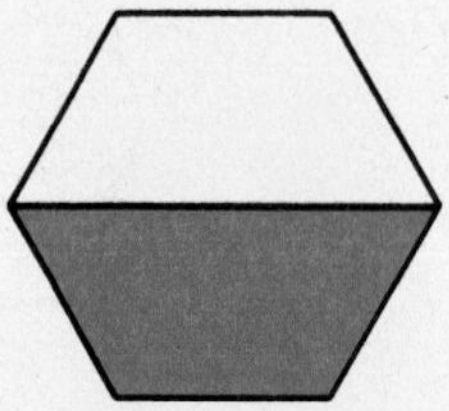

_____   _____   _____

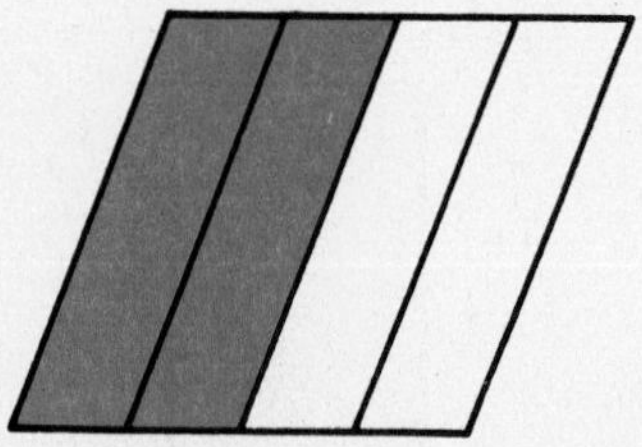

b.

_____   _____   _____

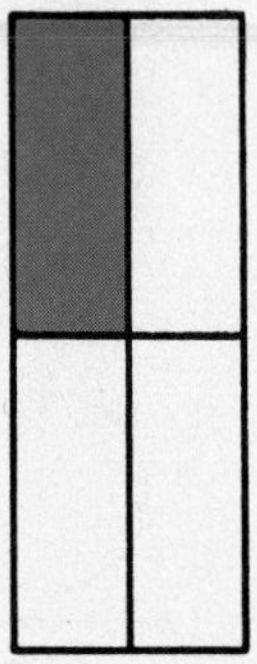

c.

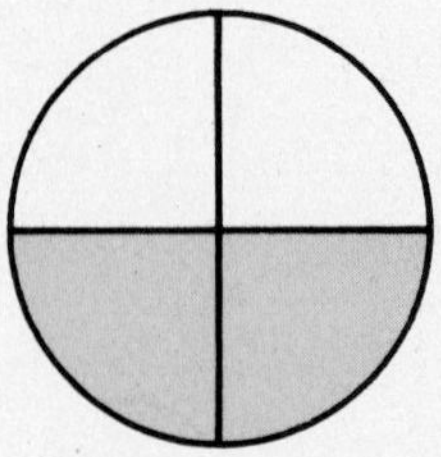

_____   _____   _____

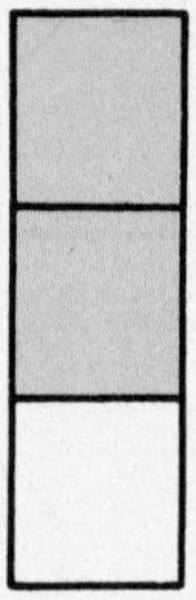

★ Challenge

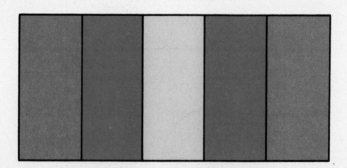

Write the fraction
that tells what part
is red. _____

Write the fraction
that tells what part
is yellow. _____

Parts of Groups

Maggie has 4 shirts.
3 of her shirts are green.
What part of the
group of shirts is green ?

$\frac{3}{4}$ ← green shirts.

← shirts in all

$\frac{3}{4}$ are green.

Ring the fraction that tells
what part of the group is green.

a.

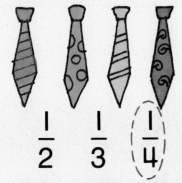

$\frac{1}{2}$　$\frac{1}{3}$　$\left(\frac{1}{4}\right)$

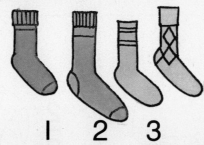

$\frac{1}{4}$　$\frac{2}{4}$　$\frac{3}{4}$

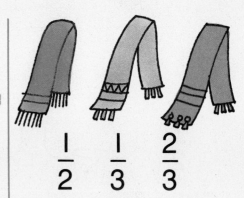

$\frac{1}{2}$　$\frac{1}{3}$　$\frac{2}{3}$

b.

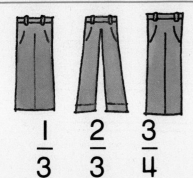

$\frac{1}{3}$　$\frac{2}{3}$　$\frac{3}{4}$

$\frac{1}{2}$　$\frac{1}{3}$　$\frac{1}{4}$

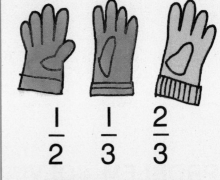

$\frac{1}{2}$　$\frac{1}{3}$　$\frac{2}{3}$

c.

$\frac{1}{4}$　$\frac{2}{4}$　$\frac{3}{4}$

$\frac{1}{4}$　$\frac{1}{3}$　$\frac{2}{3}$

$\frac{1}{4}$　$\frac{2}{4}$　$\frac{3}{4}$

Write the fraction that tells
what part of the group is green.

a.

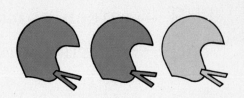 $\dfrac{2}{3}$

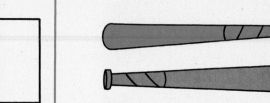

b.

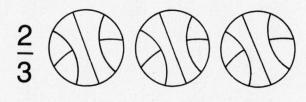

Color.

c.

$\dfrac{1}{2}$

$\dfrac{2}{3}$

d.

$\dfrac{1}{4}$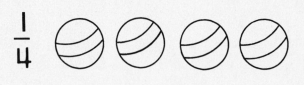

$\dfrac{1}{3}$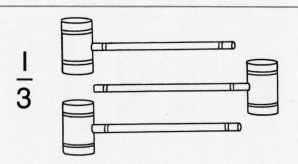

PROBLEM SOLVING

Solve.

e. Linda has **4** hats.
1 of her hats is blue.
What part of the
group of hats is
blue?

f. Craig has **3** sweaters.
2 of his sweaters are
brown. What part of
the group of sweaters
is brown?

244

Match. (pages 227-228)

a.

Match. (pages 229-230)

b.

circle   square   triangle

Ring the correct fraction. (pages 238-240)

c.

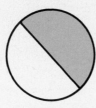
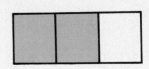

$\dfrac{1}{2}$ $\dfrac{2}{4}$ $\dfrac{3}{4}$ $\dfrac{2}{3}$ $\dfrac{1}{2}$ $\dfrac{1}{4}$ $\dfrac{2}{3}$ $\dfrac{2}{4}$ $\dfrac{1}{3}$

Write the fraction that tells what part of the group is green. (pages 243-244)

d.

Line Segments

Steve wants some fruit.
There are **3** paths.
Only one path is straight.
It is the shortest.
It is a **line segment.**

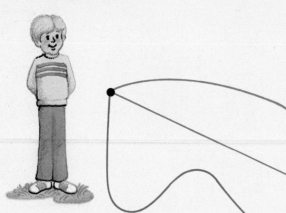

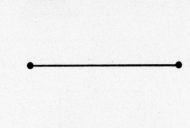

Is it a line segment?
Ring YES or NO.

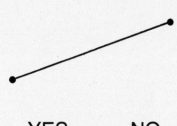

| YES | NO |

| YES | NO |

| YES | NO |

Draw as many line segments as you can.

246

Match.

a.
  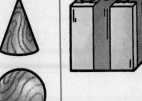   

Match.

b.

circle   triangle   rectangle

Ring the correct fraction.

c.

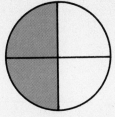   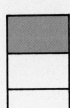 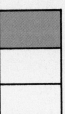   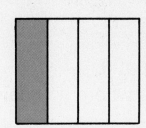

$\dfrac{1}{4}$ $\dfrac{2}{4}$ $\dfrac{2}{3}$ $\dfrac{1}{3}$ $\dfrac{2}{3}$ $\dfrac{1}{4}$ $\dfrac{2}{3}$ $\dfrac{2}{4}$ $\dfrac{1}{4}$

Write the fraction that tells what part of the group is green.

d.

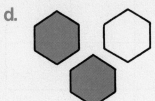

ENRICHMENT

Finding Points on a Grid

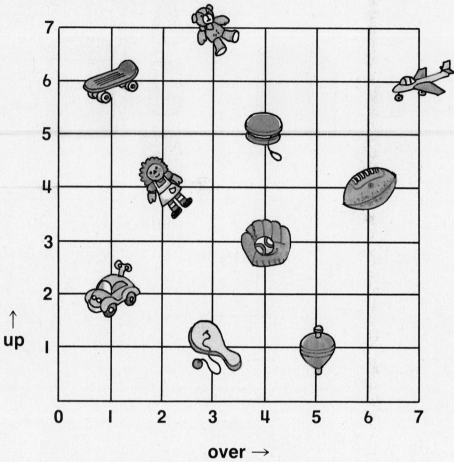

Start at 0.
Write where you can find each toy.

	→ over	up ↑
(glove)	4	3
(skateboard)		
(car)		
(yo-yo)		
(maraca)		

	→ over	up ↑
(bear)		
(airplane)		
(doll)		
(football)		
(top)		

Measurement

CHAPTER 10

GETTING STARTED

How long is each object?

The 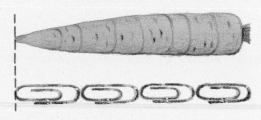 is
about **4** units long.

a.

about __4__ units

b.

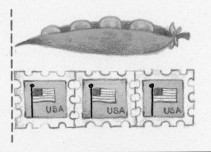

about _____ units

c.

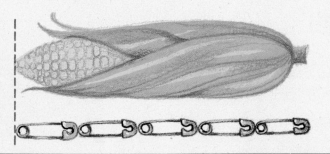

about _____ units

d.

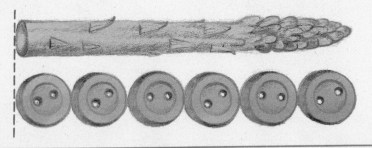

about _____ units

e.

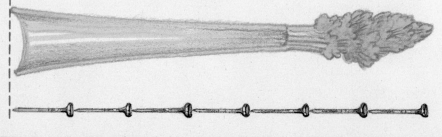

about _____ units

Centimeter

When you want to measure how long an object is,
you can use a centimeter ruler.

Measure each object to the nearest centimeter.

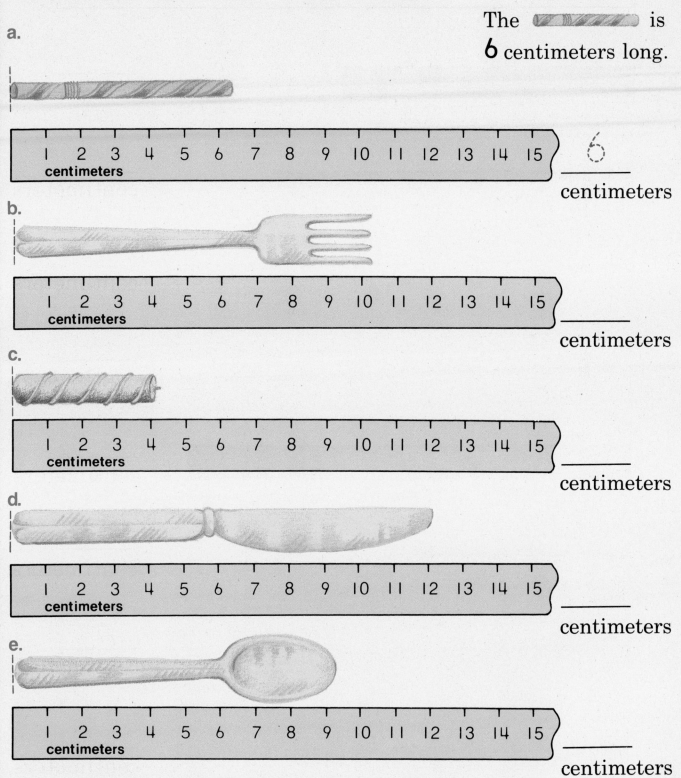

a.

The ▱▱▱▱▱ is
6 centimeters long.

6

_____ centimeters

b.

_____ centimeters

c.

_____ centimeters

d.

_____ centimeters

e.

_____ centimeters

Measure each object to the nearest centimeter.
Use your ruler.

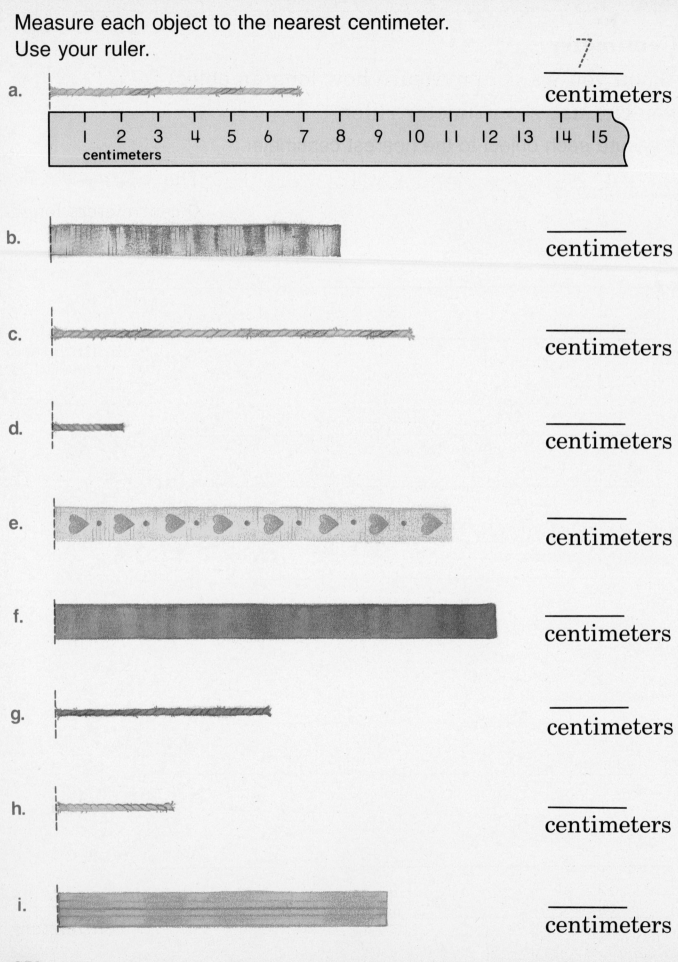

a. _____ 7 centimeters

b. _____ centimeters

c. _____ centimeters

d. _____ centimeters

e. _____ centimeters

f. _____ centimeters

g. _____ centimeters

h. _____ centimeters

i. _____ centimeters

Perimeter

How far around each figure?

a.

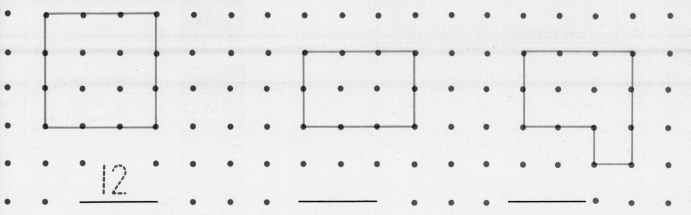

_12_ _____
centimeters

_____
centimeters

_____
centimeters

b.

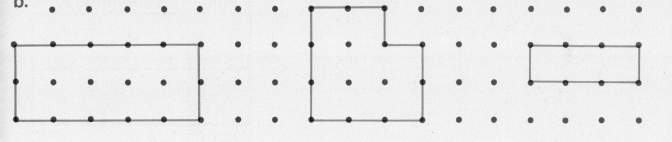

_____
centimeters

_____
centimeters

_____
centimeters

c.

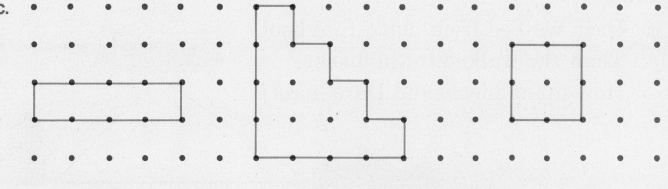

_____
centimeters

_____
centimeters

_____
centimeters

Measure each side.
How far around each figure?

a.

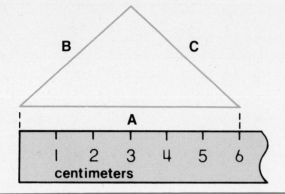

side	centimeters
A	6
B	
C	
sum	

b.

side	centimeters
D	
E	
F	
G	
sum	

c.

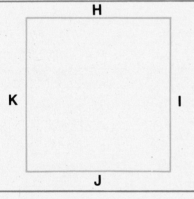

side	centimeters
H	
I	
J	
K	
sum	

PROBLEM SOLVING

Solve.

d. Dara walked from home to school.
Then she walked to the park.
How many blocks did Dara walk?

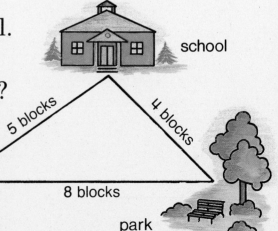

254

Area

I square unit

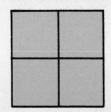

4 square units

Find how many square units.

a.

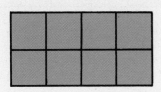

_8_ square units

_____ square units

_____ square units

b.

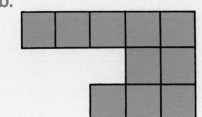

_____ square units

_____ square units

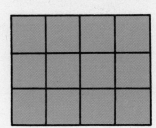

_____ square units

c.

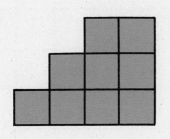

_____ square units

_____ square units

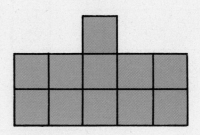

_____ square units

Draw the figures. Color them.

a. **6** square units   **8** square units   **4** square units

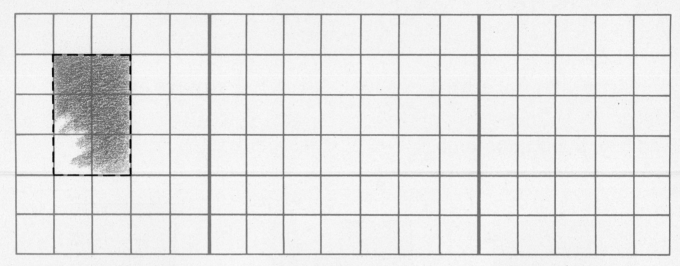

b. **7** square units   **3** square units   **10** square units

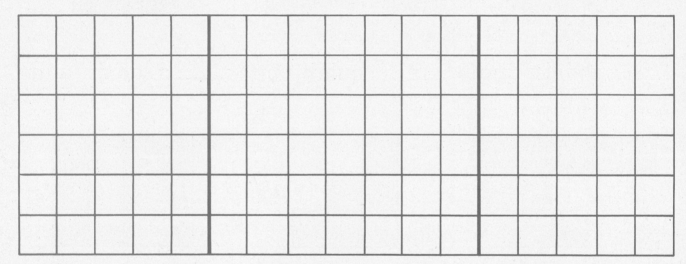

c. **9** square units   **12** square units   **14** square units

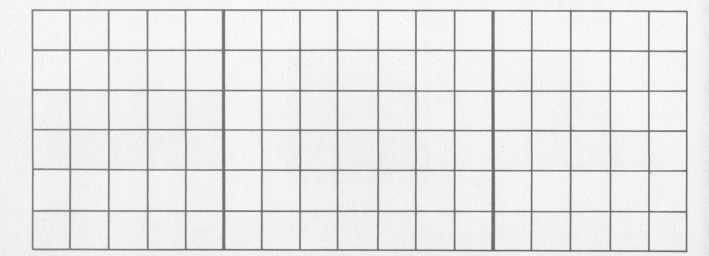

256

Liter

The liter is used to measure liquids.

about 1 liter

Does the container hold MORE or
LESS than 1 liter?

a.

MORE

(LESS)

b.

MORE

LESS

c.

MORE

LESS

d.

MORE

LESS

e.

MORE

LESS

f.

MORE

LESS

g.

MORE

LESS

h.

MORE

LESS

PROBLEM SOLVING

Geraldine made a table to show how many liters
of water some objects can hold.

object	liters
pot	2
fish tank	20
sink	60
washing machine	72

a. How much water does the fish tank hold? _____ liters

b. How much water does the washing machine hold? _____ liters

c. Which object holds the least amount of water? _____

d. How many liters of water are used to fill the sink and the fish tank? _____ liters

Skills Maintenance

Ring how much is needed.

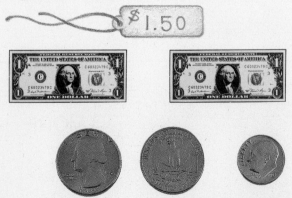

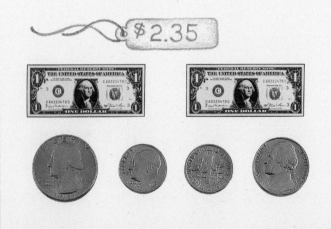

Kilogram

When you want to know how heavy an object is,
you can measure it in kilograms.

I kilogram

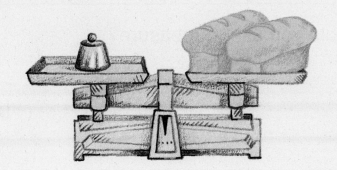

Is the object MORE or LESS than
I kilogram?

a.

(MORE)

LESS

b.

MORE

LESS

c.

MORE

LESS

d.

MORE

LESS

e.

MORE

LESS

f.

MORE

LESS

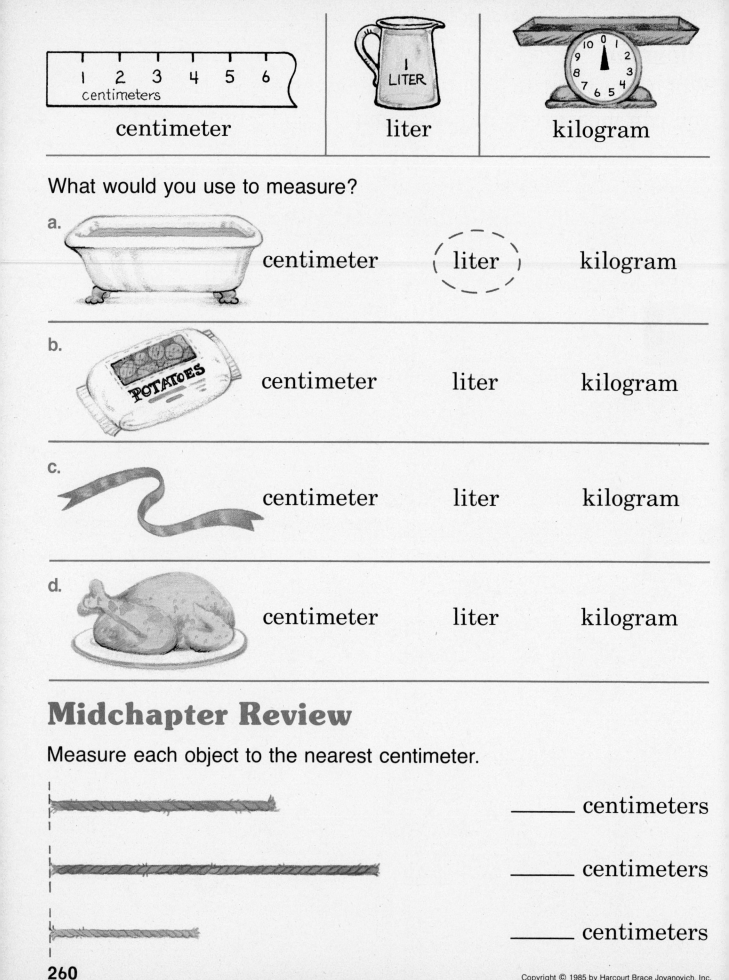

centimeter	liter	kilogram

What would you use to measure?

a. centimeter (liter) kilogram

b. centimeter liter kilogram

c. centimeter liter kilogram

d. centimeter liter kilogram

Midchapter Review

Measure each object to the nearest centimeter.

_____ centimeters

_____ centimeters

_____ centimeters

Temperature

Celsius

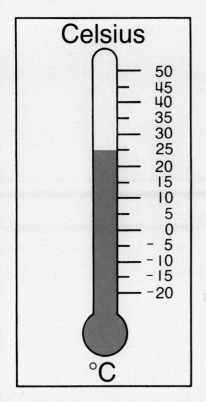

°C

We measure temperature with a thermometer. There are two kinds of thermometers. This is a Celsius thermometer.

_25_ °C

We read **25** degrees Celsius.

Write the temperature.

a.

35
30
25
20
15
10
5
0

_____ °C

b.

35
30
25
20
15
10
5
0

_____ °C

c.

35
30
25
20
15
10
5
0

_____ °C

d.

35
30
25
20
15
10
5
0

_____ °C

Fahrenheit

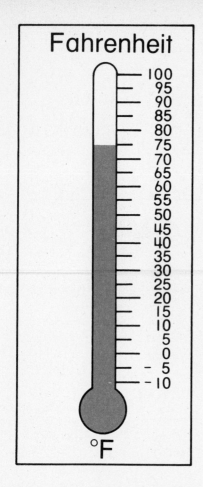

°F

We measure temperature with a thermometer. This is a Fahrenheit thermometer.

_75_ °F

We read **75** degrees Fahrenheit.

Write the temperature.

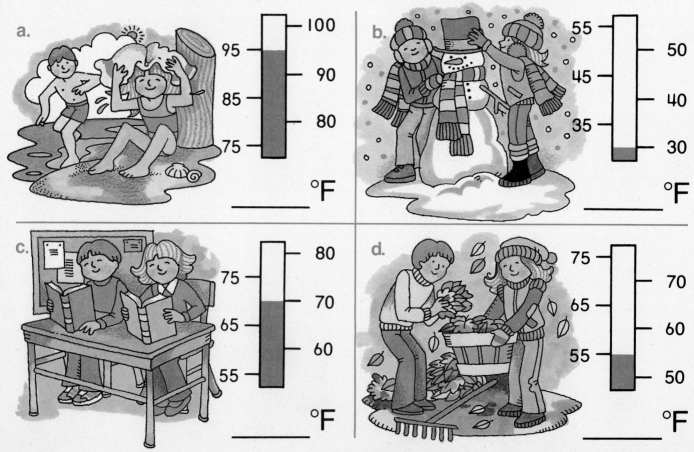

a.

_____ °F

b.

_____ °F

c.

_____ °F

d.

_____ °F

name _____

PROBLEM SOLVING

Reading Pictographs

Paper Drive

Grade	Stacks of Paper						
1	🗞	🗞	🗞				
2	🗞	🗞	🗞	🗞	🗞	🗞	🗞
3	🗞	🗞					
4	🗞	🗞	🗞	🗞	🗞		
5	🗞	🗞	🗞	🗞	🗞	🗞	
6	🗞	🗞	🗞	🗞			

a. How many 🗞 ?

Grade 1 _____   Grade 2 _____   Grade 3 _____

Grade 4 _____   Grade 5 _____   Grade 6 _____

Grades 1 and 2 _____   Grades 4 and 5 _____

b. Which grade has the most? _____

c. Which grade has the fewest? _____

Copyright © 1985 by Harcourt Brace Jovanovich, Inc.

263

Can Drive

Grade	Bags of Cans
1	🛍️ 🛍️ 🛍️ 🛍️
2	🛍️ 🛍️ 🛍️ 🛍️ 🛍️
3	🛍️
4	🛍️ 🛍️ 🛍️ 🛍️ 🛍️ 🛍️
5	🛍️ 🛍️
6	🛍️ 🛍️ 🛍️

a. How many 🛍️ ?

Grade 1 __4__   Grade 2 _____   Grade 3 _____

Grade 4 _____   Grade 5 _____   Grade 6 _____

Grades 2 and 3 _____   Grades 4 and 6 _____

b. Which grade has the most? _____

c. Which grade has the fewest? _____

Inch

You can also measure how long an object is
by using an inch ruler.

Measure each object to the nearest inch.

The 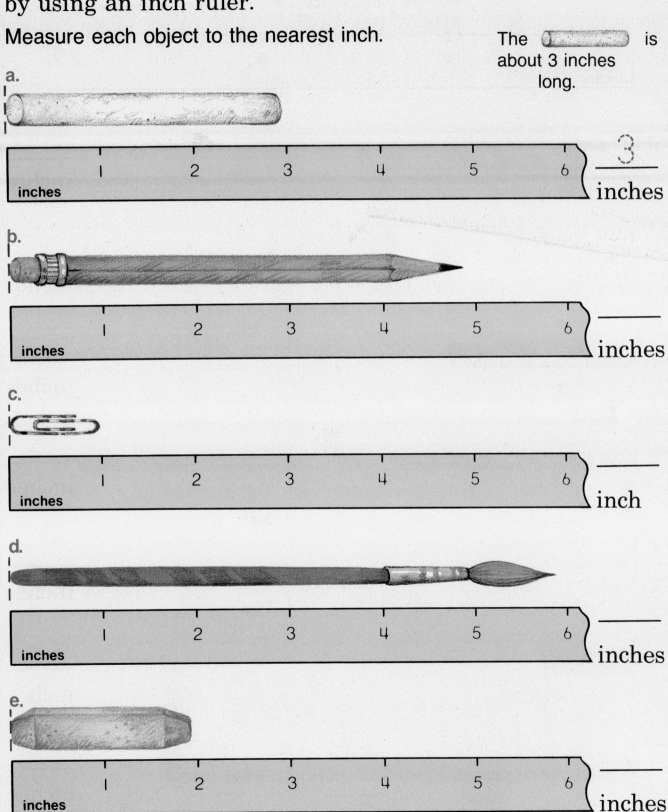 is about 3 inches long.

a.

$\dfrac{3}{\text{inches}}$

b.

$\dfrac{}{\text{inches}}$

c.

$\dfrac{}{\text{inch}}$

d.

$\dfrac{}{\text{inches}}$

e.

$\dfrac{}{\text{inches}}$

Measure each object to the nearest inch.
Use your ruler.

a.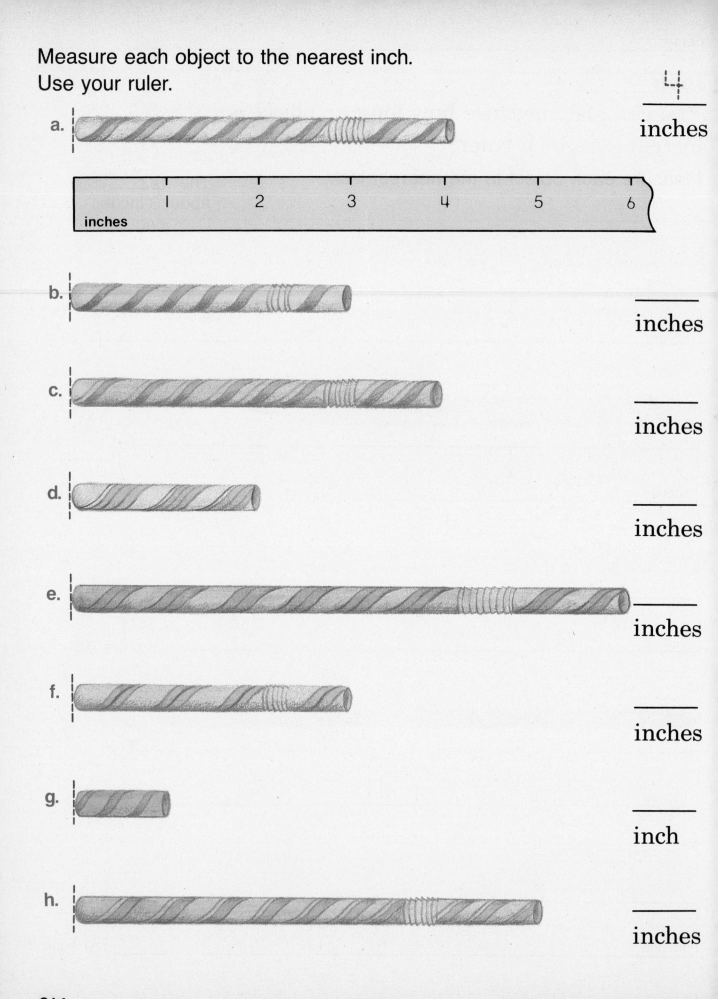

4
___
inches

inches
| 1 | 2 | 3 | 4 | 5 | 6 |
inches

b.

___
inches

c.

___
inches

d.

___
inches

e.
___
inches

f.

___
inches

g.

___
inch

h.

___
inches

Cup, Pint, and Quart

The cup, pint, and quart are also used to measure liquids.

2 cups fill **1** pint.　　　**2** pints fill **1** quart.

Ring which holds more.

a.

b.

c.

d.

e.

f.

g.

h.

2 cups = **1** pint   **2** pints = **1** quart

Color to show the same amount.

a.

b.

c.

d.

Pound

When you want to know how heavy an object is,
you can measure it in pounds.

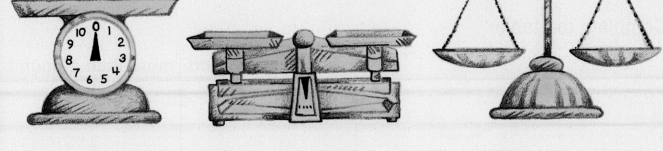

Use the scale to measure each object
in pounds.

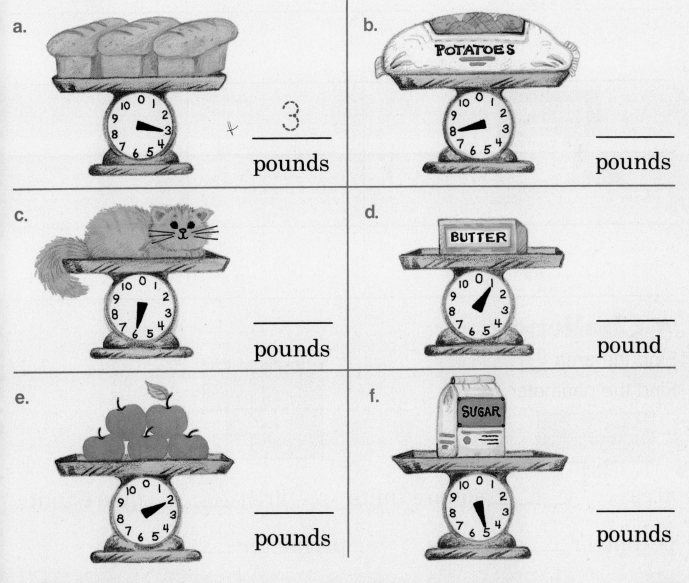

a. ✗ _3_ pounds

b. _____ pounds

c. _____ pounds

d. _____ pound

e. _____ pounds

f. _____ pounds

269

less than **l** pound **l** pound more than **l** pound

Complete the table.

	less than l pound	more than l pound
egg	X	
baby		
sock		
bookshelf		
pencil		
table		

★ Challenge

Find the area 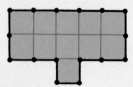.

Find the perimeter •—• .

  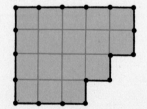

area _____ square units   area _____ square units

perimeter _____ units   perimeter _____ units

a. Measure the object to the nearest centimeter. (pages 251-252)

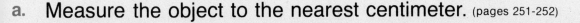

_____ centimeters

b. Does the container hold MORE or LESS than  ? (pages 257-258)

      MORE

LESS

      MORE

LESS

c. Is it MORE or LESS than 1 kilogram ? (pages 259-260)

    MORE

LESS

     MORE

LESS

d. Measure the object to the nearest inch. (pages 265-266)

_____ inches

e. Color to show the same amount. (pages 267-268)

f. Use the scale to measure each object in pounds. (pages 269-270)

 _____ pounds

 _____ pounds

271

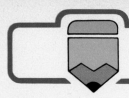

PROJECT

Meter

⌐─┐

1 centimeter

100 centimeters make **1** meter.

Measure each of these and color in the graph.

		about 1 meter or less	about 2 meters	about 3 meters	about 4 meters	about 5 meters or more
chalkboard						
teacher's desk						
bookcase						
my height						
my friend's height						

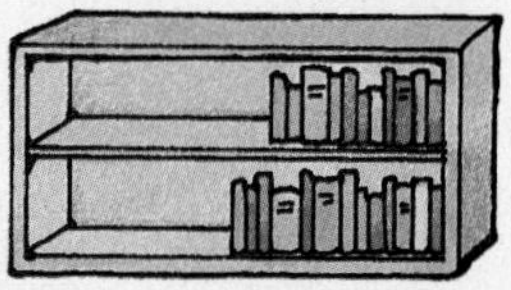

272

a. Measure the object to the nearest centimeter.

_____ centimeters

b. Does the container hold MORE or LESS than ?

   MORE

LESS

  MORE

LESS

c. Is it MORE or LESS than 1 kilogram?

 MORE

LESS

MORE

LESS

d. Measure the object to the nearest inch.

_____ inches

e. Color to show the same amount.

f. Use the scale to measure each object in pounds.

_____ pounds

_____ pounds

ENRICHMENT

Volume

I see 2 ▱.

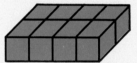 _____

Write how many .

1 layer

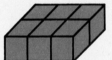

_____

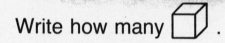 _____

2 layers

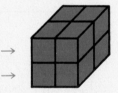

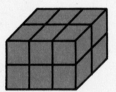

_____

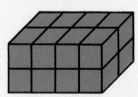 _____

3 layers

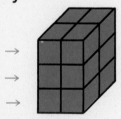

_____

 _____

274

Choose the correct answers.

1.

$$53 \\ +29$$

(A) 72
(B) 80
(C) 82
(D) not here

2.

$$76 \\ +48$$

(A) 124
(B) 114
(C) 104
(D) not here

3.

$$65¢ \\ +15¢$$

(A) 70¢
(B) 80¢
(C) 85¢
(D) not here

4.

$$94 \\ -28$$

(A) 56
(B) 60
(C) 64
(D) not here

5.

$$78 \\ -55$$

(A) 33
(B) 23
(C) 25
(D) not here

6.

$$43¢ \\ -39¢$$

(A) 12¢
(B) 14¢
(C) 4¢
(D) not here

7. The pet store has 56 fish and 28 fish tanks. How many more fish than fish tanks are there?

(A) 28
(B) 84
(C) 26
(D) not here

8. There are 45 cat toys and 39 dog toys in the pet store. How many toys in all?

(A) 6
(B) 84
(C) 80
(D) not here

9.

(A) 4:35
(B) 5:35
(C) 4:30
(D) not here

10.

(A) 3:15
(B) 9:00
(C) 9:15
(D) not here

11.

(A) 12:00
(B) 11:30
(C) 1:30
(D) not here

Choose the same shapes.

12.

(A)

(B)

(C)

(D) not here

13.

(A)

(B)

(C)

(D) not here

14.

(A) ◯

(B) ▢

(C) △

(D) not here

15.

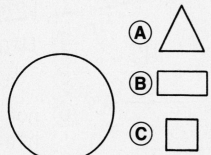

(A) △

(B) ▭

(C) ▢

(D) not here

16.

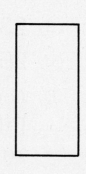

(A) ▭

(B) △

(C) ▢

(D) not here

17.

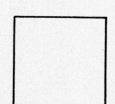

(A) △

(B) ◯

(C) ▢

(D) not here

Choose the correct answers.

18.

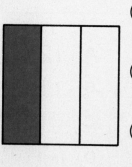

(A) $\frac{1}{3}$

(B) $\frac{2}{3}$

(C) $\frac{1}{2}$

(D) not here

19.

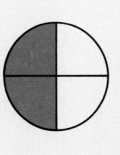

(A) $\frac{2}{3}$

(B) $\frac{1}{3}$

(C) $\frac{2}{4}$

(D) not here

20.

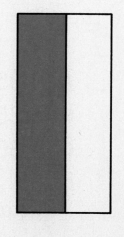

(A) $\frac{2}{3}$

(B) $\frac{1}{2}$

(C) $\frac{1}{4}$

(D) not here

276

Addition and Subtraction of Three-Digit Numbers

CHAPTER 11

GETTING STARTED

Add.

a.
$$\begin{array}{r}36\\+23\\\hline 59\end{array}$$
$$\begin{array}{r}17\\+55\\\hline 72\end{array}$$
$$\begin{array}{r}54\\+38\\\hline\end{array}$$
$$\begin{array}{r}13\\+35\\\hline\end{array}$$
$$\begin{array}{r}17\\+28\\\hline\end{array}$$
$$\begin{array}{r}57\\+\ 6\\\hline\end{array}$$

b.
$$\begin{array}{r}33\\+25\\\hline\end{array}$$
$$\begin{array}{r}46\\+15\\\hline\end{array}$$
$$\begin{array}{r}75\\+10\\\hline\end{array}$$
$$\begin{array}{r}47\\+\ 9\\\hline\end{array}$$
$$\begin{array}{r}65\\+24\\\hline\end{array}$$
$$\begin{array}{r}37\\+26\\\hline\end{array}$$

c.
$$\begin{array}{r}4\\+56\\\hline\end{array}$$
$$\begin{array}{r}70\\+11\\\hline\end{array}$$
$$\begin{array}{r}29\\+\ 5\\\hline\end{array}$$
$$\begin{array}{r}69\\+14\\\hline\end{array}$$
$$\begin{array}{r}43\\+27\\\hline\end{array}$$
$$\begin{array}{r}62\\+18\\\hline\end{array}$$

Subtract.

d.
$$\begin{array}{r}67\\-25\\\hline 42\end{array}$$
$$\begin{array}{r}70\\-35\\\hline 35\end{array}$$
$$\begin{array}{r}95\\-30\\\hline\end{array}$$
$$\begin{array}{r}64\\-58\\\hline\end{array}$$
$$\begin{array}{r}83\\-16\\\hline\end{array}$$
$$\begin{array}{r}68\\-42\\\hline\end{array}$$

e.
$$\begin{array}{r}80\\-26\\\hline\end{array}$$
$$\begin{array}{r}45\\-\ 8\\\hline\end{array}$$
$$\begin{array}{r}76\\-16\\\hline\end{array}$$
$$\begin{array}{r}39\\-26\\\hline\end{array}$$
$$\begin{array}{r}73\\-67\\\hline\end{array}$$
$$\begin{array}{r}65\\-28\\\hline\end{array}$$

f.
$$\begin{array}{r}78\\-37\\\hline\end{array}$$
$$\begin{array}{r}50\\-45\\\hline\end{array}$$
$$\begin{array}{r}63\\-48\\\hline\end{array}$$
$$\begin{array}{r}52\\-13\\\hline\end{array}$$
$$\begin{array}{r}34\\-20\\\hline\end{array}$$
$$\begin{array}{r}87\\-38\\\hline\end{array}$$

Adding Three-Digit Numbers

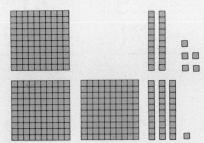

Step 1
Add the ones.

Step 2
Add the tens.

Step 3
Add the hundreds.

start
↓

hundreds	tens	ones
1	2	5
+ 2	3	1
		6

hundreds	tens	ones
1	2	5
+ 2	3	1
	5	6

hundreds	tens	ones
1	2	5
+ 2	3	1
3	5	6

Add.

↓   ↓   ↓

a.

hundreds	tens	ones
3	2	4
+ 1	3	2
4	5	6

hundreds	tens	ones
6	1	3
+	2	0

hundreds	tens	ones
8	0	3
+ 1	2	5

b.

$$\begin{array}{r} 704 \\ +145 \\ \hline \end{array} \qquad \begin{array}{r} 380 \\ +210 \\ \hline \end{array} \qquad \begin{array}{r} 725 \\ +\ 43 \\ \hline \end{array} \qquad \begin{array}{r} 500 \\ +200 \\ \hline \end{array} \qquad \begin{array}{r} 181 \\ +\ 15 \\ \hline \end{array} \qquad \begin{array}{r} 610 \\ +145 \\ \hline \end{array}$$

c.

$$\begin{array}{r} 475 \\ +214 \\ \hline \end{array} \qquad \begin{array}{r} 700 \\ +198 \\ \hline \end{array} \qquad \begin{array}{r} 425 \\ +350 \\ \hline \end{array} \qquad \begin{array}{r} 210 \\ +400 \\ \hline \end{array} \qquad \begin{array}{r} 560 \\ +134 \\ \hline \end{array} \qquad \begin{array}{r} 657 \\ +232 \\ \hline \end{array}$$

Add.

a.
$$241 + 121 = 362$$ $$534 + 62$$ $$325 + 471$$ $$615 + 242$$ $$315 + 480$$ $$700 + 215$$

b.
$$410 + 250$$ $$425 + 420$$ $$520 + 52$$ $$22 + 156$$ $$421 + 516$$ $$370 + 310$$

c.
$$169 + 530$$ $$613 + 120$$ $$736 + 253$$ $$600 + 200$$ $$382 + 15$$ $$216 + 672$$

d. $613 + 120 =$ _____ $101 + 183 =$ _____

e. $300 + 419 =$ _____ $536 + 241 =$ _____

f. $242 + 455 =$ _____ $473 + 25 =$ _____

Skills Maintenance

Write > or <.
greater than   less than

$450 \bigcirc 375$ $675 \bigcirc 780$ $200 \bigcirc 187$

$902 \bigcirc 860$ $950 \bigcirc 890$ $450 \bigcirc 540$

280

Addition with Regrouping

The school has **462** reading books and **329** math books. How many books in all?

Step 1
Add the ones.
Regroup.

start

```
  462
+ 329
    |
```

Step 2
Add the tens.

```
  462
+ 329
   91
```

Step 3
Add the hundreds.

```
  462
+ 329
  791
```

791 books in all

Add.

a.
```
  423      507      712      125      446      536
+ 159    + 238    + 169    + 237    +  24    + 218
  582
```

b.
```
  256      435      546      583      635      468
+ 107    +  29    + 235    + 108    +  38    + 419
```

c.
```
  284      358      645      619      555      705
+ 507    + 112    +  45    +  34    + 135    + 135
```

Find the sums.

a.
$$622 + 39 = 661$$
$$382 + 408$$
$$876 + 115$$
$$417 + 265$$
$$705 + 39$$
$$621 + 154$$

b.
$$202 + 183$$
$$217 + 534$$
$$150 + 239$$
$$615 + 28$$
$$563 + 29$$
$$326 + 147$$

c.
$$561 + 28$$
$$406 + 80$$
$$725 + 135$$
$$925 + 38$$
$$157 + 236$$
$$534 + 38$$

d.
$$434 + 23 + 106$$
$$533 + 142 + 217$$
$$635 + 40 + 119$$
$$105 + 322 + 419$$
$$312 + 106 + 245$$
$$53 + 200 + 418$$

PROBLEM SOLVING

Solve.

e. The school store has 245 red notebooks and 137 blue notebooks. How many notebooks in all?

f. On Monday 149 children visit the store. On Tuesday 248 children visit the store. How many children in all?

282

Adding Money

Pearl buys a cheese sandwich for $1.25 and a large bottle of juice for $1.19. How much does she spend in all?

$$\begin{array}{r} \$1.25 \\ + \ 1.19 \\ \hline \$2.44 \end{array}$$

Pearl spends $2.44 in all.

Add.

a.
$$\begin{array}{r} \$2.76 \\ + \ 3.15 \\ \hline \$5.91 \end{array}$$
$$\begin{array}{r} \$4.35 \\ + \ 2.34 \\ \hline \$6.69 \end{array}$$
$$\begin{array}{r} \$5.06 \\ + \ 2.37 \\ \hline \end{array}$$
$$\begin{array}{r} \$3.44 \\ + \ 4.23 \\ \hline \end{array}$$
$$\begin{array}{r} \$6.00 \\ + \ 2.00 \\ \hline \end{array}$$

b.
$$\begin{array}{r} \$1.48 \\ + \ .27 \\ \hline \end{array}$$
$$\begin{array}{r} \$3.64 \\ + \ 2.18 \\ \hline \end{array}$$
$$\begin{array}{r} \$6.52 \\ + \ 1.38 \\ \hline \end{array}$$
$$\begin{array}{r} \$7.28 \\ + \ 1.35 \\ \hline \end{array}$$
$$\begin{array}{r} \$2.66 \\ + \ .29 \\ \hline \end{array}$$

c.
$$\begin{array}{r} \$2.85 \\ + \ 1.07 \\ \hline \end{array}$$
$$\begin{array}{r} \$3.74 \\ + \ 4.12 \\ \hline \end{array}$$
$$\begin{array}{r} \$5.70 \\ + \ 2.18 \\ \hline \end{array}$$
$$\begin{array}{r} \$4.57 \\ + \ 4.28 \\ \hline \end{array}$$
$$\begin{array}{r} \$6.23 \\ + \ .48 \\ \hline \end{array}$$

d.
$$\begin{array}{r} \$8.57 \\ + \ 1.21 \\ \hline \end{array}$$
$$\begin{array}{r} \$2.45 \\ + \ 2.45 \\ \hline \end{array}$$
$$\begin{array}{r} \$6.39 \\ + \ .57 \\ \hline \end{array}$$
$$\begin{array}{r} \$2.75 \\ + \ 1.09 \\ \hline \end{array}$$
$$\begin{array}{r} \$1.44 \\ + \ 6.38 \\ \hline \end{array}$$

name

PROBLEM SOLVING

MENU

 Fresh Fruit $1.25

 Salad $1.42

 Hamburger Plate $2.48

Tuna Sandwich $1.63

 Egg Salad $ .75

 Milk $ .43

 Grape Juice $1.05

 Apple $ .17

Add to find the total cost.

a. Fresh Fruit Hamburger Plate $\begin{array}{r} \$1.25 \\ +\ 2.48 \\ \hline \$3.73 \end{array}$	**b.** Egg Salad Apple
c. Fresh Fruit Tuna Sandwich	**d.** Hamburger Plate Grape Juice
e. Salad Milk	**f.** Tuna Sandwich Apple

Subtracting Three-Digit Numbers

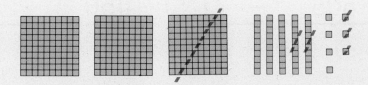

Step 1
Subtract the ones.

Step 2
Subtract the tens.

Step 3
Subtract the hundreds.

start ↓

hundreds	tens	ones
3	5	7
− 1	2	3
		4

hundreds	tens	ones
3	5	7
− 1	2	3
	3	4

hundreds	tens	ones
3	5	7
− 1	2	3
2	3	4

Subtract.

a.

↓

hundreds	tens	ones
4	3	6
− 2	2	4
2	1	2

↓

hundreds	tens	ones
2	5	7
−	2	5

↓

hundreds	tens	ones
4	6	7
− 3	2	1

b.

674	700	948	879	496	570
−531	−200	− 24	−725	−182	− 40

c.

375	963	768	895	729	674
− 22	−230	−164	−361	− 27	− 34

Subtract.

a.
$$672 - 371 = \underline{301}$$
$$928 - 605$$
$$787 - 71$$
$$960 - 450$$
$$873 - 263$$
$$987 - 354$$

b.
$$875 - 404$$
$$563 - 42$$
$$900 - 500$$
$$871 - 51$$
$$585 - 213$$
$$486 - 382$$

c.
$$140 - 30$$
$$956 - 132$$
$$342 - 41$$
$$467 - 325$$
$$968 - 405$$
$$797 - 231$$

d. $569 - 146 = \underline{}$ $958 - 232 = \underline{}$

e. $750 - 320 = \underline{}$ $892 - 472 = \underline{}$

Midchapter Review

Add.

$$251 + 327$$
$$604 + 182$$
$$512 + 34$$

$$137 + 26$$
$$408 + 257$$
$$719 + 175$$

286

Subtraction with Regrouping

There are **762** children at the baseball game. **325** are boys. How many are girls?

Step 1
You need more ones.
Regroup.
Subtract the ones.

```
  5 12
 76̷2̷
-325
   7
```

Step 2
Subtract the tens.

```
  5 12
 7̷6̷2̷
-325
  37
```

Step 3
Subtract the hundreds.

```
  5 12
 7̷6̷2̷
-325
 437
```

437 are girls.

Subtract.

a.
```
  6 16
 47̷6̷
- 38
 438
```
  580   463   235   625   834
-234 -128 - 17 -318 -519

b.
```
 634   947   876   236   562   755
-215  -128  -207  - 19  -248  -237
```

c.
```
 354   787   475   830   682   286
-128  -269  - 48  -125  -256  -129
```

Find the differences.

a.
$$
\begin{array}{r} 423 \\ -218 \\ \hline \end{array}
\qquad
\begin{array}{r} 324 \\ -15 \\ \hline \end{array}
\qquad
\begin{array}{r} 845 \\ -203 \\ \hline \end{array}
\qquad
\begin{array}{r} 925 \\ -206 \\ \hline \end{array}
\qquad
\begin{array}{r} 879 \\ -236 \\ \hline \end{array}
\qquad
\begin{array}{r} 648 \\ -29 \\ \hline \end{array}
$$

(handwritten above 423: 113; below: 205)

b.
$$
\begin{array}{r} 254 \\ -139 \\ \hline \end{array}
\qquad
\begin{array}{r} 856 \\ -328 \\ \hline \end{array}
\qquad
\begin{array}{r} 990 \\ -65 \\ \hline \end{array}
\qquad
\begin{array}{r} 789 \\ -145 \\ \hline \end{array}
\qquad
\begin{array}{r} 450 \\ -125 \\ \hline \end{array}
\qquad
\begin{array}{r} 580 \\ -120 \\ \hline \end{array}
$$

c.
$$
\begin{array}{r} 700 \\ -400 \\ \hline \end{array}
\qquad
\begin{array}{r} 356 \\ -29 \\ \hline \end{array}
\qquad
\begin{array}{r} 573 \\ -129 \\ \hline \end{array}
\qquad
\begin{array}{r} 965 \\ -108 \\ \hline \end{array}
\qquad
\begin{array}{r} 385 \\ -63 \\ \hline \end{array}
\qquad
\begin{array}{r} 482 \\ -167 \\ \hline \end{array}
$$

d.
$$
\begin{array}{r} 736 \\ -27 \\ \hline \end{array}
\qquad
\begin{array}{r} 919 \\ -306 \\ \hline \end{array}
\qquad
\begin{array}{r} 747 \\ -15 \\ \hline \end{array}
\qquad
\begin{array}{r} 554 \\ -25 \\ \hline \end{array}
\qquad
\begin{array}{r} 648 \\ -139 \\ \hline \end{array}
\qquad
\begin{array}{r} 350 \\ -127 \\ \hline \end{array}
$$

PROBLEM SOLVING

Solve.

e.

Susie's stand has **456** hats.
She sells **238**.
How many hats are left?

f.

Ron has **384** cans of
juice. He sells **126**.
How many cans of
juice are left?

288

Subtracting Money

Mindy has **$7.65.**
She buys a plant for
$3.29. How much does
she have left?

$$
\begin{array}{r}
^{5\,15} \\
\$7.\cancel{65} \\
-\ \ 3.29 \\
\hline
\$4.36
\end{array}
$$

Mindy has **$4.36** left.

Subtract.

a.
$$
\begin{array}{r}
^{2\,15} \\
\$6.\cancel{35} \\
-\ \ 2.07 \\
\hline
\$4.28
\end{array}
\qquad
\begin{array}{r}
\$3.98 \\
-\ \ 1.26 \\
\hline
\$2.72
\end{array}
\qquad
\begin{array}{r}
\$8.46 \\
-\ \ 5.17 \\
\hline
\end{array}
\qquad
\begin{array}{r}
\$7.81 \\
-\ \ 4.20 \\
\hline
\end{array}
\qquad
\begin{array}{r}
\$6.60 \\
-\ \ 3.25 \\
\hline
\end{array}
$$

b.
$$
\begin{array}{r}
\$7.54 \\
-\ \ 1.26 \\
\hline
\end{array}
\qquad
\begin{array}{r}
\$1.67 \\
-\ \ .45 \\
\hline
\end{array}
\qquad
\begin{array}{r}
\$3.46 \\
-\ \ 2.18 \\
\hline
\end{array}
\qquad
\begin{array}{r}
\$7.43 \\
-\ \ .28 \\
\hline
\end{array}
\qquad
\begin{array}{r}
\$5.79 \\
-\ \ 1.47 \\
\hline
\end{array}
$$

c.
$$
\begin{array}{r}
\$6.50 \\
-\ \ 2.29 \\
\hline
\end{array}
\qquad
\begin{array}{r}
\$7.35 \\
-\ \ .19 \\
\hline
\end{array}
\qquad
\begin{array}{r}
\$9.46 \\
-\ \ 2.07 \\
\hline
\end{array}
\qquad
\begin{array}{r}
\$8.34 \\
-\ \ .20 \\
\hline
\end{array}
\qquad
\begin{array}{r}
\$7.75 \\
-\ \ 2.46 \\
\hline
\end{array}
$$

d.
$$
\begin{array}{r}
\$5.40 \\
-\ \ 4.10 \\
\hline
\end{array}
\qquad
\begin{array}{r}
\$6.35 \\
-\ \ 1.08 \\
\hline
\end{array}
\qquad
\begin{array}{r}
\$8.75 \\
-\ \ 1.75 \\
\hline
\end{array}
\qquad
\begin{array}{r}
\$9.00 \\
-\ \ 7.00 \\
\hline
\end{array}
\qquad
\begin{array}{r}
\$4.38 \\
-\ \ 2.09 \\
\hline
\end{array}
$$

PROBLEM SOLVING

TOYS $1.38 off BIG SALE! CLOTHES $2.25 off

Subtract to find the new price.

a.

Amount off ⟶ $8.56
− 1.38
You pay $7.18

Amount off ⟶ $5.50
−
You pay

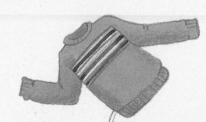

Amount off ⟶ $6.80
−
You pay

b.

Amount off ⟶ $7.48
−
You pay

Amount off ⟶ $4.99
−
You pay

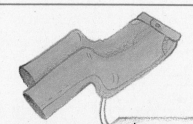

Amount off ⟶ $8.59
−
You pay

c.

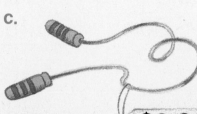

Amount off ⟶ $3.82
−
You pay

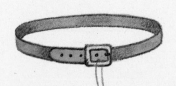

Amount off ⟶ $4.50
−
You pay

Amount off ⟶ $9.63
−
You pay

Mixed Practice

Be careful.
Watch the signs.

Add.

```
  1
 326
+215
 541
```

Subtract.

```
  3 15
 645
-328
 317
```

Add or subtract.

a.
```
 417
 457
-219
 238
```
```
 687
-355
```
```
 342
+426
```
```
 527
+ 35
```
```
 674
-237
```
```
 458
+125
```

b.
```
 535
- 26
```
```
 444
+235
```
```
 507
+ 16
```
```
 852
-431
```
```
  82
+309
```
```
 760
- 35
```

c.
```
 862
+ 28
```
```
 450
+325
```
```
 615
-  9
```
```
 786
-248
```
```
 525
- 18
```
```
 637
-127
```

d.
```
 600
-300
```
```
 583
+209
```
```
 770
- 24
```
```
  26
+148
```
```
 987
-237
```
```
 456
+237
```

Add or subtract.

a.
$$\begin{array}{r} \$1.45 \\ +\ 3.18 \\ \hline \$4.63 \end{array}$$

$$\begin{array}{r} \$4.36 \\ +\ 2.15 \\ \hline \end{array}$$

$$\begin{array}{r} \$4.23 \\ -\ 2.08 \\ \hline \end{array}$$

$$\begin{array}{r} \$7.42 \\ -\ \ .26 \\ \hline \end{array}$$

$$\begin{array}{r} \$6.38 \\ +\ 1.25 \\ \hline \end{array}$$

b.
$$\begin{array}{r} \$3.84 \\ +\ 1.09 \\ \hline \end{array}$$

$$\begin{array}{r} \$7.49 \\ -\ 3.06 \\ \hline \end{array}$$

$$\begin{array}{r} \$9.50 \\ -\ 4.25 \\ \hline \end{array}$$

$$\begin{array}{r} \$4.34 \\ +\ 5.25 \\ \hline \end{array}$$

$$\begin{array}{r} \$8.77 \\ -\ \ .38 \\ \hline \end{array}$$

c. $215 + 407 =$ _____ $748 - 328 =$ _____

d. $690 - 138 =$ _____ $384 + 608 =$ _____

e. $206 + 529 =$ _____ $933 - 507 =$ _____

★ Challenge

Follow the directions.

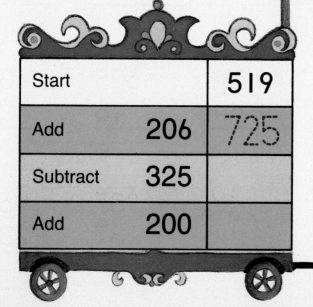

CIRCUS

Start		519
Add	206	725
Subtract	325	
Add	200	

Start		940
Subtract	635	
Add	260	
Subtract	428	

PROBLEM SOLVING

Add or Subtract?
Solve.

a. The bookstore has **557** dog books. It has **316** horse books. How many more dog books than horse books?

$$\begin{array}{r} 557 \\ -316 \\ \hline 241 \end{array}$$

b. There are **136** records on one shelf and **148** records on another shelf. How many records are there?

c. There are **245** animal books. **229** are sold. How many animal books are left?

d. Mr. Jones buys **208** storybooks and **125** sports books for the school. How many books in all?

e. There are **876** cookbooks. **239** are sold. How many cookbooks are left?

This table lists the schools in Tillytown and tells how many library books are found in each school.

School	Number of Books	School	Number of Books
Green	328	Kelly	264
Valley	412	Hill	127
Clark	645	Brown	846
Reed	130	Fox	733

How many books in all?

a.

Reed and Valley

$$\begin{array}{r} 130 \\ + 412 \\ \hline 542 \end{array}$$

b.

Clark and Hill _____

c.

Kelly and Green _____

Which school has more?
How many more?

Clark or (Brown)

$$\begin{array}{r} 846 \\ - 645 \\ \hline 201 \end{array}$$

Fox or Hill _____

Green or Clark _____

294

Add. (pages 279-284)

a.
537	645	127	706	535	138
+122	+239	+459	+ 36	+200	+257

b.
$4.56	$7.40	$5.00	$6.79	$ .36
+ 2.18	+ 1.25	+ .89	+ 2.13	+ 4.57

Subtract. (pages 285-290)

c.
435	850	594	694	843	747
− 129	− 25	− 267	− 250	− 643	− 208

d.
$7.78	$6.45	$8.43	$2.67	$6.50
− 2.39	− 3.00	− .25	− 1.09	− .36

Solve. (pages 293-294)

e. The school lunchroom has **245** sandwiches. They sold **106** . How many sandwiches are left?

f. The lunchroom has **205** orange juices and **187** grape juices. How many juices in all?

PROJECT

Maps

The parade marched around town.
Here is a map of the town.

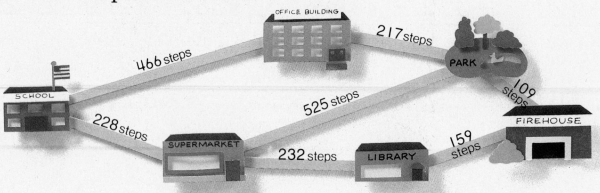

How many steps does the parade march?

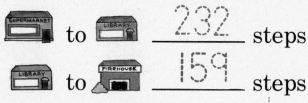 to ___232___ steps

to ___159___ steps

How many steps
in all?

$$\begin{array}{r} 232 \\ +\ 159 \\ \hline 391 \end{array}$$

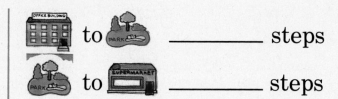 to ___ steps

to ___ steps

How many steps
in all?

 to ___ steps

to ___ steps

How many steps
in all?

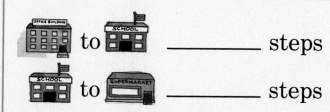 to ___ steps

to ___ steps

How many steps
in all?

Make up more problems about the map.
Give them to a friend to solve.

Add.

a.
325	509	748	675	363	610
+225	+ 82	+123	+ 19	+ 14	+158

b.
$5.04	$6.48	$4.69	$2.08	$7.15
+ 2.63	+ .27	+ 4.17	+ 6.86	+ .49

Subtract.

c.
657	458	981	346	863	764
− 139	− 256	− 35	− 117	− 649	− 26

d.
$6.52	$4.85	$8.37	$9.20	$5.86
− 4.06	− .38	− 6.27	− 1.19	− 1.17

Solve.

e. Dan collected **326** old stamps. He collected **108** new stamps. How many more old stamps than new stamps does he have?

f. Anna has **243** baseball cards. Maria has **139** baseball cards. How many cards in all?

ENRICHMENT

Expanded Form

Complete.

400	30	5	435
300	50	1	
	80		

600	20	3	
200	50	6	

100	70		172
800	10	7	

300	20	4	
	60		565
800		9	

700	10	0	
200	20	8	

600	40		648
	30	1	
700			

100	70		
	20	3	723
800		8	

500		9	549
400	50		
		9	

298

CHAPTER 12

Multiplication

GETTING STARTED

Write how many in all.

a.

$2 + 2 =$ _4_

2 twos = _4_

b.

$3 + 3 =$ _____

2 threes = _____

c.

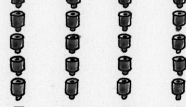

$5 + 5 + 5 + 5 =$ _____

4 fives = _____

d.

$2 + 2 + 2 + 2 + 2 =$ _____

5 twos = _____

e.

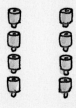

$4 + 4 =$ _____

2 fours = _____

f.

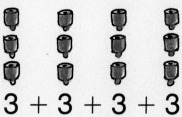

$3 + 3 + 3 + 3 =$ _____

4 threes = _____

g.

$2 + 2 + 2 =$ _____

3 twos = _____

h.

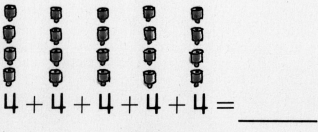

$4 + 4 + 4 + 4 + 4 =$ _____

5 fours = _____

2 as a Factor

$2 + 2 + 2 = \underline{6}$

3 twos $= \underline{6}$

$3 \times 2 = \underline{6}$

times

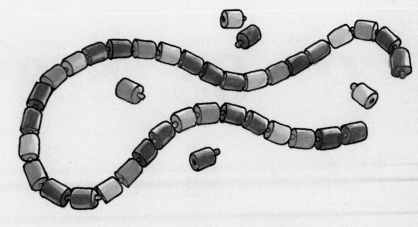

$3 \times 2 = 6$

factor   factor   product

Multiply.

a.

     $1 \times 2 = \underline{2}$

     $2 \times 2 = \underline{}$

     $3 \times 2 = \underline{}$

---

b.

 $4 \times 2 = \underline{}$

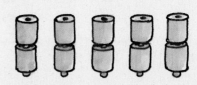 $5 \times 2 = \underline{}$

---

c. $5 \times 2 = \underline{}$ $3 \times 2 = \underline{}$ $1 \times 2 = \underline{}$

d. $2 \times 2 = \underline{}$ $4 \times 2 = \underline{}$ $5 \times 2 = \underline{}$

e. $1 \times 2 = \underline{}$ $2 \times 2 = \underline{}$ $4 \times 2 = \underline{}$

301

Find the products.

a.
$$\begin{array}{r} 2 \\ \times 1 \\ \hline 2 \end{array}$$
$$\begin{array}{r} 2 \\ \times 2 \\ \hline \end{array}$$
$$\begin{array}{r} 2 \\ \times 3 \\ \hline \end{array}$$
$$\begin{array}{r} 2 \\ \times 4 \\ \hline \end{array}$$
$$\begin{array}{r} 2 \\ \times 5 \\ \hline \end{array}$$

b.
$$\begin{array}{r} 2 \\ \times 3 \\ \hline \end{array}$$
$$\begin{array}{r} 2 \\ \times 1 \\ \hline \end{array}$$
$$\begin{array}{r} 2 \\ \times 2 \\ \hline \end{array}$$
$$\begin{array}{r} 2 \\ \times 5 \\ \hline \end{array}$$
$$\begin{array}{r} 2 \\ \times 4 \\ \hline \end{array}$$
$$\begin{array}{r} 2 \\ \times 3 \\ \hline \end{array}$$
$$\begin{array}{r} 2 \\ \times 5 \\ \hline \end{array}$$

c.
$$\begin{array}{r} 2 \\ \times 4 \\ \hline \end{array}$$
$$\begin{array}{r} 2 \\ \times 2 \\ \hline \end{array}$$
$$\begin{array}{r} 2 \\ \times 5 \\ \hline \end{array}$$
$$\begin{array}{r} 2 \\ \times 1 \\ \hline \end{array}$$
$$\begin{array}{r} 2 \\ \times 3 \\ \hline \end{array}$$
$$\begin{array}{r} 2 \\ \times 4 \\ \hline \end{array}$$
$$\begin{array}{r} 2 \\ \times 2 \\ \hline \end{array}$$

d.
$$\begin{array}{r} 2 \\ \times 1 \\ \hline \end{array}$$
$$\begin{array}{r} 2 \\ \times 4 \\ \hline \end{array}$$
$$\begin{array}{r} 2 \\ \times 2 \\ \hline \end{array}$$
$$\begin{array}{r} 2 \\ \times 5 \\ \hline \end{array}$$
$$\begin{array}{r} 2 \\ \times 3 \\ \hline \end{array}$$
$$\begin{array}{r} 2 \\ \times 1 \\ \hline \end{array}$$
$$\begin{array}{r} 2 \\ \times 4 \\ \hline \end{array}$$

Skills Maintenance

Count by twos and fives.

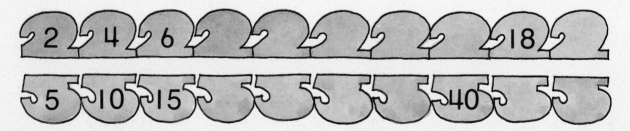

2 4 6   18

5 10 15   40

302

3 as a Factor

Multiply.

a.

$1 \times 3 = \underline{}$ $2 \times 3 = \underline{}$ $3 \times 3 = \underline{}$

b.

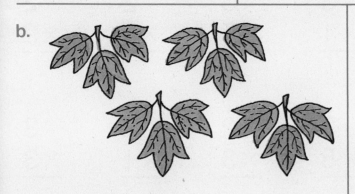 

$4 \times 3 = \underline{}$ $5 \times 3 = \underline{}$

c. $3 \times 3 = \underline{}$ $1 \times 3 = \underline{}$ $2 \times 3 = \underline{}$

d. $4 \times 3 = \underline{}$ $5 \times 3 = \underline{}$ $3 \times 3 = \underline{}$

e. $2 \times 2 = \underline{}$ $4 \times 2 = \underline{}$ $1 \times 2 = \underline{}$

f. $5 \times 3 = \underline{}$ $3 \times 2 = \underline{}$ $5 \times 2 = \underline{}$

g. $2 \times 3 = \underline{}$ $1 \times 2 = \underline{}$ $4 \times 2 = \underline{}$

h. $2 \times 2 = \underline{}$ $4 \times 3 = \underline{}$ $1 \times 3 = \underline{}$

i. $5 \times 2 = \underline{}$ $3 \times 3 = \underline{}$ $5 \times 3 = \underline{}$

Find the products.

a.
$$\begin{array}{r} 3 \\ \times 1 \\ \hline 3 \end{array}$$
$$\begin{array}{r} 3 \\ \times 2 \\ \hline \end{array}$$
$$\begin{array}{r} 3 \\ \times 3 \\ \hline \end{array}$$
$$\begin{array}{r} 3 \\ \times 4 \\ \hline \end{array}$$
$$\begin{array}{r} 3 \\ \times 5 \\ \hline \end{array}$$

b.
$$\begin{array}{r} 3 \\ \times 3 \\ \hline \end{array}$$
$$\begin{array}{r} 3 \\ \times 2 \\ \hline \end{array}$$
$$\begin{array}{r} 3 \\ \times 4 \\ \hline \end{array}$$
$$\begin{array}{r} 3 \\ \times 1 \\ \hline \end{array}$$
$$\begin{array}{r} 3 \\ \times 5 \\ \hline \end{array}$$
$$\begin{array}{r} 2 \\ \times 4 \\ \hline \end{array}$$
$$\begin{array}{r} 2 \\ \times 2 \\ \hline \end{array}$$

c.
$$\begin{array}{r} 3 \\ \times 4 \\ \hline \end{array}$$
$$\begin{array}{r} 3 \\ \times 1 \\ \hline \end{array}$$
$$\begin{array}{r} 2 \\ \times 2 \\ \hline \end{array}$$
$$\begin{array}{r} 3 \\ \times 5 \\ \hline \end{array}$$
$$\begin{array}{r} 2 \\ \times 3 \\ \hline \end{array}$$
$$\begin{array}{r} 2 \\ \times 1 \\ \hline \end{array}$$
$$\begin{array}{r} 3 \\ \times 3 \\ \hline \end{array}$$

d.
$$\begin{array}{r} 2 \\ \times 5 \\ \hline \end{array}$$
$$\begin{array}{r} 3 \\ \times 2 \\ \hline \end{array}$$
$$\begin{array}{r} 2 \\ \times 4 \\ \hline \end{array}$$
$$\begin{array}{r} 1 \\ \times 2 \\ \hline \end{array}$$
$$\begin{array}{r} 3 \\ \times 3 \\ \hline \end{array}$$
$$\begin{array}{r} 2 \\ \times 3 \\ \hline \end{array}$$
$$\begin{array}{r} 2 \\ \times 5 \\ \hline \end{array}$$

PROBLEM SOLVING

Solve.

e.

5 carts

3 in each

How many
in all?

f.

2 bags

3 in each

How many
in all?

304

4 as a Factor

Multiply.

a.

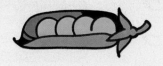

$1 \times 4 = \underline{4}$

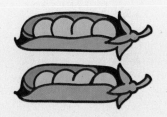

$2 \times 4 = \underline{}$

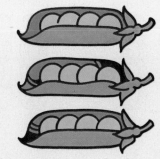

$3 \times 4 = \underline{}$

b.

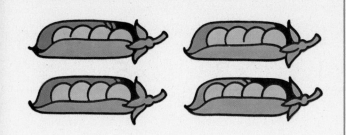

$4 \times 4 = \underline{}$

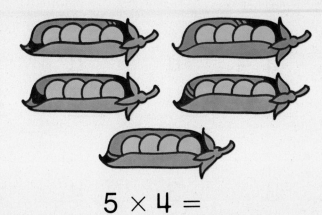

$5 \times 4 = \underline{}$

c. $3 \times 4 = \underline{12}$　　$5 \times 4 = \underline{}$　　$1 \times 4 = \underline{}$

d. $2 \times 4 = \underline{}$　　$4 \times 4 = \underline{}$　　$3 \times 4 = \underline{}$

e. $5 \times 3 = \underline{}$　　$3 \times 2 = \underline{}$　　$5 \times 2 = \underline{}$

f. $1 \times 3 = \underline{}$　　$5 \times 4 = \underline{}$　　$2 \times 4 = \underline{}$

g. $4 \times 4 = \underline{}$　　$1 \times 4 = \underline{}$　　$4 \times 3 = \underline{}$

h. $2 \times 2 = \underline{}$　　$4 \times 2 = \underline{}$　　$3 \times 3 = \underline{}$

i. $1 \times 2 = \underline{}$　　$2 \times 3 = \underline{}$　　$5 \times 3 = \underline{}$

Find the products.

  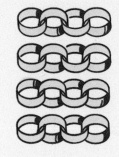  

a.
$$4 \times 1$$
$$4$$
$$4 \times 2$$
$$4 \times 3$$
$$4 \times 4$$
$$4 \times 5$$

b.
$$4 \times 2$$
$$4 \times 4$$
$$4 \times 5$$
$$4 \times 1$$
$$4 \times 3$$
$$3 \times 5$$
$$3 \times 2$$

c.
$$3 \times 4$$
$$3 \times 1$$
$$4 \times 4$$
$$2 \times 4$$
$$2 \times 2$$
$$3 \times 3$$
$$4 \times 3$$

d.
$$2 \times 1$$
$$2 \times 5$$
$$4 \times 5$$
$$3 \times 2$$
$$4 \times 1$$
$$4 \times 2$$
$$2 \times 3$$

PROBLEM SOLVING
Solve.

e. 3 boxes.

4 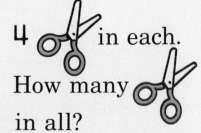 in each.

How many in all?

f. 5 bags.

2 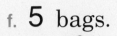 in each.

How many 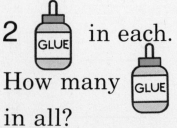 in all?

5 as a Factor

Multiply.

a.

$1 \times 5 = \underline{5}$

$2 \times 5 = \underline{}$

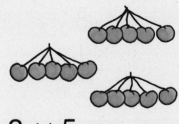

$3 \times 5 = \underline{}$

b.

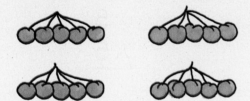

$4 \times 5 = \underline{}$

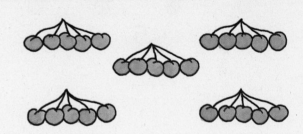

$5 \times 5 = \underline{}$

c. $2 \times 5 = \underline{10}$ $4 \times 5 = \underline{}$ $5 \times 5 = \underline{}$

d. $3 \times 5 = \underline{}$ $1 \times 5 = \underline{}$ $3 \times 5 = \underline{}$

e. $1 \times 4 = \underline{}$ $4 \times 4 = \underline{}$ $3 \times 3 = \underline{}$

f. $5 \times 5 = \underline{}$ $2 \times 3 = \underline{}$ $2 \times 5 = \underline{}$

g. $4 \times 2 = \underline{}$ $4 \times 5 = \underline{}$ $2 \times 2 = \underline{}$

h. $1 \times 5 = \underline{}$ $5 \times 3 = \underline{}$ $5 \times 4 = \underline{}$

i. $3 \times 2 = \underline{}$ $4 \times 3 = \underline{}$ $2 \times 4 = \underline{}$

Find the products.

a.

$$\begin{array}{r} 5 \\ \times 1 \\ \hline 5 \end{array}$$

$$\begin{array}{r} 5 \\ \times 2 \\ \hline \end{array}$$

$$\begin{array}{r} 5 \\ \times 3 \\ \hline \end{array}$$

b.

$$\begin{array}{r} 5 \\ \times 4 \\ \hline \end{array}$$

$$\begin{array}{r} 5 \\ \times 5 \\ \hline \end{array}$$

c.
$$\begin{array}{r} 5 \\ \times 3 \\ \hline 15 \end{array}$$
$$\begin{array}{r} 5 \\ \times 5 \\ \hline \end{array}$$
$$\begin{array}{r} 5 \\ \times 4 \\ \hline \end{array}$$
$$\begin{array}{r} 5 \\ \times 2 \\ \hline \end{array}$$
$$\begin{array}{r} 5 \\ \times 1 \\ \hline \end{array}$$
$$\begin{array}{r} 3 \\ \times 2 \\ \hline \end{array}$$
$$\begin{array}{r} 4 \\ \times 3 \\ \hline \end{array}$$

d.
$$\begin{array}{r} 5 \\ \times 5 \\ \hline \end{array}$$
$$\begin{array}{r} 1 \\ \times 2 \\ \hline \end{array}$$
$$\begin{array}{r} 5 \\ \times 2 \\ \hline \end{array}$$
$$\begin{array}{r} 4 \\ \times 4 \\ \hline \end{array}$$
$$\begin{array}{r} 3 \\ \times 3 \\ \hline \end{array}$$
$$\begin{array}{r} 4 \\ \times 3 \\ \hline \end{array}$$
$$\begin{array}{r} 5 \\ \times 1 \\ \hline \end{array}$$

e.
$$\begin{array}{r} 4 \\ \times 1 \\ \hline \end{array}$$
$$\begin{array}{r} 3 \\ \times 4 \\ \hline \end{array}$$
$$\begin{array}{r} 5 \\ \times 4 \\ \hline \end{array}$$
$$\begin{array}{r} 3 \\ \times 5 \\ \hline \end{array}$$
$$\begin{array}{r} 4 \\ \times 5 \\ \hline \end{array}$$
$$\begin{array}{r} 3 \\ \times 1 \\ \hline \end{array}$$
$$\begin{array}{r} 5 \\ \times 3 \\ \hline \end{array}$$

f.
$$\begin{array}{r} 2 \\ \times 2 \\ \hline \end{array}$$
$$\begin{array}{r} 5 \\ \times 2 \\ \hline \end{array}$$
$$\begin{array}{r} 4 \\ \times 2 \\ \hline \end{array}$$
$$\begin{array}{r} 2 \\ \times 4 \\ \hline \end{array}$$
$$\begin{array}{r} 4 \\ \times 5 \\ \hline \end{array}$$
$$\begin{array}{r} 5 \\ \times 5 \\ \hline \end{array}$$
$$\begin{array}{r} 5 \\ \times 2 \\ \hline \end{array}$$

308

0 and 1 as Factors

The product of any number and 1 is that number.

$3 \times 1 = 3$

$$\begin{array}{r} 1 \\ \times 5 \\ \hline 5 \end{array}$$

The product of any number and 0 is 0.

$2 \times 0 = 0$

$$\begin{array}{r} 0 \\ \times 4 \\ \hline 0 \end{array}$$

Find the products.

a.
$$\begin{array}{r} 1 \\ \times 0 \\ \hline 0 \end{array} \quad \begin{array}{r} 1 \\ \times 1 \\ \hline \end{array} \quad \begin{array}{r} 1 \\ \times 2 \\ \hline \end{array} \quad \begin{array}{r} 1 \\ \times 3 \\ \hline \end{array} \quad \begin{array}{r} 1 \\ \times 4 \\ \hline \end{array} \quad \begin{array}{r} 1 \\ \times 5 \\ \hline \end{array} \quad \begin{array}{r} 1 \\ \times 4 \\ \hline \end{array}$$

b.
$$\begin{array}{r} 0 \\ \times 0 \\ \hline \end{array} \quad \begin{array}{r} 0 \\ \times 1 \\ \hline \end{array} \quad \begin{array}{r} 0 \\ \times 2 \\ \hline \end{array} \quad \begin{array}{r} 0 \\ \times 3 \\ \hline \end{array} \quad \begin{array}{r} 0 \\ \times 4 \\ \hline \end{array} \quad \begin{array}{r} 0 \\ \times 5 \\ \hline \end{array} \quad \begin{array}{r} 0 \\ \times 2 \\ \hline \end{array}$$

c.
$$\begin{array}{r} 1 \\ \times 5 \\ \hline \end{array} \quad \begin{array}{r} 1 \\ \times 2 \\ \hline \end{array} \quad \begin{array}{r} 0 \\ \times 5 \\ \hline \end{array} \quad \begin{array}{r} 1 \\ \times 1 \\ \hline \end{array} \quad \begin{array}{r} 0 \\ \times 0 \\ \hline \end{array} \quad \begin{array}{r} 0 \\ \times 4 \\ \hline \end{array} \quad \begin{array}{r} 1 \\ \times 3 \\ \hline \end{array}$$

d.
$$\begin{array}{r} 0 \\ \times 1 \\ \hline \end{array} \quad \begin{array}{r} 0 \\ \times 3 \\ \hline \end{array} \quad \begin{array}{r} 5 \\ \times 1 \\ \hline \end{array} \quad \begin{array}{r} 3 \\ \times 1 \\ \hline \end{array} \quad \begin{array}{r} 1 \\ \times 0 \\ \hline \end{array} \quad \begin{array}{r} 2 \\ \times 1 \\ \hline \end{array} \quad \begin{array}{r} 4 \\ \times 1 \\ \hline \end{array}$$

Find the products.

a.
$\begin{array}{r} 0 \\ \times 2 \\ \hline \end{array}$
$\begin{array}{r} 1 \\ \times 3 \\ \hline \end{array}$
$\begin{array}{r} 5 \\ \times 3 \\ \hline \end{array}$
$\begin{array}{r} 4 \\ \times 5 \\ \hline \end{array}$
$\begin{array}{r} 3 \\ \times 2 \\ \hline \end{array}$
$\begin{array}{r} 0 \\ \times 4 \\ \hline \end{array}$
$\begin{array}{r} 5 \\ \times 5 \\ \hline \end{array}$

b.
$\begin{array}{r} 1 \\ \times 1 \\ \hline \end{array}$
$\begin{array}{r} 2 \\ \times 4 \\ \hline \end{array}$
$\begin{array}{r} 3 \\ \times 3 \\ \hline \end{array}$
$\begin{array}{r} 2 \\ \times 3 \\ \hline \end{array}$
$\begin{array}{r} 5 \\ \times 2 \\ \hline \end{array}$
$\begin{array}{r} 4 \\ \times 4 \\ \hline \end{array}$
$\begin{array}{r} 0 \\ \times 1 \\ \hline \end{array}$

c.
$\begin{array}{r} 2 \\ \times 2 \\ \hline \end{array}$
$\begin{array}{r} 1 \\ \times 5 \\ \hline \end{array}$
$\begin{array}{r} 0 \\ \times 3 \\ \hline \end{array}$
$\begin{array}{r} 5 \\ \times 4 \\ \hline \end{array}$
$\begin{array}{r} 0 \\ \times 0 \\ \hline \end{array}$
$\begin{array}{r} 5 \\ \times 1 \\ \hline \end{array}$
$\begin{array}{r} 4 \\ \times 3 \\ \hline \end{array}$

d.
$\begin{array}{r} 0 \\ \times 5 \\ \hline \end{array}$
$\begin{array}{r} 1 \\ \times 4 \\ \hline \end{array}$
$\begin{array}{r} 1 \\ \times 2 \\ \hline \end{array}$
$\begin{array}{r} 3 \\ \times 4 \\ \hline \end{array}$
$\begin{array}{r} 3 \\ \times 5 \\ \hline \end{array}$
$\begin{array}{r} 4 \\ \times 2 \\ \hline \end{array}$
$\begin{array}{r} 1 \\ \times 0 \\ \hline \end{array}$

Midchapter Review

Multiply.

$2 \times 5 = $ _____ $4 \times 3 = $ _____ $3 \times 0 = $ _____

$4 \times 1 = $ _____ $0 \times 5 = $ _____ $3 \times 3 = $ _____

Multiplication in Any Order

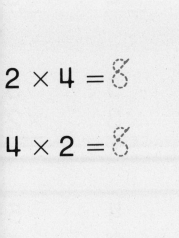

$2 \times 4 = 8$

$4 \times 2 = 8$

$$\begin{array}{r} 3 \\ \times 4 \\ \hline 12 \end{array} \qquad \begin{array}{r} 4 \\ \times 3 \\ \hline 12 \end{array}$$

You can multiply two numbers in either order.
The product is always the same.

Multiply.

a. $2 \times 3 = \underline{6}$ $5 \times 4 = \underline{}$ $3 \times 5 = \underline{}$

  $3 \times 2 = \underline{6}$ $4 \times 5 = \underline{}$ $5 \times 3 = \underline{}$

b. $4 \times 1 = \underline{}$ $0 \times 2 = \underline{}$ $5 \times 2 = \underline{}$

  $1 \times 4 = \underline{}$ $2 \times 0 = \underline{}$ $2 \times 5 = \underline{}$

c. $1 \times 3 = \underline{}$ $4 \times 2 = \underline{}$ $0 \times 4 = \underline{}$

  $3 \times 1 = \underline{}$ $2 \times 4 = \underline{}$ $4 \times 0 = \underline{}$

d. $3 \times 0 = \underline{}$ $1 \times 2 = \underline{}$ $4 \times 3 = \underline{}$

  $0 \times 3 = \underline{}$ $2 \times 1 = \underline{}$ $3 \times 4 = \underline{}$

Practice your multiplication facts.

a.
$$\begin{array}{r} 4 \\ \times 5 \\ \hline 20 \end{array}$$
$$\begin{array}{r} 5 \\ \times 4 \\ \hline \end{array}$$
$$\begin{array}{r} 3 \\ \times 3 \\ \hline \end{array}$$
$$\begin{array}{r} 5 \\ \times 1 \\ \hline \end{array}$$
$$\begin{array}{r} 3 \\ \times 4 \\ \hline \end{array}$$
$$\begin{array}{r} 4 \\ \times 2 \\ \hline \end{array}$$
$$\begin{array}{r} 0 \\ \times 3 \\ \hline \end{array}$$

b.
$$\begin{array}{r} 1 \\ \times 3 \\ \hline \end{array}$$
$$\begin{array}{r} 2 \\ \times 4 \\ \hline \end{array}$$
$$\begin{array}{r} 2 \\ \times 2 \\ \hline \end{array}$$
$$\begin{array}{r} 5 \\ \times 2 \\ \hline \end{array}$$
$$\begin{array}{r} 4 \\ \times 4 \\ \hline \end{array}$$
$$\begin{array}{r} 5 \\ \times 3 \\ \hline \end{array}$$
$$\begin{array}{r} 3 \\ \times 2 \\ \hline \end{array}$$

c.
$$\begin{array}{r} 0 \\ \times 5 \\ \hline \end{array}$$
$$\begin{array}{r} 0 \\ \times 0 \\ \hline \end{array}$$
$$\begin{array}{r} 1 \\ \times 1 \\ \hline \end{array}$$
$$\begin{array}{r} 2 \\ \times 4 \\ \hline \end{array}$$
$$\begin{array}{r} 4 \\ \times 1 \\ \hline \end{array}$$
$$\begin{array}{r} 4 \\ \times 3 \\ \hline \end{array}$$
$$\begin{array}{r} 5 \\ \times 5 \\ \hline \end{array}$$

d.
$$\begin{array}{r} 3 \\ \times 3 \\ \hline \end{array}$$
$$\begin{array}{r} 2 \\ \times 5 \\ \hline \end{array}$$
$$\begin{array}{r} 1 \\ \times 5 \\ \hline \end{array}$$
$$\begin{array}{r} 3 \\ \times 1 \\ \hline \end{array}$$
$$\begin{array}{r} 2 \\ \times 2 \\ \hline \end{array}$$
$$\begin{array}{r} 0 \\ \times 4 \\ \hline \end{array}$$
$$\begin{array}{r} 2 \\ \times 3 \\ \hline \end{array}$$

e.
$$\begin{array}{r} 1 \\ \times 2 \\ \hline \end{array}$$
$$\begin{array}{r} 1 \\ \times 4 \\ \hline \end{array}$$
$$\begin{array}{r} 0 \\ \times 2 \\ \hline \end{array}$$
$$\begin{array}{r} 2 \\ \times 1 \\ \hline \end{array}$$
$$\begin{array}{r} 5 \\ \times 2 \\ \hline \end{array}$$
$$\begin{array}{r} 5 \\ \times 4 \\ \hline \end{array}$$
$$\begin{array}{r} 3 \\ \times 4 \\ \hline \end{array}$$

★ **Challenge**

Write the missing numbers.

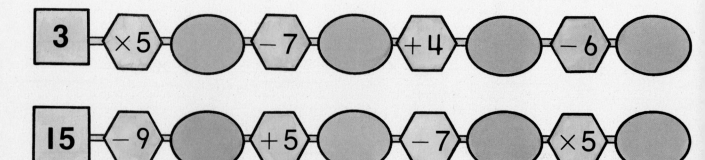

312

PROBLEM SOLVING

Multiplication

Solve.

a. There are 5 .

4 are on each.

How many

in all?

$$\begin{array}{r} 4 \\ \times\, 5 \\ \hline 20 \end{array}$$

b. Jeff has 4 .

4 are in each.

How many

in all?

---

c. Mrs. Rogers has 3 .

5 are on each.

How many

in all?

d. There are 5 .

Each has 2 .

How many

in all?

---

e. There are 2 .

Each has 4 .

How many

in all?

f. There are 3 .

3 are on each.

How many

in all?

---

g. Mike sees 3 .

Each holds 2 .

How many

in all?

h. Jenny has 3 .

Each has 4 .

How many

in all?

Multiply to find the cost.

a.

5¢

Buy 2.

$$\begin{array}{r} 5¢ \\ \times\ 2 \\ \hline 10¢ \end{array}$$

2¢

Buy 4.

4¢

Buy 3.

b.

3¢

Buy 2.

4¢

Buy 4.

2¢

Buy 1.

c.

5¢

Buy 1.

3¢

Buy 3.

4¢

Buy 5.

d.

2¢

Buy 4.

5¢

Buy 5.

3¢

Buy 4.

Mixed Practice

Add. Subtract. Multiply.

$$\begin{array}{r} 5 \\ +2 \\ \hline 7 \end{array} \qquad \begin{array}{r} 5 \\ -2 \\ \hline 3 \end{array} \qquad \begin{array}{r} 5 \\ \times 2 \\ \hline 10 \end{array}$$

Be careful. Watch the signs.

Add, subtract, or multiply.

a.
$$\begin{array}{r} 3 \\ +6 \\ \hline 9 \end{array} \qquad \begin{array}{r} 4 \\ \times 2 \\ \hline \end{array} \qquad \begin{array}{r} 12 \\ -\ 8 \\ \hline \end{array} \qquad \begin{array}{r} 5 \\ \times 3 \\ \hline \end{array} \qquad \begin{array}{r} 6 \\ +7 \\ \hline \end{array} \qquad \begin{array}{r} 2 \\ \times 1 \\ \hline \end{array} \qquad \begin{array}{r} 9 \\ -4 \\ \hline \end{array}$$

b.
$$\begin{array}{r} 4 \\ \times 0 \\ \hline \end{array} \qquad \begin{array}{r} 4 \\ +9 \\ \hline \end{array} \qquad \begin{array}{r} 13 \\ -\ 6 \\ \hline \end{array} \qquad \begin{array}{r} 9 \\ +8 \\ \hline \end{array} \qquad \begin{array}{r} 3 \\ \times 4 \\ \hline \end{array} \qquad \begin{array}{r} 17 \\ -\ 8 \\ \hline \end{array} \qquad \begin{array}{r} 5 \\ +3 \\ \hline \end{array}$$

c.
$$\begin{array}{r} 15 \\ -\ 8 \\ \hline \end{array} \qquad \begin{array}{r} 3 \\ \times 2 \\ \hline \end{array} \qquad \begin{array}{r} 5 \\ +6 \\ \hline \end{array} \qquad \begin{array}{r} 14 \\ -\ 7 \\ \hline \end{array} \qquad \begin{array}{r} 5 \\ \times 4 \\ \hline \end{array} \qquad \begin{array}{r} 6 \\ +8 \\ \hline \end{array} \qquad \begin{array}{r} 7 \\ -4 \\ \hline \end{array}$$

d.
$$\begin{array}{r} 3 \\ \times 3 \\ \hline \end{array} \qquad \begin{array}{r} 4 \\ +6 \\ \hline \end{array} \qquad \begin{array}{r} 9 \\ -9 \\ \hline \end{array} \qquad \begin{array}{r} 16 \\ -\ 7 \\ \hline \end{array} \qquad \begin{array}{r} 7 \\ +8 \\ \hline \end{array} \qquad \begin{array}{r} 5 \\ \times 1 \\ \hline \end{array} \qquad \begin{array}{r} 4 \\ \times 4 \\ \hline \end{array}$$

e.
$$\begin{array}{r} 7 \\ +5 \\ \hline \end{array} \qquad \begin{array}{r} 11 \\ -\ 4 \\ \hline \end{array} \qquad \begin{array}{r} 0 \\ \times 3 \\ \hline \end{array} \qquad \begin{array}{r} 5 \\ \times 5 \\ \hline \end{array} \qquad \begin{array}{r} 18 \\ -\ 9 \\ \hline \end{array} \qquad \begin{array}{r} 8 \\ +8 \\ \hline \end{array} \qquad \begin{array}{r} 15 \\ -\ 6 \\ \hline \end{array}$$

Add, subtract, or multiply.

a. $2 \times 2 = \underline{4}$ $7 + 3 = \underline{}$ $12 - 4 = \underline{}$

b. $8 + 5 = \underline{}$ $16 - 8 = \underline{}$ $4 + 7 = \underline{}$

c. $1 \times 4 = \underline{}$ $2 + 7 = \underline{}$ $5 \times 2 = \underline{}$

d. $11 - 6 = \underline{}$ $0 \times 1 = \underline{}$ $9 + 5 = \underline{}$

e. $3 \times 5 = \underline{}$ $13 - 9 = \underline{}$ $3 + 8 = \underline{}$

f. $9 - 2 = \underline{}$ $4 \times 3 = \underline{}$ $14 - 6 = \underline{}$

Write +, −, or ×.

g. $5 \;\boxed{+}\; 2 = 7$ $1 \;\bigcirc\; 1 = 1$ $9 \;\bigcirc\; 3 = 6$

h. $14 \;\bigcirc\; 9 = 5$ $8 \;\bigcirc\; 4 = 4$ $5 \;\bigcirc\; 4 = 20$

i. $9 \;\bigcirc\; 9 = 18$ $5 \;\bigcirc\; 0 = 0$ $16 \;\bigcirc\; 9 = 7$

j. $6 \;\bigcirc\; 9 = 15$ $5 \;\bigcirc\; 5 = 10$ $3 \;\bigcirc\; 4 = 12$

k. $7 \;\bigcirc\; 7 = 0$ $3 \;\bigcirc\; 2 = 6$ $9 \;\bigcirc\; 3 = 12$

l. $4 \;\bigcirc\; 2 = 8$ $5 \;\bigcirc\; 6 = 11$ $8 \;\bigcirc\; 3 = 5$

PROBLEM SOLVING

Choosing the Operation

Ring the correct example for each question.
Then solve.

a. There are **5** clowns in the circus.
Each clown wears **2** hats.
How many hats are there in all?

$$\begin{array}{r} 2 \\ +5 \\ \hline \end{array}$$

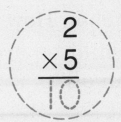

b. There are **9** horses in the ring.
There are **4** dogs in the ring.
How many more horses than dogs?

$$\begin{array}{r} 9 \\ -4 \\ \hline \end{array}$$
$$\begin{array}{r} 9 \\ +4 \\ \hline \end{array}$$

c. Anita buys **3** cans of orange juice
and **5** cans of grape juice.
How many cans of juice in all?

$$\begin{array}{r} 3 \\ +5 \\ \hline \end{array}$$
$$\begin{array}{r} 3 \\ \times 5 \\ \hline \end{array}$$

d. Fred had **15** balloons.
He sold **8** balloons.
How many balloons were left?

$$\begin{array}{r} 15 \\ +\ 8 \\ \hline \end{array}$$
$$\begin{array}{r} 15 \\ -\ 8 \\ \hline \end{array}$$

e. **4** tigers are in the cage.
Each tiger will do **3** tricks.
How many tricks will they do in all?

$$\begin{array}{r} 3 \\ \times 4 \\ \hline \end{array}$$
$$\begin{array}{r} 3 \\ +4 \\ \hline \end{array}$$

f. Neil buys a drink for **55¢** and
an apple for **27¢**.
How much does he spend in all?

$$\begin{array}{r} 55¢ \\ -27¢ \\ \hline \end{array}$$
$$\begin{array}{r} 55¢ \\ +27¢ \\ \hline \end{array}$$

Add, subtract, or multiply to solve.

a.

There are **4** teams running in the race. **5** children are on each team. How many children are there in all?

$$\begin{array}{r} 4 \\ \times 5 \\ \hline 20 \end{array}$$

b.

There are **12** girls in the race. There are **8** boys in the race. How many more girls than boys?

c.

There are **9** bags of popcorn and **8** bags of peanuts sold at the race. How many bags are sold in all?

d.

Each race takes **5** minutes. How long will **3** races take?

e.

There are **26** children watching the race. **11** children go home. How many children are left?

f.

8 girls and **8** boys win prizes for running in the race. How many children win prizes in all?

318

name

Division Readiness

6 hats.

2 hats in each group.

There are 3 groups of 2.

Ring groups of 2.

a.

How many groups of 2 are in 4? ___2___

b.

How many groups of 2 are in 8? _____

c.

How many groups of 2 are in 10? _____

d.

How many groups of 2 are in 6? _____

e.

How many groups of 2 are in 2? _____

f.

How many groups of 2 are in 12? _____

Ring groups of 3.

a.

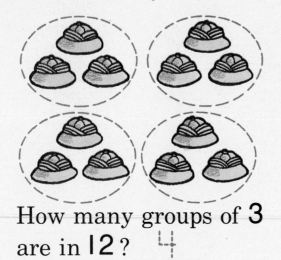

How many groups of 3 are in 12? ____4____

b.

How many groups of 3 are in 9? _____

c.

How many groups of 3 are in 6? _____

d.

How many groups of 3 are in 15? _____

Ring groups of 4.

e.

How many groups of 4 are in 8? _____

f.

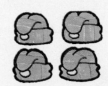

How many groups of 4 are in 12? _____

name

More Division Readiness

6 trains.

3 groups.

There are 2 trains in each group.

a.

4 trucks in 2 groups. How many trucks in each group? ___2___

b.

8 cars in 4 groups. How many cars in each group? _____

c.

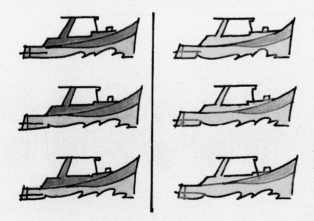

6 boats in 2 groups. How many boats in each group? _____

d.

8 sleds in 2 groups. How many sleds in each group? _____

a.

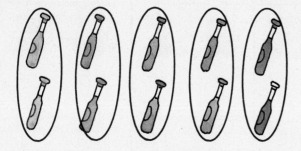

10 bats in 5 groups.
How many bats in each
group? _2_

b.

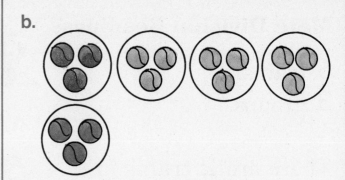

15 balls in 5 groups.
How many balls in each
group? _____

c.

10 rockets in 2 groups.
How many rockets in each
group? _____

d.

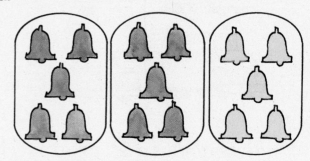

15 bells in 3 groups.
How many bells in each
group? _____

e.

12 dolls in 4 groups.
How many dolls in each
group? _____

f.

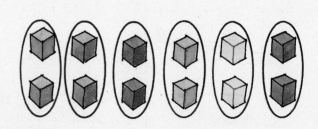

12 blocks in 6 groups.
How many blocks in each
group? _____

Multiply. (pages 301-312)

a. $2 \times 4 =$ _____ $3 \times 3 =$ _____ $5 \times 3 =$ _____

b. $2 \times 3 =$ _____ $5 \times 0 =$ _____ $2 \times 2 =$ _____

c.
$$\begin{array}{r} 4 \\ \times 1 \\ \hline \end{array} \quad \begin{array}{r} 5 \\ \times 2 \\ \hline \end{array} \quad \begin{array}{r} 4 \\ \times 3 \\ \hline \end{array} \quad \begin{array}{r} 0 \\ \times 4 \\ \hline \end{array} \quad \begin{array}{r} 5 \\ \times 5 \\ \hline \end{array} \quad \begin{array}{r} 4 \\ \times 4 \\ \hline \end{array} \quad \begin{array}{r} 5 \\ \times 4 \\ \hline \end{array}$$

Add, subtract, or multiply. (pages 315-316)

d.
$$\begin{array}{r} 6 \\ +5 \\ \hline \end{array} \quad \begin{array}{r} 4 \\ \times 2 \\ \hline \end{array} \quad \begin{array}{r} 9 \\ -3 \\ \hline \end{array} \quad \begin{array}{r} 4 \\ \times 5 \\ \hline \end{array} \quad \begin{array}{r} 7 \\ +8 \\ \hline \end{array} \quad \begin{array}{r} 14 \\ -9 \\ \hline \end{array} \quad \begin{array}{r} 2 \\ \times 1 \\ \hline \end{array}$$

Add, subtract, or multiply to solve. (pages 313-314, 317-318)

e.

There are 3 .
5 are in each.
How many  in all?

f.

There are **8** red pens.
There are **9** blue pens.
How many pens in all?

Ring groups of 3. (pages 319-320 321-322)

g.

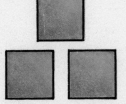

How many groups of **3**
are in **6**? _____

h.

8 stars in **4** groups.
How many stars in
each group? _____

Even and Odd Numbers

Complete the pattern.

Even Numbers		Odd Numbers

2

4

___

___

___

10

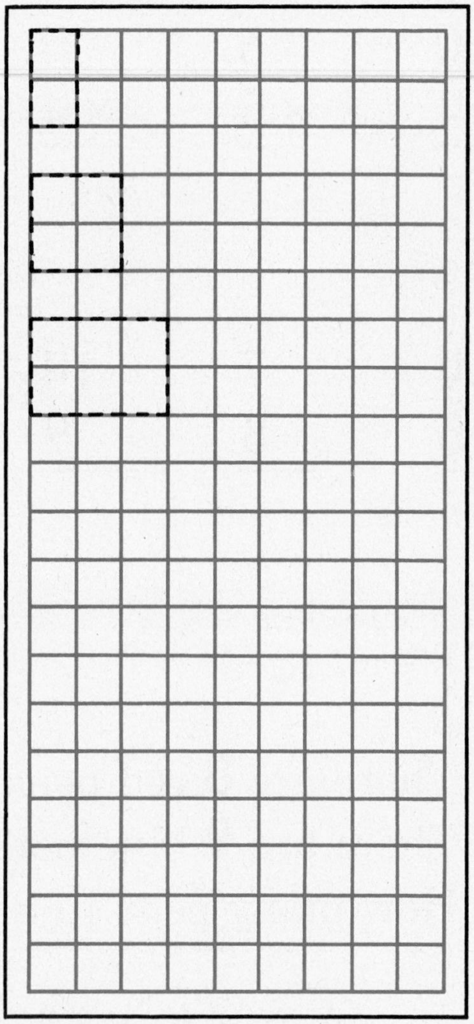

___

___

1

3

___

___

___

11

___

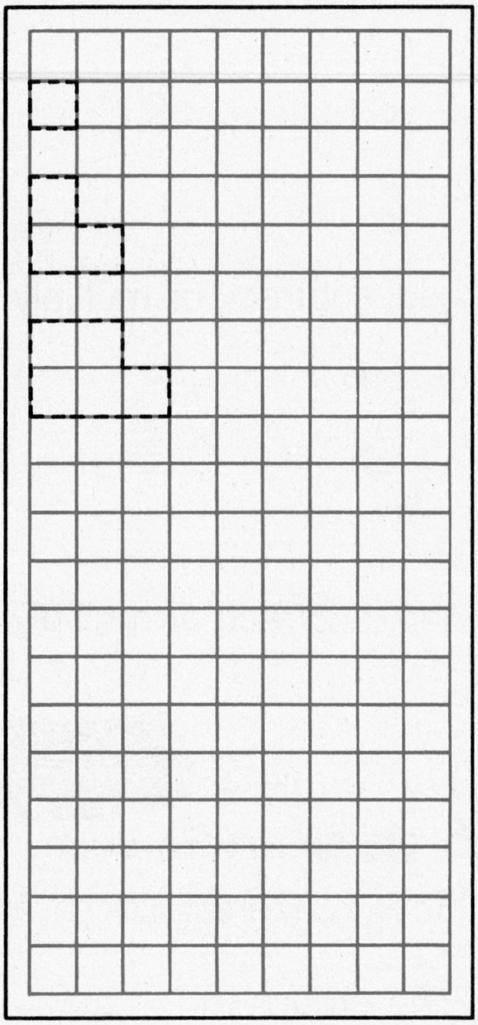

Write the missing numbers.

Even Numbers	2	4			12				20
Odd Numbers	1		7				15		

Multiply.

a. $2 \times 1 = $ _____ $5 \times 2 = $ _____ $3 \times 3 = $ _____

b. $5 \times 4 = $ _____ $1 \times 1 = $ _____ $0 \times 2 = $ _____

c.
$$\begin{array}{r} 5 \\ \times 1 \\ \hline \end{array} \qquad \begin{array}{r} 5 \\ \times 3 \\ \hline \end{array} \qquad \begin{array}{r} 2 \\ \times 2 \\ \hline \end{array} \qquad \begin{array}{r} 4 \\ \times 4 \\ \hline \end{array} \qquad \begin{array}{r} 3 \\ \times 2 \\ \hline \end{array} \qquad \begin{array}{r} 4 \\ \times 3 \\ \hline \end{array} \qquad \begin{array}{r} 4 \\ \times 1 \\ \hline \end{array}$$

Add, subtract, or multiply.

d.
$$\begin{array}{r} 5 \\ +3 \\ \hline \end{array} \qquad \begin{array}{r} 3 \\ \times 4 \\ \hline \end{array} \qquad \begin{array}{r} 9 \\ -2 \\ \hline \end{array} \qquad \begin{array}{r} 5 \\ \times 5 \\ \hline \end{array} \qquad \begin{array}{r} 8 \\ +6 \\ \hline \end{array} \qquad \begin{array}{r} 4 \\ -4 \\ \hline \end{array} \qquad \begin{array}{r} 4 \\ \times 2 \\ \hline \end{array}$$

Add, subtract, or multiply to solve.

e. There are **2**
4 are on each.
How many in all?

f. Rich buys **4** books.
Carol buys **5** books.
How many books in all?

Ring groups of 2.

g.

How many groups of
2 are in **6**? _____

h.

9 triangles in **3** groups.
How many triangles in
each group? _____

name

ENRICHMENT

Multiplication Tables

Complete each multiplication table.

X	0	1	2	3	4	5
0	0					
1						
2				6		
3						
4					16	
5			10			

X	4	2	0	5	1	3
	12				3	
5					5	
1						
		8		20		
0				0		
		4				2

Copyright © 1985 by Harcourt Brace Jovanovich, Inc.

SKILLS MAINTENANCE

Choose the correct answers.

1.
$$\begin{array}{r} 9 \\ +8 \\ \hline \end{array}$$
Ⓐ 15
Ⓑ 18
Ⓒ 17
Ⓓ not here

2.
$$\begin{array}{r} 14 \\ -6 \\ \hline \end{array}$$
Ⓐ 8
Ⓑ 10
Ⓒ 6
Ⓓ not here

3.
$$\begin{array}{r} 5 \\ 3 \\ +7 \\ \hline \end{array}$$
Ⓐ 13
Ⓑ 14
Ⓒ 15
Ⓓ not here

4.
$$\begin{array}{r} 26 \\ +48 \\ \hline \end{array}$$
Ⓐ 64
Ⓑ 68
Ⓒ 74
Ⓓ not here

5.
$$\begin{array}{r} 36 \\ +49 \\ \hline \end{array}$$
Ⓐ 95
Ⓑ 85
Ⓒ 75
Ⓓ not here

6.
$$\begin{array}{r} 62 \\ -48 \\ \hline \end{array}$$
Ⓐ 12
Ⓑ 14
Ⓒ 16
Ⓓ not here

7.
$$\begin{array}{r} 88 \\ -49 \\ \hline \end{array}$$
Ⓐ 39
Ⓑ 49
Ⓒ 40
Ⓓ not here

8.
$$\begin{array}{r} 245 \\ +439 \\ \hline \end{array}$$
Ⓐ 674
Ⓑ 684
Ⓒ 784
Ⓓ not here

9.
$$\begin{array}{r} 345 \\ -136 \\ \hline \end{array}$$
Ⓐ 219
Ⓑ 309
Ⓒ 209
Ⓓ not here

10.
$$\begin{array}{r} 506 \\ +217 \\ \hline \end{array}$$
Ⓐ 703
Ⓑ 723
Ⓒ 733
Ⓓ not here

11.
$$\begin{array}{r} 5 \\ \times 5 \\ \hline \end{array}$$
Ⓐ 0
Ⓑ 20
Ⓒ 15
Ⓓ not here

12.
$$\begin{array}{r} 3 \\ \times 5 \\ \hline \end{array}$$
Ⓐ 15
Ⓑ 20
Ⓒ 8
Ⓓ not here

Choose the correct answers.

13.

- (A) 103
- (B) 130
- (C) 310
- (D) not here

14.

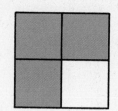

- (A) $\frac{1}{3}$
- (B) $\frac{3}{4}$
- (C) $\frac{1}{4}$
- (D) not her

15.

- (A) 4:45
- (B) 3:15
- (C) 4:15
- (D) not here

16.

48¢
+35¢

- (A) 13¢
- (B) 83¢
- (C) 73¢
- (D) not here

17.

Michelle sells 27 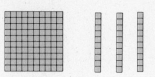 for the school play. Harold sells 19. How many in all?

- (A) 8
- (B) 45
- (C) 46
- (D) not here

18.

Ruth has 18. Barbara has 7. How many more does Ruth have than Barbara?

- (A) 25
- (B) 9
- (C) 11
- (D) not here

19.

Don buys 4 cans of balls. There are 3 balls in each can. How many balls in all?

- (A) 12
- (B) 7
- (C) 1
- (D) not here

20.

Ken has 85¢. He spends 49¢. How much money does he have left?

- (A) $1.3
- (B) 36¢
- (C) 44¢
- (D) not here

Extra Practice

SET 1 (pages 1–11)

Add.

a.
$$
\begin{array}{r} 2 \\ +6 \\ \hline \end{array} \quad
\begin{array}{r} 5 \\ +5 \\ \hline \end{array} \quad
\begin{array}{r} 7 \\ +2 \\ \hline \end{array} \quad
\begin{array}{r} 6 \\ +1 \\ \hline \end{array} \quad
\begin{array}{r} 5 \\ +3 \\ \hline \end{array} \quad
\begin{array}{r} 4 \\ +2 \\ \hline \end{array} \quad
\begin{array}{r} 9 \\ +1 \\ \hline \end{array}
$$

b.
$$
\begin{array}{r} 8 \\ +2 \\ \hline \end{array} \quad
\begin{array}{r} 9 \\ +0 \\ \hline \end{array} \quad
\begin{array}{r} 1 \\ +7 \\ \hline \end{array} \quad
\begin{array}{r} 3 \\ +7 \\ \hline \end{array} \quad
\begin{array}{r} 3 \\ +4 \\ \hline \end{array} \quad
\begin{array}{r} 4 \\ +5 \\ \hline \end{array} \quad
\begin{array}{r} 0 \\ +5 \\ \hline \end{array}
$$

SET 2 (pages 15–22)

Subtract.

c.
$$
\begin{array}{r} 8 \\ -6 \\ \hline \end{array} \quad
\begin{array}{r} 10 \\ -4 \\ \hline \end{array} \quad
\begin{array}{r} 5 \\ -5 \\ \hline \end{array} \quad
\begin{array}{r} 9 \\ -2 \\ \hline \end{array} \quad
\begin{array}{r} 10 \\ -7 \\ \hline \end{array} \quad
\begin{array}{r} 6 \\ -2 \\ \hline \end{array} \quad
\begin{array}{r} 8 \\ -1 \\ \hline \end{array}
$$

d.
$$
\begin{array}{r} 9 \\ -4 \\ \hline \end{array} \quad
\begin{array}{r} 8 \\ -4 \\ \hline \end{array} \quad
\begin{array}{r} 10 \\ -2 \\ \hline \end{array} \quad
\begin{array}{r} 7 \\ -6 \\ \hline \end{array} \quad
\begin{array}{r} 6 \\ -0 \\ \hline \end{array} \quad
\begin{array}{r} 7 \\ -3 \\ \hline \end{array} \quad
\begin{array}{r} 9 \\ -3 \\ \hline \end{array}
$$

PROBLEM SOLVING (pages 13–14, 23–24)

Solve.

e. 6  are eating.

4 are swimming.

How many in all?

f. There are 10 .

3 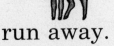 run away.

How many are left?

Extra Practice

SET 3 (pages 38–48)

Write the numbers.

a.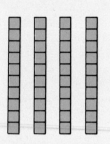

b.  ____

Write the missing numbers.

c.

77	78	◯	◯	81	◯	◯	84	◯	◯

SET 4 (pages 49–58)

Count by twos.

d. __24__ , __26__ , ____ , ____ , ____ , ____ , ____

Write > or < .

e. 12 ◯ 17   43 ◯ 40   18 ◯ 23

f. 67 ◯ 66   75 ◯ 85   91 ◯ 92

PROBLEM SOLVING (pages 51–52)

Write + or − .

g. 5 ◯ 4 = 9   8 ◯ 3 = 5   6 ◯ 2 = 8

h. 7 ◯ 3 = 4   5 ◯ 1 = 6   9 ◯ 2 = 7

name

Extra Practice

chapter 3

SET 5 (pages 65–72)

Add.

a.
$$3 + 8 \quad 7 + 5 \quad 5 + 9 \quad 6 + 7 \quad 9 + 2 \quad 7 + 7 \quad 8 + 4$$

b.
$$6 + 6 \quad 5 + 6 \quad 9 + 4 \quad 6 + 8 \quad 4 + 7 \quad 5 + 8 \quad 3 + 9$$

SET 6 (pages 73–82)

Subtract.

c.
$$13 - 7 \quad 14 - 9 \quad 12 - 5 \quad 14 - 6 \quad 11 - 7 \quad 13 - 4 \quad 12 - 6$$

d.
$$14 - 8 \quad 13 - 5 \quad 11 - 2 \quad 12 - 8 \quad 14 - 7 \quad 12 - 9 \quad 11 - 3$$

PROBLEM SOLVING (pages 83–84)

Choose ADD or SUBTRACT. Then solve.

e. 13 trucks are parked. 6 trucks drive away. How many trucks are left?

ADD or SUBTRACT

f. 9 cars are red. 5 cars are blue. How many cars in all?

ADD or SUBTRACT

331

name
Extra Practice

chapter
4

SET 7 (pages 89–95)

Add or subtract.

a.
15	16	9	18	9	8	17
− 8	− 7	+8	− 9	+6	+8	− 9

b.
15	17	9	16	15	7	16
− 6	− 8	+9	− 8	− 7	+9	− 9

SET 8 (pages 96–106)

Complete the addition sentences.

c. 8 + ____ = 17   7 + ____ = 15   9 + ____ = 16

Add.

d.
6	7	4	5	8	6	3
0	1	2	3	1	2	6
+9	+8	+6	+9	+6	+1	+7

PROBLEM SOLVING (pages 97–98, 103–104)

Solve.

e.

17 girls are hiking.

8 boys are hiking.

How many more girls

than boys are hiking?

f.

6 children are on the boat.

9 more children join them.

How many children

are on the boat in all?

332

Copyright © 1985 by Harcourt Brace Jovanovich, Inc.

Extra Practice

SET 9 (pages 114–120)

Write the numbers.

a.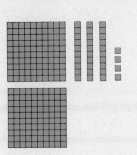

_____

b.

_____

c.

_____

d.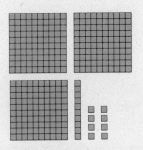

_____

SET 10 (pages 121–126)

Write the missing numbers.

e.

831	832							839	

f.

586					591	592			

Count by fives.

g. _135_ , _140_ , _____ , _____ , _____ , _____

h. _400_ , _____ , _____ , _____ , _____ , _425_

Extra Practice

SET II (pages 127–131)

Write > or < .

a. 745 $\bigcirc$ 850   114 $\bigcirc$ 86   640 $\bigcirc$ 700

b. 900 $\bigcirc$ 895   275 $\bigcirc$ 175   324 $\bigcirc$ 323

PROBLEM SOLVING (pages 125–126)

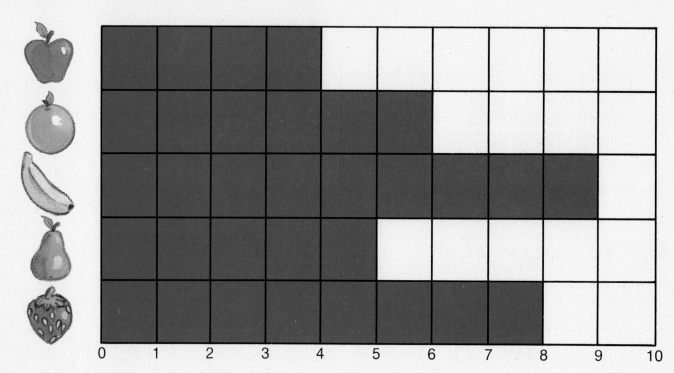

Write how many of each.

c.   _____   d.   _____

e. _____   f.   _____

Extra Practice

SET 12 (pages 135–140)

What time is it?

a.

_____ _____ _____

b.

_____ _____ _____

SET 13 (pages 141–146)

Ring the correct time.

c.

3:05   2:05   8:25   5:40   1:25   2:25

d.

8:10   2:40   12:35   11:35   6:50   7:50

Extra Practice

SET 14 (pages 147–158)

Write how much money.

a.

_____ ¢

b.

_____ ¢

c.

$ _____

d.

$ _____

PROBLEM SOLVING (pages 151–152)

Write how many cents.
Do you have enough?
Ring YES or NO.

e.

_____ ¢

32¢

YES
NO

f.

_____ ¢

45¢

YES
NO

g.

_____ ¢

28¢

YES
NO

h.

_____ ¢

25¢

YES
NO

SET 15 (pages 169–178)

Add.

a.
$$
\begin{array}{r} 45 \\ +54 \\ \hline \end{array}
\qquad
\begin{array}{r} 60 \\ +18 \\ \hline \end{array}
\qquad
\begin{array}{r} 33 \\ +52 \\ \hline \end{array}
\qquad
\begin{array}{r} 6 \\ +40 \\ \hline \end{array}
\qquad
\begin{array}{r} 21 \\ +43 \\ \hline \end{array}
\qquad
\begin{array}{r} 12 \\ +45 \\ \hline \end{array}
$$

b.
$$
\begin{array}{r} 65 \\ +25 \\ \hline \end{array}
\qquad
\begin{array}{r} 38 \\ +16 \\ \hline \end{array}
\qquad
\begin{array}{r} 57 \\ +8 \\ \hline \end{array}
\qquad
\begin{array}{r} 46 \\ +27 \\ \hline \end{array}
\qquad
\begin{array}{r} 48 \\ +39 \\ \hline \end{array}
\qquad
\begin{array}{r} 79 \\ +17 \\ \hline \end{array}
$$

SET 16 (pages 179–186)

Add.

c.
$$
\begin{array}{r} 47 \\ +81 \\ \hline \end{array}
\qquad
\begin{array}{r} 60 \\ +49 \\ \hline \end{array}
\qquad
\begin{array}{r} 72 \\ +43 \\ \hline \end{array}
\qquad
\begin{array}{r} 93 \\ +54 \\ \hline \end{array}
\qquad
\begin{array}{r} 50 \\ +80 \\ \hline \end{array}
\qquad
\begin{array}{r} 74 \\ +92 \\ \hline \end{array}
$$

d.
$$
\begin{array}{r} 68 \\ +54 \\ \hline \end{array}
\qquad
\begin{array}{r} 79 \\ +41 \\ \hline \end{array}
\qquad
\begin{array}{r} 86 \\ +65 \\ \hline \end{array}
\qquad
\begin{array}{r} 38 \\ +99 \\ \hline \end{array}
\qquad
\begin{array}{r} 57 \\ +43 \\ \hline \end{array}
\qquad
\begin{array}{r} 88 \\ +76 \\ \hline \end{array}
$$

PROBLEM SOLVING (pages 187–188)

Solve.

e.
Lucy collects 36 shells.
Robert collects 29 shells.
How many shells in all?

f.
There are 21 girls and 19 boys in the art club.
How many children in all?

Extra Practice

SET 17 (pages 195–200)

Subtract.

a.
$$56 - 24$$ $$75 - 30$$ $$68 - 18$$ $$47 - 21$$ $$94 - 33$$ $$89 - 72$$

b.
$$37 - 15$$ $$48 - 41$$ $$59 - 4$$ $$78 - 35$$ $$86 - 52$$ $$99 - 31$$

SET 18 (pages 201–210)

Subtract.

c.
$$82 - 36$$ $$64 - 27$$ $$73 - 18$$ $$81 - 6$$ $$90 - 36$$ $$52 - 39$$

d.
$$57 - 49$$ $$41 - 19$$ $$95 - 27$$ $$62 - 48$$ $$56 - 28$$ $$85 - 76$$

PROBLEM SOLVING (pages 211–212)

Solve.

e. There are 35 girls and 26 boys on the team. How many more girls than boys are there?

f. There are 46 children in the band. 28 are boys. How many girls are in the band?

Extra Practice

SET 19 (pages 225–230)

Ring the objects that are the same shape.

a.

b.

c.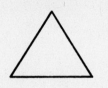

SET 20 (pages 231–238)

How many sides and corners?

d.

_____ sides   _____ sides   _____ sides

_____ corners   _____ corners   _____ corners

Ring the correct fractions.

e.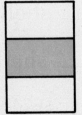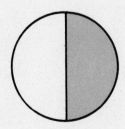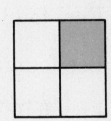

$\frac{1}{2}$ $\frac{1}{3}$ $\frac{1}{4}$ $\frac{1}{2}$ $\frac{1}{3}$ $\frac{1}{4}$ $\frac{1}{2}$ $\frac{1}{3}$ $\frac{1}{4}$

Extra Practice

SET 21 (pages 239–244)

Ring the correct fractions.

a.

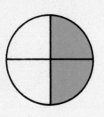 $\dfrac{3}{4}$ $\dfrac{1}{3}$ $\dfrac{2}{4}$

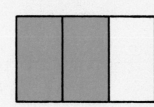 $\dfrac{1}{3}$ $\dfrac{2}{3}$ $\dfrac{2}{4}$

$\dfrac{2}{4}$ $\dfrac{2}{3}$ $\dfrac{3}{4}$

Write the fraction that tells
what part of the group is blue.

b.

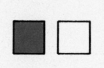

PROBLEM SOLVING (pages 233–234)

Name	Lee	Kimi	Earl	Lisa	Carl	Jane
Shells Found	8	9	10	7	6	12

Complete.

c. Earl found _____ shells.

d. Jane found _____ shells.

e. Lee found _____ shells.

f. Kimi found _____ shells.

Lisa found _____ shells.

Carl found _____ shells.

How many shells did Lee
and Lisa find in all? _____

How many shells did Kimi
and Carl find in all? _____

Extra Practice

SET 22 (pages 250–256)

Measure each object to the nearest centimeter.

a.    _____ centimeters

b.    _____ centimeters

Find how many square units.

c.

             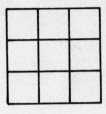

_____ square units | _____ square units | _____ square units

SET 23 (pages 257–260)

What would you use to measure?

d.    centimeter   liter   kilogram

e.   centimeter   liter   kilogram

f.    centimeter   liter   kilogram

Extra Practice

SET 24 (pages 265–270)

Measure each object to the nearest inch.

a.  _____ inches

b. _____ inches

Ring which holds more.

c.

PROBLEM SOLVING (pages 263–264)

Name	Books Read					
Mike	■	■				
Diane	■	■	■			
Pablo	■	■	■	■	■	■
Lamont	■	■	■	■	■	
Pam	■	■	■	■		

How many ■ ?

d. Pablo _____   Pam _____   Mike _____

Extra Practice

SET 25 (pages 279–284)

Add.

a.
$$
\begin{array}{r} 637 \\ +150 \end{array}
\qquad
\begin{array}{r} 408 \\ +341 \end{array}
\qquad
\begin{array}{r} 253 \\ +132 \end{array}
\qquad
\begin{array}{r} 642 \\ +\ 36 \end{array}
\qquad
\begin{array}{r} 512 \\ +347 \end{array}
\qquad
\begin{array}{r} 40 \\ +126 \end{array}
$$

b.
$$
\begin{array}{r} 413 \\ +309 \end{array}
\qquad
\begin{array}{r} 674 \\ +219 \end{array}
\qquad
\begin{array}{r} 35 \\ +425 \end{array}
\qquad
\begin{array}{r} 217 \\ +336 \end{array}
\qquad
\begin{array}{r} 608 \\ +\ 49 \end{array}
\qquad
\begin{array}{r} 853 \\ +128 \end{array}
$$

SET 26 (pages 285–290)

c.
$$
\begin{array}{r} 948 \\ -234 \end{array}
\qquad
\begin{array}{r} 849 \\ -206 \end{array}
\qquad
\begin{array}{r} 675 \\ -425 \end{array}
\qquad
\begin{array}{r} 784 \\ -\ 82 \end{array}
\qquad
\begin{array}{r} 441 \\ -120 \end{array}
\qquad
\begin{array}{r} 563 \\ -211 \end{array}
$$

d.
$$
\begin{array}{r} 875 \\ -419 \end{array}
\qquad
\begin{array}{r} 750 \\ -216 \end{array}
\qquad
\begin{array}{r} 362 \\ -154 \end{array}
\qquad
\begin{array}{r} 648 \\ -\ 29 \end{array}
\qquad
\begin{array}{r} 725 \\ -306 \end{array}
\qquad
\begin{array}{r} 940 \\ -138 \end{array}
$$

PROBLEM SOLVING (pages 293–294)

Solve.

e. There are 193 books on the first shelf. There are 206 books on the second shelf. How many books in all?

f. The school has 480 math books and 365 science books. How many more math books than science books are there?

SET 27 (pages 300–310)
Multiply.

a. $2 \times 2 =$ _____ $4 \times 3 =$ _____ $3 \times 2 =$ _____

b. $1 \times 4 =$ _____ $2 \times 5 =$ _____ $5 \times 1 =$ _____

c.
$$\begin{array}{c} 0 \\ \times 2 \\ \hline \end{array} \quad \begin{array}{c} 1 \\ \times 1 \\ \hline \end{array} \quad \begin{array}{c} 4 \\ \times 5 \\ \hline \end{array} \quad \begin{array}{c} 3 \\ \times 1 \\ \hline \end{array} \quad \begin{array}{c} 2 \\ \times 4 \\ \hline \end{array} \quad \begin{array}{c} 3 \\ \times 0 \\ \hline \end{array} \quad \begin{array}{c} 5 \\ \times 3 \\ \hline \end{array}$$

SET 28 (pages 311–322)
Ring groups of 2.

d.

How many groups
of **2** are in **4** ? _____

e.

How many groups
of **2** are in **8** ? _____

PROBLEM SOLVING (pages 313–314, 317–318)
Solve.

f.
Lisa has **4** shirts.
Each shirt has **5**
buttons. How many
buttons in all?

g.
There are **2** bags of
apples. Each bag has
3 apples. How many
apples in all?

4
B 5
C 6
D 7
E 8
F 9
G 0
H 1
I 2
J 3

344

0 1 2

3 4 5

6 7 8

9 10 +
−
=

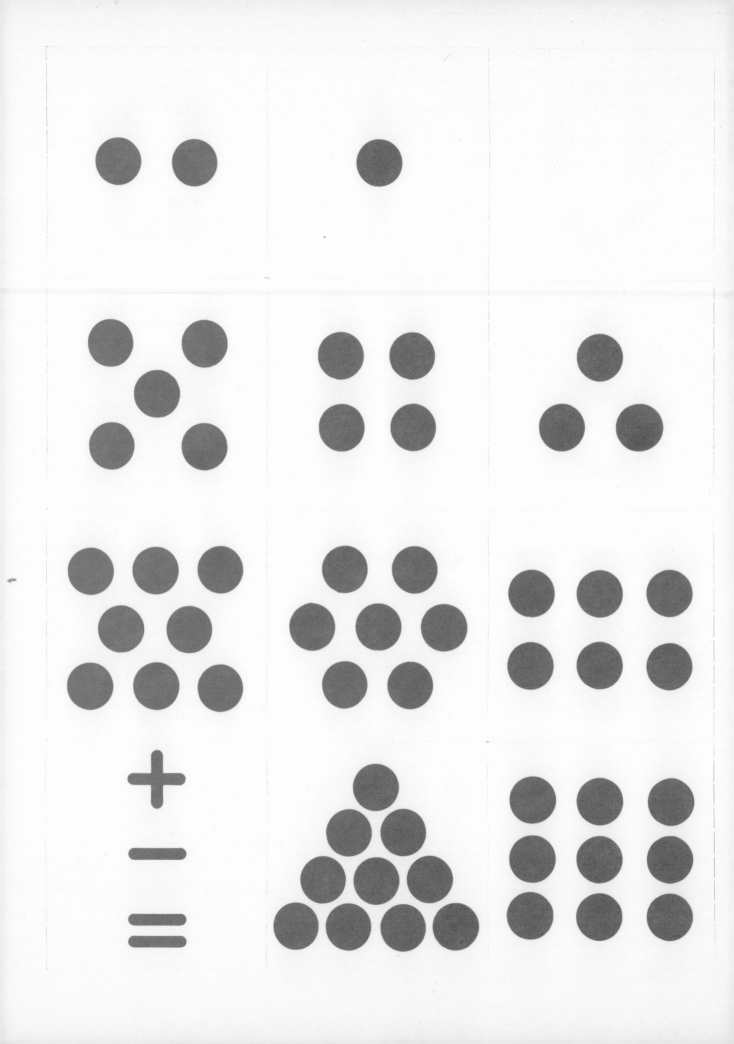

ones

hundred

tens

hundred

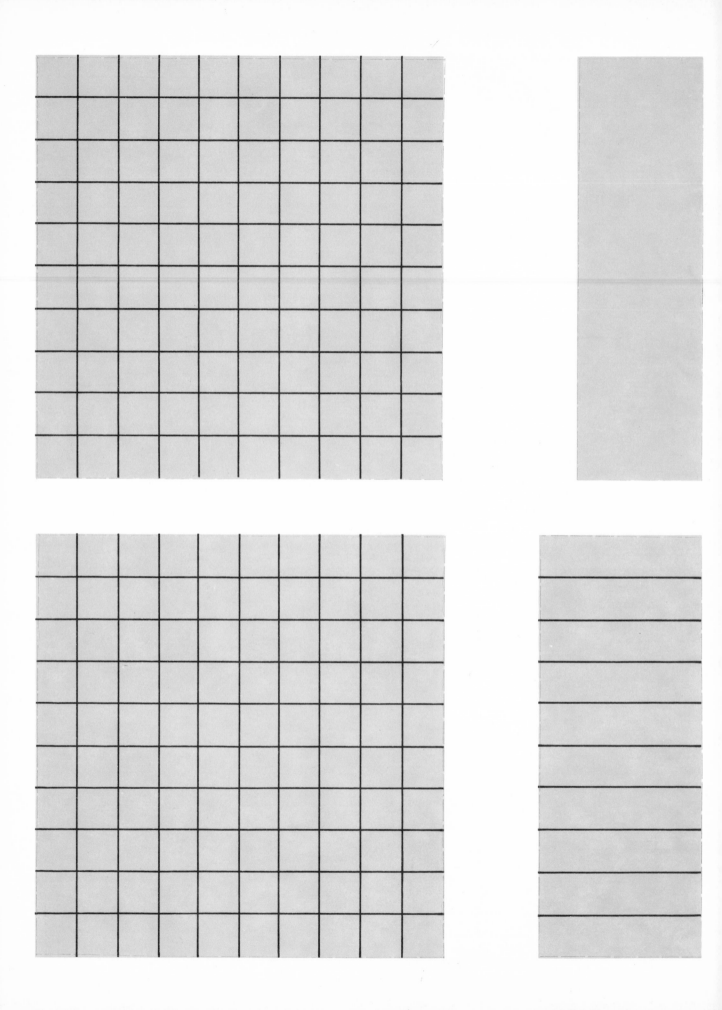

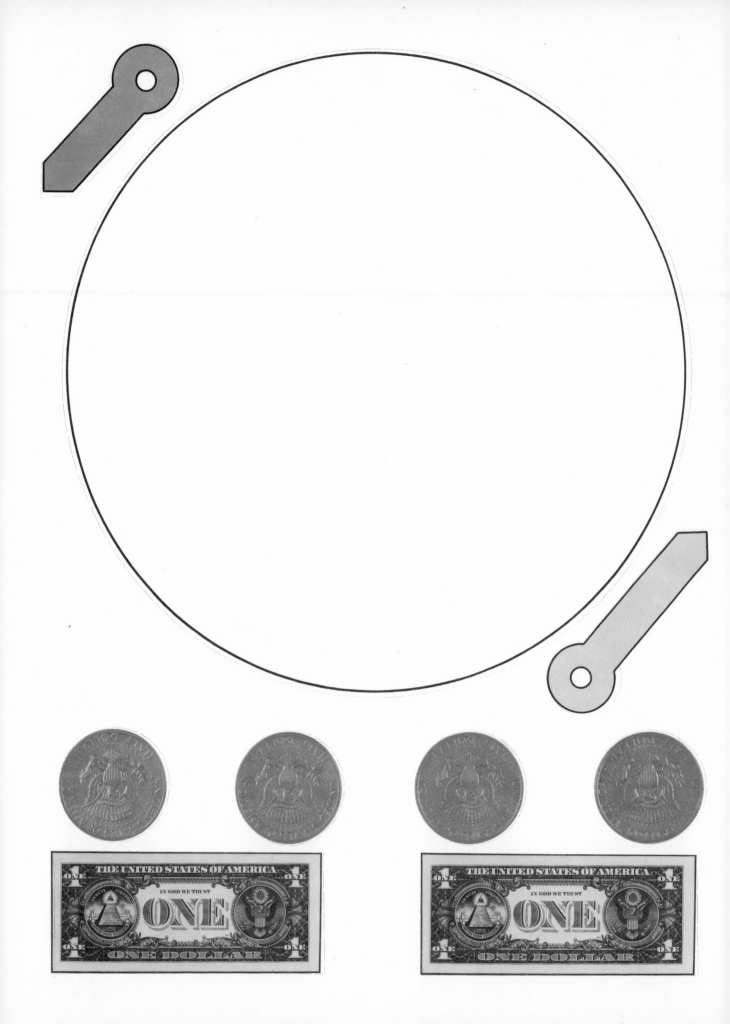

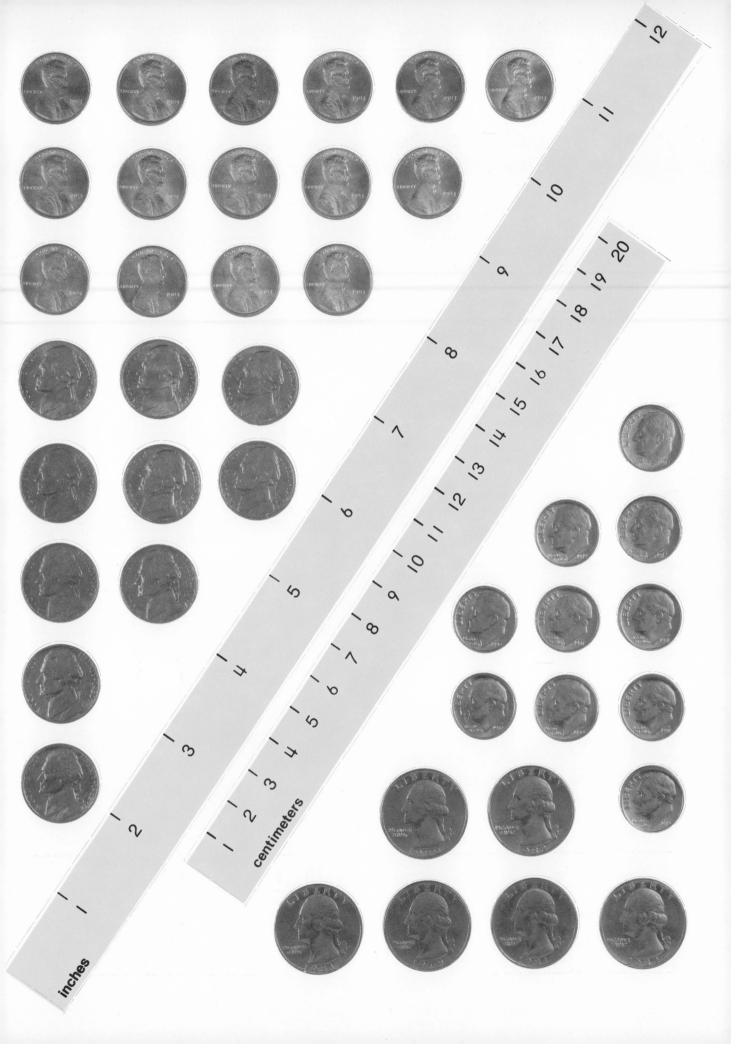

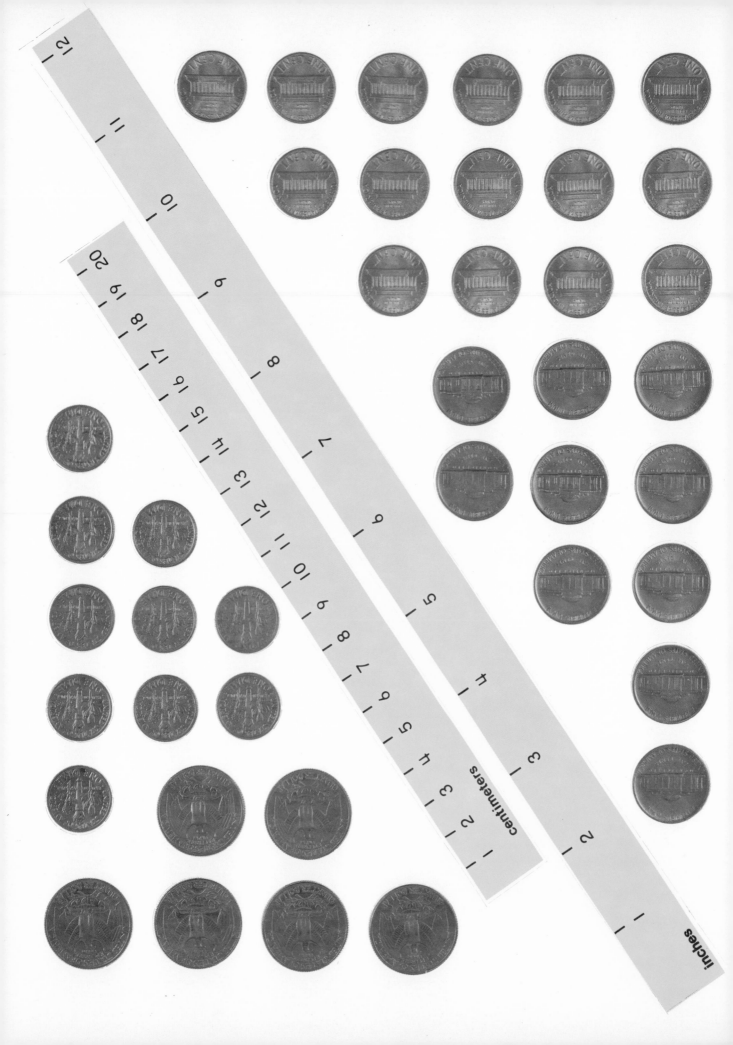